⤞ Endorsements ⤝

Swimming Upstream is the engrossing story of a young woman, divorced, who struggles to care for herself and her children, get a higher education, and attain self-realization. Must read for those who are on a like journey.

–Shirley Sikes, author of *Suns Go Down*

In this poignant tale Richardson piques the reader's interest with the glamour of a year in Paris, married life in Bogota, Colombia, and the failure of her marriage in Marblehead, Massachusetts. With the keen eye of the filmmaker that she eventually becomes, she catches the local color and characteristic speech patterns in each setting.

–Mary Ellen Barnes, author of *The Road to Mt. Lemmon*,
Teresa and the Cowboy, Un Cuento de Amor Tucsonense

SWIMMING UPSTREAM

SWIMMING UPSTREAM

A Memoir

Constance Richardson

Published by Wheatmark®
1760 E. River Road, Suite 145
Tucson, Arizona 85718 U.S.A.
www.wheatmark.com

ISBN: 978-1-60494-489-1
LCCN: 2010930435

For Hans
&
Aunt Fiz (1914–2007)

Swimming Upstream covers a period in my life from the mid-nineteen fifties through the early nineteen seventies. The events are as accurate as I could reconstruct them, and my feelings about them are still vivid. It's also true that memories are, in themselves, subjective.

Swimming Upstream is populated with people I knew and members of my family. At one person's request and to protect another's identity, their names were changed, as were names of all physicians. In an early scene two minor characters were invented so their conversation could shed light on domestic and political issues in post-World War II France. Otherwise it's a true story.

"When you do something,
you should burn yourself completely,
like a good bonfire,
leaving no trace of yourself."

Shunryu Suzuki
Zen Mind, Beginner's Mind

⤳ Acknowledgements ⤳

I thank Mary Ellen Barnes, Ellie Nelson, Bert Steves, Molly McKinney, Shirley Sikes, and Terry Ambrose of the St. Phillips Writer's Workshop.

Thanks to Shirley Sikes, Michaele Lockhart, Glenda Taylor, William Don Carlos, and Penny Porter of the Easy Writers critique group.

Thanks to Carol Kardon for her rendition of Clement Greenberg's painting critique.

I thank editors Michael Garrett, Allen Kates, Michaele Lockhart (French), and The Editorial Department.

⇥ Contents ⇤

⊹ Contents ⊹

⇒1⇐

Boys, men everywhere. Of course, there were females in the group, too, but it was the men I was drawn to, or they to me, and they seemed to materialize out of the shadows everywhere we went.

At eighteen I was the youngest member on the political science tour, which consisted of twenty-two people: graduate students, older citizens, and tour leader Dr. Louis Wasserman. We visited six countries in six weeks, often staying in government facilities.

In Holland we stayed in rooms adjacent to the royal palace, and in Bonn we spent the night in a monastery. Having broken a strap on my sandal, I found a cobbler near the monastery who would fix it. When I went to his shop the next day, there was a sign on the door saying it was closed. Realizing it was Sunday, I collapsed on a bench outside the shop. I had only one other pair of shoes—the ones I was wearing; they pinched and had already caused a painful blister. We were leaving this afternoon for Denmark. What to do? I lowered my head to my lap, clasped my arms around my knees, and considered options.

A young man about my age rolling a bicycle tire approached and sat down next to me. He had on a blue short-sleeve shirt and dirty shorts. His hands had grease stains, but he had a wide smile. Raising his eyebrows, he appeared concerned. I pointed at the closed cobbler's shop next door, then at my right foot, then again at the shop. He said something in German that I didn't understand.

"My shoe!" I wailed. "We're leaving in an hour."

"I'm sorry. My English is, um, not practice, *ja*?" he said.

I took off my right shoe and showed him the blister. "Do you know the cobbler?"

"*Ja*. He—how say?—fish?" he said, throwing an imaginary fishing line over his head.

"Fishing?

He nodded, "Always Sunday."

"Can you get him to open his shop?" I asked.

He shrugged his shoulders but smiled hopefully.

I got up, explaining that I had to pack and get ready to leave. He stuck out his right hand.

"I am Dieter."

"Constance," I said, shaking his.

He walked beside me the several blocks to the monastery. Leaning the bicycle tire against the building, he said, "I find your shoe."

Giving Dieter the tag for my shoe, I smiled encouragingly before turning to go inside, thinking I'd never see him—or my sandal—ever again.

Most of us had ascended and taken our seats in the bus that was taking us to the airport. The doors closed. From my window seat I spotted Dieter running toward us waving something over his head.

"Halt, halt," he yelled.

I went forward and had the driver open the door, where a breathless Dieter handed me my shoe, its cobbler's tag still attached.

"Thank you, Dieter," I cried.

The pneumatic door closed. I waved at him through my window until we turned onto the highway. Nobody had done such a thoughtful thing for me without wanting something in return.

In Copenhagen on top of the hall tower, I met a tall Englishman with light brown hair lecturing to a group of students. Outgoing, he projected easy authority coupled with a sense of humor.

I faked a coughing fit to get his attention.

"Are you going to be all right?" he asked after thumping me on the back.

Sputtering a thank-you for his concern, I learned his name was Mark Flynn.

Mark joined us for lunch the next day and was introduced to everyone. Dr. Wasserman invited Mark to join us at General Field Marshal Montgomery's house in England the following week.

After visiting Montgomery's house and library, where Mark more or less conducted the presentation, he asked if I might leave the group for a day or two to visit London. Dr. Wasserman gave his blessing.

Mark took me to Harrow, a prestigious boys public school where he spent his elementary school years. I heard stories about English hazing, not unlike hazing in American preparatory schools. We visited Corpus Christi College at Oxford University, where he completed a baccalaureate degree; we also saw his former apartment. He knew so much history it made my head spin. Filled with admiration, I was also ashamed of my ignorance and wished we were on a more equal footing. For the first time, I wanted to go back to school. At my request, Mark bought several books by Evelyn Waugh to whet my appetite for satire.

When he invited me to Cornwall, England, for the weekend to meet his parents, I accepted and arranged to rejoin my group in London on Monday morning. I wondered about the invitation. Wasn't it a sign that he was smitten? One didn't invite just anyone home.

Over that weekend I picked up funny vibes from his parents, which led me to believe they didn't like one another. The animosity was ever so controlled underneath polite chitchat. I brought this up with Mark, who said his mother was "eternally dissatisfied, no matter what." If, by this remark, Mark exhibited a certain callousness toward his mother, he showed only kindness and empathy toward his father. Mr. Flynn senior was headmaster of The Old Ride, an English public school in Buckinghamshire.

What I remember most about Cornwall was how much the terrain resembled the northern California coastline near my home, Green Gulch Ranch. Unadorned round, green hills, often kissed by fog or rain, rolled steeply to the sea. On my second and last night there, without any spoken intentions to see one another again, I crept into his bedroom, awakened him, and blurted out my feelings.

"I can't stand not ever seeing you again."

He mustn't have known just what to do or say. Not wanting to diminish or crush such a tender spirit, he still must have weighed his words carefully. Holding me in his arms, he whispered, "I'd be taking so much and giving so little."

What did he mean? Didn't he realize I was still a virgin? What I meant was that never seeing him again was unthinkable. I burst into sobs and wiped my tears with his striped pajama sleeve. Finally I went back to my room and fell into the sleep of the young and innocent who believe in tomorrows.

The next morning I rejoined my tour group in London. From there, we boarded a train to Dover and then took a boat across the English Channel to Calais, then another train to Paris. We arrived at night on July 13 at the

Gare du Nord and went by bus to a simple hotel on the Left Bank near the Arab quarter, our last leg of the trip before heading home.

The elevator broken, I climbed to the fourth floor to my small room and fell into bed, relieved to be going home but also sad that the trip was almost over.

The next morning a shaft of sunlight from the window struck my face. I tried to orient myself—my suitcase and raincoat on a chair, shoes nearby. A folding screen shielded a toilet and small sink in one corner. I glanced at my watch; it showed it was a bit before 8 a.m. Suddenly the telephone rang its hollow double French tone.

When I answered, a woman's voice said, *"Bonjour Mademoiselle, deux hommes sont ici pour vous."*

"Moi?"

"Oui"

"Merci."

I looked out the small window. Two young men, well dressed in three-piece suits, were standing in the street. One held flowers. I opened the window and leaned out.

"Constance?"

"Yes."

"We're your cousins. I'm Arnaud. This is Patrick."

"Hello."

"We're coming up!"

I raced into some clothes, brushed my hair, and splashed cold water on my face, slicking my eyebrows with a finger.

Someone knocked. I opened the door. Arnaud thrust forth the bouquet of flowers, which I took and placed in the small sink. Arnaud had a naughty smile and dark hair, and his cologne smelled wonderful. Patrick was blond and seemed shy.

"How are we cousins?" I asked.

"Your grandfather's sister married our grandfather," Arnaud said.

"Who?"

"Aunt Constance, married *Count Odon de Lubersac*. She's our grandmother."

I let this sink in. "I'm named after her."

"We know," they said in unison.

I had heard the stories about my mother's years in Europe, her escape from a horrid English boarding school and flight to Paris to her favorite

4

aunt, Constance. I didn't know I had actual relatives, but their children, who were my cousins, stood right before me. I lucked out!

They explained that today, July 14, was a very special day in France. In 1789 a revolutionary mob stormed the Bastille, the king's prison, marking the beginning of the French Revolution. On the first anniversary, people gathered to celebrate what became known as Bastille Day. Tonight there would be dancing in the streets and in the bistros all over Paris. They asked if I would join them later, telling me it might be dangerously full of drunk, wild people, fireworks and mobs. I'd need their protection.

Excitedly, I agreed and we arranged to meet just after 5 p.m. Then they were gone, leaving behind a sophisticated aroma of cologne and French Gauloises cigarettes.

Arnaud navigated a little Renault through many small streets in the Latin Quarter, a cigarette dangling from his mouth. Patrick yelled "*gauche,*" then "*droit, droit!*" as the car turned this way and that. Thrust first to the right, then the left, I held on to the back of the driver's seat as Paris unfolded through the windows. We passed the *Palais du Luxembourg,* all lighted up, then the *Boulevard Saint Michel,* with cafés full of people. Several people stepped right in front of the car. Arnaud shouted, stepped on the break and peeled left around them. There were so many people laughing and gesturing everywhere.

In Montparnasse, Arnaud parked in an alley off the boulevard. I followed them into a crowded bistro, and we pushed to the brass-railed bar. Arnaud shouted an order to the bartender while Patrick escorted me to a small table in the back. Although it was so noisy I couldn't hear what Patrick said, at least we could sit. Arnaud joined us with three glasses of beer and a menu, which they discussed in rapid-fire French.

Arnaud kept eyeing a woman dressed in a tight skirt and top standing near our table. She had frizzy black hair, an incredibly long neck, and small, tight breasts. It was obvious she wore no bra, because her breasts jiggled when she laughed. Within earshot, Arnaud and Patrick discussed her in English.

"*Mon vieux,* she's a whore."

"No, she's a model."

"Two hundred francs she's a whore."

"Three hundred francs she isn't."

Arnaud tapped her on the shoulder and asked her something in French, which was later translated to me as "My brother says you are a movie star. Are you?"

Her boyfriend told Arnaud to go fuck himself, at which point we ordered more beers and food from a middle-aged waiter with a white napkin slung over his arm. As we sipped our beers, the couple moved away from us.

Arnaud told me this place was a hotbed for political demonstrations by students. Our waiter arrived carrying a tray with a basket of bread, butter and assorted cold cuts, brie, and a small dish of fruit. He left and reappeared with plates, mustard, forks, and knives. I was famished. We all were.

It was good to be eating in this Paris bistro with these French cousins-by-marriage, whom I hadn't known existed until that morning. We got another round of beer. Suddenly the room burst into *La Marseillaise*. People sang *"Allons enfants de la patrie,"* to the accompaniment of an accordion. I'd heard the song but didn't know the words, so I hummed the melody. It was impossible not to join in.

Soon people were forming a conga line through the bistro and out into the street, kicking alternating feet out every sixth beat. Ta-ta-ta-ta-ta-*ta*. Ta-ta-ta-ta-ta-*ta*. I lost sight of Arnaud, whom I last saw holding on to the waist of the dark-haired woman with the skin-tight clothes. Patrick was ahead of me. A tall man over six feet tall was holding on to me. I felt his breath on my shoulder. He whispered something in guttural French that I didn't understand, then something I did, *"Très jeune."*

I said, *"Je ne parle pas Francais."*

Everyone was dancing a conga line down the middle of the street. There must have been fifty or sixty people, all dancing and singing to the beat: ta-ta-ta-ta-ta-*ta*. I felt rivulets of sweat on my neck and bodice. Now hot, I felt tired.

Slowly, the conga line wound down and then dissipated. I bent over in an effort to get blood to my brain. The man behind me touched my shoulder. I straightened up, sucking in my breath. He wiped a large hand across his sweaty mouth and jaw and smiled. We both laughed. He was lanky and well built, with small hips, broad shoulders, and long legs. His muscles rippled. Soft yellow hairs on his forearms caught the light. The hair on his head was wavy, light brown, thick. He looked the way a man should; he was also a complete stranger. Suddenly, he reached out with one hand and flipped my hair up and away from my neck. I liked his touch. Next, he took a matchbook from his pocket. He wrote on the inside cover and pressed the matchbook into my right palm as he stroked it with his finger. I jerked my hand from his and ran back into the lighted bistro. Finding our old table, I crumpled into a chair.

Why did I run away? I looked at the matchbook. Inside was written a strange name, an address, and telephone number. I shoved it into my dress pocket before Arnaud and Patrick returned. Later, in the back seat of the Renault on our way to the hotel, I felt the matchbook in my pocket and wondered who he was.

Saturday brought glorious weather: clear blue sky with occasional fluffy clouds. Dr. Wasserman and the group were going to visit a museum, and I watched them consult maps as they prepared to navigate the Parisian Metro system.

Arnaud arrived before noon to bring me to a luncheon at Aunt Jackie's, Arnaud and Patrick's stepmother, who is married to their father, Uncle Jacques. He arrived early to take me to a special place before the lunch. He wouldn't tell me where. He said, "Wait and see, a beautiful surprise."

I jumped into the Renault and we headed south toward the Seine river and, beyond it, the Right Bank. We crossed a beautiful bridge to an island called Ile de la Cité right in the heart of Paris. Parking the car, we walked past the Notre Dame Cathedral and its flying buttresses, through the park and out to where the island ended in a point in the Seine. We sat on a bench under a tree. A barge drifted lazily by with laundry drying on the wheelhouse, then another with a cat and a deck filled with junk. A man fished from the *quai* in front of us. The air was permeated with smells of newly cut grass mixed with the Seine's unique essence and occasional whiffs of cigarette smoke from passersby. Arnaud bought me a gift, *Le Grand Bal du Printemps*, by Jacques Prévert, a booklong poem about springtime in Paris with photographs. He took my hand in his as we looked at the book together, he translating the French into English and explaining where the photographs were taken. He put an arm around my shoulder, which felt romantic.

"My little American cousin, don't ever change. Promise?" he said.

"I won't change. I promise."

Then Arnaud kissed me. His mouth was soft and warm, his lips enveloping mine. When our lips parted he whispered, *"Ne change pas, ma petite."*

With one kiss, he made me feel so special.

No. 199 Avenue Victor Hugo was a handsome building. We ascended the elevator to the fourth floor and entered to see many people standing in a receiving line. They all seemed honored that I had come.

Arnaud presented me to Great-Aunt Constance, a tall, thin patrician woman who resembled her brother, my grandfather. She had a lovely smile and beautiful white hair.

Next I was introduced to Jackie, then to Jacques, Mimi and Raoul, and finally to a line of children of various ages and heights and their governess, Mlle. Bouchard. Everyone's English was perfect. We were ushered to the dining room, to a table set with an elaborate array of utensils and glassware. I was seated to the right of Uncle Jacques in the place of honor. Aunt Constance was on Jacques' left. A butler served the first course: jellied consommé with a poached egg in the middle and a slice of lemon on a large soup plate. I wondered how in the world did the poached egg get into the middle. I watched to see who would start first. When everyone had been served, Jackie lifted a spoonful to her lips, which was the signal for everyone to follow. The soup spoon was incredibly heavy. I wondered if it could be some sort of serving implement. I noticed that Aunt Constance, who sat directly opposite me, had a spoon the same size.

When the first course was finished, the soup plates were removed and clean plates were put in front of each of us. The butler served each person fish, new potatoes, and peas from a large platter. Then he poured white wine. All the while, the conversation was directed toward me.

"My dear, tell us all about your mother and George and the ranch."

I related news about George's latest range cattle and the Australian grasses he was trying to establish to make permanent pastures where we had brush. I was repeating an automatic script I'd heard many times so I could concentrate on not making a gaffe in my table manners. I told them my mother loved teaching illiterates how to read and write and adored her vegetable garden. Uncle Raoul seemed surprised.

"You mean your mother, Hopie, is digging in a garden?" he said.

"It's mostly Andrew, the gardener."

"Ahh."

The children at the other end of the table smiled sweetly.

When lunch was finished, we adjourned to the living room for coffee and tea, which Aunt Jackie served from a gigantic silver service. The children passed the coffee and tea. Everyone was terribly polite, which I found exhausting. I was asked about the tour. What countries had we visited, who were the other group members, who was leading it? Suddenly I heard myself say, "Dr. Wasserman teaches political science. The House Un-American Activities Committee accused him of being a Communist, which led to his losing that job. But now he teaches at San Francisco State and he's a really good friend of Mom's."

There was sudden silence. I shouldn't have mentioned anything about the House Un-American Activities Committee or Communists. But I did. Anyway, it was true.

Suddenly Uncle Raoul abruptly stood and said, " Well, your mother was quite something."

He recounted the time she ran away from her dreadful English boarding school to their house.

"She hid under a large bed and rolled from one side to the other as the chauffeur tried to pull her out."

"Really?" I asked. "How old was she?"

"My age. We were about sixteen or seventeen. Hopie wouldn't come out until they promised her she wouldn't have to go back to England."

I loved hearing these stories about when mom was young because she sounded so human, like me.

After lunch it was decided I'd go with Great-Aunt Constance, Uncle Raoul and Aunt Mimi to No. 1 rue Charles-Lamoureaux, just a few blocks away. They wanted to show me their apartment and introduce me to Guy and Chantal, Raoul and Mimi's son and daughter-in-law. We would telephone Arnaud when the visit was concluded, and he'd take me back to the Left Bank.

No. 1 rue Charles Lamoureaux sat on the corner of the blocklong street. Aunt Constance lived on the first floor, and Raoul and Mimi lived on the fourth. We all got into the small elevator, a polished brass cage encased in glass, which slowly ascended. (The first floor in France is really the floor above the ground floor.) We deposited Great-Aunt Constance at her front door. Everyone kissed everyone on both cheeks before parting.

Julie, the maid, opened the door and explained to Mimi that Madame la Comtesse and Monsieur le Comte were not in. I was aware that she addressed Aunt Mimi with "Madame" and referred to Guy and Chantal by their full titles. It was such a foreign and strange custom that I felt as if I'd arrived on a movie set.

The apartment was vast, wrapping 360 degrees around a courtyard. The living room was sumptuously furnished with matching velvet sofas, upholstered period chairs, lacquered inlaid tables with marble tops, and hand-carved and gilded framed paintings on wood-paneled walls. Over each of the double doors leading to a small balcony above rue Charles-Lamoureaux were floor-length brocade curtains with roped and tasseled tiebacks.

I'd never been in anything as fine except a museum. Our two-story California ranch house had linoleum and cork floors, and the windows had no curtains. Our dining area was an eight-foot-long wooden table with backless benches for seating in the kitchen.

A mini tour of the apartment with Mimi revealed two smaller bedrooms and an adjoining bath on one side of the living room, and the master bedroom, sitting room, and double bathroom on the other. Each of the bathrooms had a bidet.

"Raoul teases me for having over eight meters of closet space," she said, indicating the hallway outside the master suite with floor-to-ceiling storage. She smiled and checked my reaction.

I had no idea how to respond. She and I came from different worlds. I'd never heard of the Paris Collections or her favorite design house, Balmain. I didn't know what was so amusing about eight meters of closet space. Perhaps it was only her way of trying to be friendly. I was a girl who has driven cattle through brush in cold, damp fog during spring roundup. I could churn butter and yodel like hell, but I didn't know a thing about French culture or the subtleties of this kind of conversation.

We completed the tour by passing through the storage hall and servants staircase, the kitchen, and the dining room. Meanwhile, Raoul, who spoke American English with no trace of an accent, dug up some old photographs of my mother. There was something familiar about Raoul, which made it seem I'd always known him. It dawned on me then that he must have been 6-foot-4. My mother, aunt, great-aunt, and grandfather are all over six feet tall, and they all have the same bone structure: large, even features, square jaws, and naturally curly hair, although Raoul's was receding.

He patted the arm of his chair and I perched on it as we looked at the black and white snapshots. In one, my mother was standing in front of a French country house. About my age, she wore jodhpurs and a white shirt and held a riding crop, her golden hair catching the light. Her body's stance said, "Ta-da, here I am!" My mother was quite shy even though she was beautiful. Another showed her standing next to my father, who wore a beret and held a small white dog. They looked so dapper in Bohemian 1930s outfits.

"This was taken in the garden off rue Notre Dames des Champs, where they lived," he said. I figured it must have been taken in 1931 or '32, just before my older brother, Turo, was born.

"We liked Arthur very much," said Raoul. He had actually known my beloved father! This cemented our bond.

Suddenly, we heard the front door opening and closing, followed by high heels clicking on the parquet. A heavy male footstep followed. A high-pitched voice rang out. *"Cheri, nous sommes ici finalement!"* Chantal, a large, pregnant, dark-haired woman wearing bright red lipstick and lacquered nails swept in and planted a kiss on Mimi's cheek, then on Raoul's, and finally on mine. Guy, who looked like a younger version of his father, carried two armfuls of packages and crossed the living room to shake my hand.

"Hello, Constance. Nice to meet you. Sorry we're late. We lost the time."

He sat on a sofa and dropped the bundles onto the carpet. Chantal plopped next to him and began to speak in rapid-fire French while pulling items from the packages, holding them up and passing them to Mimi. This must be a first grandchild. Mimi's eyes lighted up as Chantal, like a magician, reached into a bag and pulled out an adorable yellow and white outfit, then a crib blanket with embroidery, then a baby's hat, a tiny sweater and soft white booties.

"Here, Consie." Chantal handed me the hat and tiny sweater. I felt like a giant holding such small articles of clothing. All the packages were now empty and their contents proudly displayed on laps, the tips of chairs, and sofas. Chantal's English was minimal, but her warmth needed no translation.

Raoul picked up the telephone and dialed. I heard a short exchange in French and deduced that Arnaud was on his way, so I began polite rounds of thank-yous and goodbyes. Ten minutes later when the doorbell buzzed, I kissed everyone on each cheek and took the stairs down, a safer alternative to the antique elevator. Arnaud was waiting outside, smoking a cigarette. He opened the passenger door of the Renault. He was so quiet during the ride to the hotel that I thought I might have inconvenienced him and said so.

"No, no, it's quite all right," he replied. We fell silent again. I was longing for the same closeness we had on the *quai* earlier. Although polite, he appeared to be in a hurry. As he maneuvered through Paris intersections, crossed bridges, and finally arrived in front of my hotel, I didn't think I could verbalize my confused feelings. Why had he given me a book of poems and kissed me earlier? Had his feelings changed in the space of a few hours? I was learning that interesting men are not so easily understood. On the sidewalk where Arnaud deposited me, I placed my hand on his shoulder and thanked him.

"It was my pleasure," he said. I waved as he drove away.

Only later, alone in my room, did I acknowledge that Arnaud had brushed me off. Still, the beautiful book I held was tangible evidence that I hadn't imagined his tenderness or the wonderful feelings he evoked in me.

On Sunday morning, Dr. Wasserman called early. He and my mother had had a long telephone conversation. I found him in the hotel dining room moments later. I'd been so busy with relatives I never knew existed that I'd almost forgotten about the tour group.

Dr. Wasserman and I sat at a small table with coffee, baguettes, butter, and jam.

"Your Uncle Raoul called Hope to say they would love to have you stay with them for a year," he said. "You could have the spare bedroom in their flat. Your mother wants to leave it up to you." In case I decided to come home, she wanted to confirm our return flight schedules.

I was stunned. A whole year in Paris? How could I resist? Who wouldn't jump at the chance?

⟫2⟪

It was August that I became ensconced in the smaller of the two guest bedrooms in Raoul and Mimi's flat. The cozy room had a single bed with a bedside table, a tall carved-wooden armoire, a writing desk and lamp, a comfortable chair, and my own small balcony over rue Charles-Lamoureux. The routine I settled into included a breakfast tray brought by Julie, with coffee, a slice of baguette, butter, and jam. Lunch was a sit-down meal in the dining room, at which Raoul presided before departing again for the office. Dinner was always more casual, featuring lighter fare. After dinner we might play cards, talk about the news of the day, or entertain Aunt Constance or friends. We might read or study before heading to our bedrooms to sleep. Julie made my bed every day, and each evening she turned down the bed linens and placed my pajamas on top. My dirty clothes disappeared and reappeared clean and folded. I had only what I packed for the six-week trip, but I'd written and asked my mother to send sweaters, jeans, and shoes. I was expecting a footlocker to arrive any day, and I was enjoying being spoiled.

August in Paris apparently is a Paris without Parisians. They all seemed to be on holiday. The city was filled with camera-slung, shorts-clad, plaid-shirted, middle-aged, mostly American but also some German tourists, the latter identifiable by their athletic sandals. They were everywhere.

Otherwise it was a sort of lazy settling-in period for Raoul, Mimi, and me. August also brought the couture showings in Paris for the fall season. Paris couturiers still set fashion trends, and these were reported by editors and sent by wire service to magazine headquarters and fashion centers around the world.

One Wednesday, Mimi announced she was going to the Pierre Cardin show in the afternoon and invited me. We arrived at Pierre Cardin's on the Faubourg St. Honore via taxi for a 3 p.m. show. Mimi presented her invitation inside the door, and we were seated in the front row and given a program. My goodness, I thought, Mimi's invitation to sit in the first row means she's a VIP. Mimi chatted with a few ladies already seated and then whispered in my ear, "Pierre Cardin is very young and his specialty is suits."

I hoped I was invisible in my ordinary cotton print dress and scruffy sandals. Mimi must have been somewhat embarrassed to be escorting me. I noted a couple of photographers with flash cameras and others in the back rows with pen and pad poised who must have been reporters or fashion editors of women's magazines.

The show opened with a tall dark-haired model wearing a bright orange wool jersey blouse tucked into slim, tapered tweed slacks. Other models rapidly appeared, one after the other, strutting, their hips thrust forward. They wore combinations of suit jackets with billowy backs and varied collars, most of which were closely fitted in front without pinching the waist. Skirts had big release box pleats in front, and some had small pleats on the sides. I loved these feminine and wearable ensembles. The last model wore a violet velvet suit trimmed with mink, leading a white Russian wolfhound on a leash. I imagined the dog suddenly marking its territory on the runway and stifled the urge to laugh. Flashbulbs created a dizzying strobe effect while a muffled round of applause from gloved hands demurely signaled the end of the show.

During the taxi ride home, I thanked Aunt Mimi for inviting me. "The clothes are so beautiful, Aunt Mimi. Are they very expensive?"

Mimi nodded and told me we only went to the Cardin show for fun; she would never buy anything there. "He's too, too *je ne sais quoi.*" She circled one gloved hand as if it could pluck the desired word from the air, "*nouveau.*"

The next day we were off to see the Christian Dior collection. To my relief, we didn't have front-row seats, and I relaxed behind two rows of attendees.

The audience around me gasped as the models appeared. Flat-chested as little girls, they paraded in loose-fitting sheaths or tube-like columns with narrow-shouldered bodices, some with belts slung around the hips. The bosom was out and the flat look was in. With my curves, I could never fit into one of those tubes and didn't think I wanted to.

In juxtaposition with the austere sheaths were a group of circus-girl dresses, all beaded or pleated of soft pink tulle below long torso tops and quite short skirts. The crowd loved this group, oohing and aahing, indicating that this was an important collection, but I couldn't figure out why.

The previous day's Pierre Cardin collection was exciting, but this one was disappointing. Who would want to wear a circus-girl dress anyway?

14

Maybe a midget, not me. The worst part was the realization that I could never hope to be fashionable without the wherewithal to buy a single outfit. I expressed this as diplomatically as I could to Mimi, who explained, "French women are very, very clever at finding a seamstress who copies an original, or a figure-flattering chic style. You must learn to do this, too."

One rainy afternoon during the latter half of August, we left to spend the weekend at Maucreux, Raoul and Mimi's château. An hour from Paris, we turned off the main highway onto a one-lane dirt road that soon arrived in the middle of a barnyard. Here we stopped to collect eggs, butter, and milk from a ruddy-cheeked woman wearing a yellow rain slicker and muddy boots. We continued about a half-mile along the rutted, mud-filled lane up a hill to the château. Maucreux, a two-story building of white lime-stone, sat on a slight rise surrounded by farmland and forests. Its courtyard was covered with fine gravel lined with boxwood hedges that framed a low retaining wall, beyond which lay fields and forests.

Inside the entry hall we removed our raincoats and handed them to a smallish man named Gérôme.

"Bon après midi, Madame la Comtesse, Monsieur le Comte, Mademoiselle."

On the wall adjacent to a sweeping staircase hung a tapestry at least two stories tall, and to the right was a large salon. Taking our things upstairs we proceeded down a hallway with rooms on either side. Mimi opened the door to one and said, "This is the blue room." She opened the door to the next. "This is the yellow room." The walls of both rooms were covered in a French toile fabric with matching curtains and bedspreads. Finding the yellow room cheerful, I plunked my duffle on the bed.

"Why do you have this big house?" I asked Mimi.

"We love to come on weekends. Once a year we have a hunt," she said.

I wondered what in the world Raoul, Mimi, and I would do during the next twenty-four hours in the middle of nowhere. I decided to investigate the grounds and then soak in a hot bath before dinner.

Although damp, the walk was invigorating, and the air was filled with that particular smell of wet boxwood, hay, and grass. I saw that much of the land surrounding the château was cultivated.

While meandering, I revisited how I had come to be here on a yearlong visit. Ever since my father died in 1946 when I was ten, I'd felt at sea, without anchor. My mind flashed back to our family's relocation from the East Coast to the West Coast in 1947 just after Dad's funeral. I didn't realize that my parents were separated at the time of my father's death, because the World War II years and separation from Dad were synonymous.

He died suddenly, accidentally in Tucson, Arizona, and my mother married George Wheelwright, a Navy commander, that same year. He and his two kids, Mike and George, moved in with us. From there we all moved to Green Gulch Ranch, in northern California, just ten miles north of the Golden Gate Bridge. Little did I know then that this 860-acre ranch would become famous.

I remembered my first day in fifth grade at Dominican, my new Catholic school twelve miles from home. I wore my new blue and white check uniform and saddle shoes. My mother drove that day. Eventually she joined a carpool, often complaining about the long commute.

One afternoon that first week, realizing I'd missed the carpool or it had missed me, I took a taxi home, proud that I remembered how to direct the cab twelve miles back. When I ran inside to get money for the driver, Turo and Georgie laughed with glee as my stepfather asked incredulously, "You took *a taxi* home?"

When he went to pay the taxi driver, my brothers snickered and made me feel I'd done a stupid thing that cost a small fortune. I was only eleven years old. How was I supposed to get home?

That night I cried myself to sleep, missing Dorothy, my beloved nanny, whom we'd left behind in Connecticut. She wouldn't have let them get away with saying mean things about me. I could hear her thick Welsh accent shaming the boys, "Who gives you two the right to judge yur little sister? Sounds to me like yur desperately tryin' to elevate yur own importance. So mind yur P's and Q's!"

But she wasn't there. The visceral impact of having lost Dot created what felt like a giant empty hole in my middle as I rocked back and forth on the bed, crying for the two people I loved the most, Dot and Dad.

I wiped away new tears before noticing I'd wandered into an old apple orchard, whose rotten fruit was scattered underneath dripping boughs. Fermenting smells drifted up from the soggy ground. I noticed a dryish-looking boulder under some branches of an old tree and sat down, wondering what would happen to me now while also remembering the next painful occurrence I experienced in California.

I was sent to board at Miss Branson's School for Girls, an exclusive day and boarding school in Marin County. If I hadn't been sent there as punishment, I might have liked it or even excelled. Since that was not the case, I smoked anything I could find to propel my exodus and succeeded.

The reason I was sent there in the first place was an innocent gesture on my part that my parents interpreted as a product of cunning and lying. On Easter Sunday I had refused to join the family at church, preferring to go for a horseback ride. The memory was so clear and real that I could almost smell the sagebrush and eucalyptus and feel the sun on my shoulders as I cinched up the saddle around Nimba's girth. We headed up the narrow canyon trail to where it joined the fire road at the top of the gulch. There the trail met Highway 1 before turning into a fire road south, meandering its way along the southerly rim of our hills. Spectacular views of San Francisco Bay and the top of the Golden Gate Bridge peeked through rounded green hills. That time of year was my favorite. Blue lupine and California poppies dotted the soft green of sagebrush and bright green grass. The air was crisp with the scent of California laurel.

Just as Nimba and I reached the junction of Highway 1 and the fire road, an old Ford with John, an Army guy I knew from hanging out with kids at Muir Beach, was heading west to the beach. I hollered and waved until John pulled over to the shoulder.

"Want to meet my horse?" I shouted.

I showed him how to let her sniff his hand and how to stroke her neck and talk real quiet, no jerky movements. He was just getting the gist of it when a car pulled over behind John's. My stepfather stormed from behind the wheel, shouting at the top of his lungs. He grabbed the reins and ordered me to dismount, shouting at John to leave, adding, "This isn't the last you'll hear from me!"

John hunched his shoulders forward and made fast for his car.

"You can't be trusted to ride home," he said, mounting my horse and sending me to the car, where my mother had gotten behind the wheel. I felt shamed, and didn't understand what I had done wrong.

The next day, outraged at the unfairness, I was delivered to Miss Branson's School as a boarder.

In retrospect, I realized that I was sent there because I was a girl who matured early and they were afraid of any boys who showed a non-scholastic interest in me. One had made a model airplane with my name across the four-foot wingspan; another gave me a pretty dresser set with a comb, a brush, and a mirror.

"You can't accept expensive gifts from boys," my mother told me, making me give them back.

After being expelled from Miss Branson's, I was shuffled around. First to the Santa Cruz Valley School in Tumacaccori, Arizona. Then Stevens College in Colombia, Missouri. Finally to San Jose State College in San Jose, California, where I got all A's in the fall semester. Spring semester, when I discovered surfing and parties, my GPA dropped to C.

Then I met Steve, an older architecture student in a drawing class, and I latched on to him for dear life. Nice and protective, he made me feel safe, something I hadn't felt since we moved from the East Coast to California. Missing Steve when classes ended, I told my mother I wanted to marry him. She immediately arranged for me to go to Europe on a group tour led by their friend, Dr. Wassermann. Within two weeks I had a passport and a ticket.

Noticing that the drizzle had lifted but left a low blanket of fog along the ground, I got up from my hard perch and retraced my steps from the orchard to the château and a hot bath.

After dinner Mimi, Raoul, and I retired to the salon, where a cozy fire cast flickering shadows around the room, rendering it more intimate. Gérôme served brandy and coffee. I took brandy only. Raoul began to talk about the years during the German occupation of Paris, which led to a harrowing story of his and Mimi's arrests by five members of the Gestapo one morning at rue Charles Lamoureaux in the fall of 1943.

"I had been part of an elite French underground unit under the command of Mr. Balleshofsky, a Russian by birth and a French citizen trained in military intelligence." He swirled the cognac around his glass and took a sip. "Two American fliers claimed they had parachuted from a doomed aircraft three days prior. When a farmer discovered them hiding in his barn, he spoke to them without revealing whether he would or could help them. He needed to speak to a local magistrate."

At this point Mimi got up to go to bed, while Raoul was on fire to continue. He began pacing back and forth in front of me, pausing from time to time to take sips from his cognac snifter.

He explained how he was chosen to conduct the interrogation because of his nearly perfect American English.

"If anyone could detect an impostor, I could. We brought the men to a local church at night under a cloak of secrecy and separated them."

"And then what?"

"All day long, I questioned each one—they were separate, far enough away that they couldn't hear me question the other."

Raoul asked the separated men the same questions. What had they eaten for breakfast the day their flight left, for lunch, the evening before? Where was their unit stationed? What U.S. city or town did they hail from? As the day wore on, they were asked progressively more detailed questions. Their stories jibed.

"We were convinced they were American fighter pilots."

"They were, weren't they?"

His lips curled cryptically before he continued.

"Our French underground unit arranged a 'pickup.' On a specific night at such and such location with only flashlights outlining a landing strip, an allied aircraft would pick them up and fly them out of France." Raoul stopped pacing and looked straight at me, hands clasped behind his back. "My final task was to make certain the fliers were at the right spot at the right time. Everything went smoothly. The plane landed. The men boarded, and the plane took off. Two days later Mimi and I were awakened with the muzzle of a gun against our faces and shouts in German. 'Wacht auf!.' After we threw on some clothes, they took us in separate cars to *Fresnes* prison, where we were separated. Thank God Mimi didn't know anything about my resistance activities."

"What happened then?" I gasped.

Mimi spent two and a half months in a cell with three other women while Raoul was interrogated and eventually convicted, he said. "We were loaded into a cattle-car train—standing room only. Jews, POWs, civilians. No food, no toilet stops. In other words, you shat where you stood. The train stopped every now and then in the middle of nowhere. The dead were off-loaded, and we were given water; then the train proceeded. After more than three days, the train arrived at Buchenwald, near Weimar, Germany.

"We were housed in barracks with a capo, usually a common criminal, sometimes a Jew, who lived at one end of the barrack. Capos were successful at surviving. We had to sew our number on the jacket and a little triangle, according to classification. Green for criminals, blue for murderers, red for political—mine was red—pink for homosexuals, and yellow for the lowest, the Jews. Beds were stacked, two to each bed."

"It sounds horrible," I said.

"The only thing worse was to be shot."

Raoul managed to keep alive in the camp, he said, by playing politics with the Jewish capo who ran the day-to-day operations inside his block. By getting on this person's good side, he was assigned the duty of harvesting cabbages, not shoveling corpses into a pit. If he had been assigned the latter job, he risked being shot and dumped into the pit along with the corpses. The Germans killed witnesses.

"I learned how to slice a loaf of bread with a spoon. Can you believe that?"

"How in the world?"

Raoul made slicing motions with his right thumb and forefinger on an imaginary loaf of bread. "When you're starving, you invent. Thin slices last longer."

Tears began streaming down my cheeks.

"We ate so much cabbage that now, any time I smell it, I gag. Today, August 27, is the tenth anniversary of the liberation of Paris, with a big parade from the Étoile down the Champs-Élysées to the Place de la Concorde. The Garde Republicaine, veterans of the Resistance groups, soldiers, American and British detachments all march in remembrance of ten years ago when General Charles de Gaulle, surrounded by Resistance leaders, also walked down the Champs-Élysées of liberated Paris."

"Were you there?" I asked.

"No. I was still in Buchenwald. We hadn't been freed."

When Allied forces liberated Buchenwald, 6-foot-4 Raoul weighed only 93 pounds.

As we both climbed the stairs to our bedrooms, I didn't feel I could express my horror and sorrow at what he had endured. Speechless, I hugged him good night on the landing. He passed a thumb over my wet cheek and muttered, "Good night, *ma petite*."

Had I at long last found another father?

3

September arrived. In the *New York Herald Tribune, Paris Edition,* I read that Hurricane Dolly had slammed the East Coast. Hearing news about home made me feel less of an expatriate even if that news was about the East Coast.

This was a busy time for me. I had to enroll in French classes and learn how to get from where I lived in the sixteenth *arrondisement* to the Left Bank. The footlocker with my clothes arrived, and it was wonderful to see my faded Levis, worn pajamas, and sweaters and smell my leather cowboy boots. Mimi was less than thrilled. While I was out one morning, she had Julie dispose of the Levis and other offending clothing. When I discovered what she had done, I was shocked, feeling *I* had been discarded.

"Not at all appropriate for a young lady. *Pas une jupe, mon Dieu!*" Mimi cried.

No skirt? I haven't worn one in two years. That night I wrote my mother, emotions exploding over the pages.

> "Mimi had the maid throw out most of the clothes you sent. All she cares about is how you look, not what you're like inside."

I pleaded to come home, signing it "Tearfully, your loving daughter."

The next day Mimi took me to Bon Marché, a large two-story department store, to find "one black-tie dress, one *jupe*, two pair of shoes, and one day dress." Aunt Constance's chauffeur drove us.

The salesgirl, who brought out a large assortment of cocktail dresses, was Mimi's regular personal shopper. The most becoming dress was a dark blue and black jacquard velvet décolleté with a fitted bodice and a flared skirt, an inverted pleat and a crinoline underskirt. As I slipped it over my head and felt its weight slide over my hips and hug my waist and breasts,

I felt transformed. Small jacquard bows topped the shoulder straps. I felt beautiful. Mimi ordered it. Next we went to the casual-clothes section. The skirt we chose was a midcalf length A-lined gray tweed wool. The "day" dress was chocolate wool jersey with long sleeves, a contrasting black collar and cuffs, and a soft gathered skirt. On the street level in the shoe department, we selected a pair of dressy pumps and a pair of black walking shoes. At home I spread the new clothes on my bed and tried them all on again and admired myself, feeling like an emerging butterfly.

Raoul instructed me how to take the Metro from Trocadero to Raspail, where the Alliance Française language school was located. All I had to do was get myself there, give them a check, which Mimi handed me, and begin my first day of French classes. "You will make lots and lots of friends," she chimed.

Paris was experiencing a heat wave, so I wore my lightest summer dress and a backpack. Clutching a Paris map, I marched off, turned right on rue de Pomereu and then left on rue de Longchamp to Avenue D'Eylau, which ran into the Place du Trocadero. Paris is deceiving. Much of it is laid out in star shapes with streets shooting off from rotaries. It's not at all like New York or San Francisco, whose streets and avenues are laid out in perpendicular rows and numbered accordingly.

My walk was about seven long blocks, roughly fifteen minutes at a fast clip. Downstairs in the Metro, I double-checked my destination by using the Metro map aid on the wall. You depressed a button over the desired destination and the appropriate route lighted up, indicating which train to take. I depressed the button over "Raspail." The Orange Line lighted up, with the final destination "Nation." I paid my token and waited for a train marked "Nation." I'd memorized our phone number in case I got lost: *Passy soisante huite, soisante neuf.*

Several trains arrived and left before one marked "Nation" came and I got on. With only five other people, I easily found a seat. I'd memorized that I must get off on the tenth stop. Cooler underground than outside, there was a warm wind generated by the train's speed through the tunnels. By the time we reached Raspail, people were standing in the aisles. I detrained and climbed a long flight of stairs to the boulevard.

In no time I found the school's entry on the side of a building with a large sign that read "Alliance Française." Many students were milling in the hallways. I made my way to the cashier's booth.

"Good morning. I'm here for French classes."

"*Bonjour, Mademoiselle*," the lady behind the glass window said. I didn't understand one other thing she said. She handed me a form to fill out. Name, address, telephone number, nationality.

When I handed her the completed form with the check, she stamped it and gave me a receipt. Then she pointed toward a room down the hall where students were entering. I followed and sat at the back. A middle-aged woman with jet-black hair introduced herself as Mme. du Charme. "*Je parle Francaise seulement,*" she told us. She spoke slowly and repeated everything, gesturing. Somehow I understood what she said or thought I did. She asked the class to guess how many native languages were represented. One look around the room confirmed that there were many. Mme. du Charme walked to a large world map unfurled in front of the blackboard. Each time a person said his nationality, she pointed to that country on the map and called out the French name of that country. We were a little United Nations. I was the only American.

At the end of two hours, we were given a book, instructed which pages to read by tomorrow, and dismissed for the day. Too shy to speak to anyone, I made my way back to the Metro and retraced the route I took that morning.

I arrived home just after noon in time for lunch, having taken what amounted to a first small but important first step for this former cowgirl! The rest of the week passed more or less the same way.

I was learning to pronounce the food Julie served.

"Would you like *coquille meunière* or *filet de sole*?" asked Mimi as she planned the day's menu. Would I prefer *a tête de veau* or *coq au vin* tomorrow? For dessert, do I prefer *pêche Melba, fruit compote,* or *tarte maison*?

Raoul had become a terrible tease, calling me his *petit bête,* "his little beast." His idea of educating me was to have me learn the Seven Wonders of the World and the twelve labors of Hercules and to recite them. He loved to march into my room each morning, open the metal shutters over the full-length windows, and shout, "*Ma bête,* name me just three of the seven wonders!"

"Ah, the Pyramids, the Hanging Gardens of Babylon, and the Temple of Zeus." It was almost automatic.

"And where is the Temple of Zeus?"

"Is it in Olympia?"

"Yes. Very good, very good." And he left to shower and dress while I sneaked another few winks.

Arnaud telephoned to invite me to a picnic that Saturday at the Faures' country house, La Chartre. He would pick me up at around ten. He asked me to wear what I wore the day we first met. I thought I'd worn a pair of hot pink pedal pushers with a matching top that were the rage in California and that Mimi hadn't found and discarded. The tight-fitting pants stopped midcalf. I asked if that's what he remembered.

"*Oui, oui. Délicieux!*"

The thought of seeing Arnaud again delighted me, and a picnic sounded informal and fun. My family often had picnics at the beach near our ranch; even though it meant getting smoke in your eyes and sand in your food, they were always memorable.

Saturday was a beautifully warm day, and we drove with the windows down, singing at the top of our lungs. He taught me all the words to *La Marseillaise*, and I taught him *Home on the Range*.

Upon arriving I noticed a shady lawn and a long linen-covered table on which were bottles of wine, platters of food with silver covers, plates, and cutlery. Strolling about were elegantly dressed ladies in high heels and gentlemen in jackets and ties nibbling hors-d'oeuvres and sipping wine. I felt totally out of place in my attire.

Arnaud left me at the edge of the lawn and trotted off to greet the assembled guests. Heads turned in my direction and I heard laughter. Were they laughing at me? I wanted to evaporate but seemed cemented in place, unable to move for what seemed an elastic time warp. Then I abruptly turned as if I'd forgotten something and walked toward the car. Once out of view, I detoured down the driveway to the other side of the house. There I stumbled into a walled flower garden where I took refuge among rows of gladiolas and roses. What a fool I was! Did Arnaud deliberately get me to wear these ridiculous clothes so I'd be the laughingstock, to provide amusement? My California provincialism was for their amusement. Picnic? If this was a picnic, I was the Empress of Russia. I was so angry that my face felt as if it had been hot-washed in nettles. I hated him!

"Constance," I heard Arnaud call. "Con*stance*." Louder now. Arnaud's head appeared in the doorway of the garden wall. "What are you doing here?"

"I have a headache."

"Everyone wants to meet you. Please come."

"No!"

He approached me. "*Pourquoi, ma petite cousine?*"

"Don't call me that! You rat! I hate you. Go away." I grasped a clump of dirt and hurled it in his direction.

He extended both arms, palms upturned, scrunched his shoulders to his ears, turned, and left.

Fueled by adrenaline, I decided to join the proceedings on the lawn for long enough to get myself a plate of food, a glass of wine, a napkin, a fork, and a knife. Then I sat under a tree on the grass without speaking to a single soul.

On the way home, I didn't say a word to Arnaud, who chain-smoked all the way. In front of *my building* he said, "*Il faut avoir confiance en moi, Constance.*" I'm supposed to *trust* him? Fat chance!

I eyed him coldly, turned, and entered the lobby.

A routine developed over the weeks, with French classes each morning and sightseeing or exploring in the afternoons. Dinner was always at rue Charles-Lamoureux, and occasionally in the evening we went to the opera, a concert or a film.

I met another uncle, Raoul's younger brother, François, and his wife, Laetitia, who lived a floor below us. Considering herself a princess, Laetitia thought she married beneath her because François was only a count. Raoul teased her mercilessly about the nouveau title bestowed on her family by Napoleon in honor of General Joachim Murat, Laetitia's great-uncle. Laetitia had an original royal saddle blanket with embroidered Napoleonic gold bees casually draped across her Empire sofa. Whenever Raoul visited, he flicked at the bees, calling them "damn flies." Laetitia, wise to the bait, just laughed.

Laetitia had a younger brother, Napo, short for Napoleon, a prince and man about town. It was decided that Napo should take me out for an evening to expose me to customs and manners befitting gentlemen and ladies. The day before this arranged date, I was a nervous wreck about what to wear. Mimi said to wear "*mon aprez midi dress—le chocolat—avec le* dressy shoe."

The doorbell rang. Julie opened the door and Napo, a heavy-set older man in his thirties with black hair and a moustache, walked in. He gave Mimi the obligatory French peck on both cheeks, hugged Raoul, and took my hand.

"*Enchanté*," he murmured.

In his car he asked where I'd like to dine.

"I don't care."

"*Alors,* I know a place with good beef steak."

"Oh, I love steak."

"Tell me, Constance, what do you do here? In Paris?"

I explained that I was taking French at the Alliance Francaise and that I'd learned to navigate the Metro, which took forty-five minutes each way. I told him I thought Paris was very beautiful. Thank goodness we arrived before I ran out of things to say.

The restaurant was tiny, with a sign over the marquee that read "Napoleon's." Napo escorted me by the arm and led me to a small cloth-covered table near a window. I was dying to ask if the restaurant's owner knew who he was, but I didn't want to appear unsophisticated. He was named after Napoleon Bonaparte, but that's all I knew. Napo ordered snails and steak and a bottle of wine. I ordered steak.

"*Alors,* Constance, and what will you do then?"

"When?"

"*En générale.* Do you plan to study law? Medicine?"

"I'm not sure. I haven't really thought about it."

"Ah-ha."

"And you, Napo, what do you do?"

"*Moi?* I manage affairs, family affairs. We have property here."

Thank goodness the waiter brought bread and wine, so his attention momentarily shifted.

"Constance, do you enjoy history?"

"I'm afraid I don't know very much."

"I see. I see. *Savez-vous que Napoleon* was important? *Par example,* he created the Legion of Honor, the Bank of France, and he changed the stupid French laws. *Il y a quelque chose* called *le Code Napoleon.* Modern law, it comes from *le Code Napoleon. Savez-vous?*"

Do I know this? How would I know? If he was trying to make me feel inferior, he was succeeding.

The snails arrived, twelve in an oval dish covered in parsley and butter. Napo deftly handled a small snail holder and quickly devoured five of them, motioning for me to try one.

"Where was I?" he continued.

"Modern law."

"*Oui. Oui.* Law. He was brilliant. He had defeat—how you say?— because of the rain. Only that *je suis sûr.*"

"I don't understand."

"I bore you, *pardonnez-moi.*"

Shaking my head in disagreement, I was glad that our dinner arrived at that point and the waiter filled our wine glasses. Looking back, I wonder at my naivete at that age. I might have voiced what I really thought: The boring conversation, mostly about Napoleon, who was dead and buried, was making me want to scream. However, my polite façade prevailed.

The steak was delicious, as were the fried potatoes, and the Bordeaux offered a perfect counterbalance to the steak.

"Thank you for inviting me. It's delicious."

"*Pas du tout, pas du tout. Mon plaisir.*"

Napo ordered fruit tarts and coffee. We enjoyed these in relative silence, paid our bill, and left.

On the way home, Napo drove past Les Invalides to point out where Napoleon was buried under the dome. I made a promise to visit Les Invalides one day soon, and then we arrived back at rue Charles-Lamoureux. Napo escorted me into the elevator and into the flat. He and Raoul stepped into Raoul's study and closed the door. I heard Napo say in French, "You can't have a conversation with her. You can't sleep with her. What are you going to do with her?"

I crept to my room in humiliation.

⇒4⇐

The day was cold and gray. The walk from rue Charles-Lamoureux to the Trocadero chilled me that morning. My book bag was slung across my left shoulder. Not owning gloves, I jammed my hands deep into the coat pockets as near to the warmth of my body as possible and tried to keep the bag from slipping off my shoulder. The ash trees along the small streets and the larger boulevard had been pollarded, as I assumed they were each fall. They now appeared to be a mutated species with bulbous, sideways growth.

Fall had definitely left Paris. Happy, cheerful faces disappeared, too. Passersby kept their eyes on the sidewalk in front of them or stared over my head. The Faure household on Avenue Victor Hugo retreated into a self-contained entity, into which I was rarely invited. Arnaud no longer addressed me in anything but a condescending manner when our paths did cross.

Aunt Mimi made small talk, but the vapid conversation was depressing: What hat to wear with what dress? What a terrible cook so-and-so had hired. How silly the crossword puzzle was today. Even Julia, the maid, was dismissing. What once seemed the dream of a lifetime was now just lonely. Uncle Raoul was suddenly the only bright, funny spot in my life. I would be cautious from now on about any further attempts to turn me into a French lady. I would concentrate on learning French and rejoining my family, whom I suddenly realized I missed horribly.

I hurried toward the warmth of the Metro, hoping to find Frances. Frances Wister, an American girl from New Jersey, had just signed up at the Alliance the week before. She also lived with a French family in the Sixteenth Arrondisement, which was why we both took the same route each morning.

Greeting me as I descended into the Métro was a tsunami of hot air against my downward momentum. Frances stood on the platform below.

"I need to buy a winter coat, but I don't know where. Do you?" she said.

"Mimi does. I'll ask her."

The train marked "Nation" squealed to a stop. Its pneumatic doors slid open and we got on.

"I'm supposed to meet a friend of my brother's after class. Do you want to come?"

"Sure. Who?"

"Alan Sedgwick. He and Billy went to Andover. Alan's in an intern program."

The train inched forward and suddenly picked up speed as it rumbled through the tunnel toward Passy, then to Bir-Hakeim. I'd memorized all the stops between Trocadero and Raspail.

"Frances, I've come to the conclusion my relatives live in the past."

"Oh?"

I told her about the dreadful dinner date with Prince Napo, how he thought that because I couldn't carry on an intelligent conversation and since he couldn't sleep with me, what was he supposed to do? How gauche. Frances thought it was funny.

"Don't you realize the French think everything French is superior? Next on their list is sex. A French woman is supposed to be well versed in culture, art and history. She is also supposed to be a virgin before she marries. After that she can do whatever she wants. What did he look like anyway?"

"Swarthy. Five o'clock shadow."

"Pompous?"

"Yes. Loves to hear himself talk."

We burst out laughing. Then, somberly, Frances said, "My living situation is so different. It's sad really. Mme Pucheu—I have a room in their house—is the widow of Pierre Pucheu, who was executed after World War II."

"Executed?"

Frances nodded. "He was high up in the Vichy government during the Occupation. Apparently he gave the Germans some French hostages. Mme Pucheu thinks he didn't have a choice, that he was forced to pick them. They executed him anyway. It's all rather depressing. Madame has no friends to speak of, and I think she depends on the money from my room and board."

"How awful. You'll have to come around *chez moi*. Raoul and Mimi are superficial, but it's not depressing, and the food is good."

Our stop was next. We agreed to meet after class.

I telephoned home to say I wouldn't be there for *le déjeuner* today. Julie, who answered the telephone, sounded curious to know why, but her station in life prevented her from asking.

We walked down Boulevard Raspail, cut across the Luxembourg Gardens, and made our way to the Café Tournon. Frances waved at a gentleman behind the glass enclosure, who stood. Inside, he embraced Frances.

Alan had an intense, somewhat fleshy face with penetrating eyes. He was dressed in a buttoned-down white oxford shirt, a narrow nondescript tie and a Harris Tweed jacket. His camel overcoat lay over a chair. I noticed Lucky Strikes on the table.

"Alan, this is Constance. She's spending a year in Paris with her uncle and aunt."

We shook hands.

"We last saw each other two summers ago in Dark Harbor, wasn't it?" Frances asked him.

"Yup," Alan answered. "Billy and I took your dad's boat down to the Cape and back. He didn't come on that cruise."

"That's because it was the summer Mom was diagnosed."

"Right. Sorry. How is she?"

"Okay, in remission. You're never cured, you know."

Alan kept glancing out the window to the street. "I'm expecting a friend—another American. I met him at La Rose Rouge, where Juliette Greco sings. He's lonely, a regular guy. Ah, that's him now."

Alan waved at a dark-haired man wearing wrinkled trousers, an oversize sweater, and a dark blue scarf that hid most of his face.

Julian unwound the long scarf, revealing shoulder-length black hair. He had an angular face with high cheekbones, deep-set eyes and full lips that broadened into a wide smile.

"Julian, meet Frances and Constance. What'll you have? Milk?"

Shaking his head, Julian said, "A beer."

While Julian shook hands, Alan motioned to the waiter and turned to the women, explaining, "Mendés-France is promoting milk. He claims 16,000 people die each year from cirrhosis of the liver. He thinks he can get the French to give up wine and drink milk, pandering to his own constituency, Normandy, the cow district."

"Not to mention that wine is France's best product and export. The whole thing is retarded," concluded Julian.

"Jules, you seem a bit frazzled. What's up?"

"Finances. Every month. *Pas un sou.*"

I asked, "Isn't it exciting to be on your own?"

"*Au contraire.* I'm dependent on my father's check each month and barely get by."

"That's pretty independent, compared to my situation," I said.

Julian smiled. "Want to trade? Some days cat food looks pretty good."

Frances listened without saying a word, but her eyes took everything in. I thought about our different realities. Julian ran out of money even though his father supported him. Frances lived with the poor widow of an executed WWII collaborator who needed her rent money. Although on one hand I felt secure at Raoul and Mimi's, on the other I felt alienated by their materialistic values.

Drifting back to the present, I heard Alan and Julian discussing French politics.

". . . apathetic. They thought the end of occupation would bring a new prosperity. Instead, it brought disillusionment, unemployment, and a long war in Indochina," Alan said.

"Tell me! I feel guilty by association—being an American and part of a grand conspiracy called the Marshall Plan to take control of Europe. Can you believe such rubbish?"

"I can. Mendes-France is doing the right things, but he's not popular enough. They'll cross him in the assembly."

"Maybe not."

"He knows France can't afford its colonies. France has wasted 80 percent of its aid on Indochina, for Chrissake. What about all who have died there?"

"Close to 100,000."

"Dienbienphu was a disaster!"

Alan looked at Frances, then me. "Ladies, are we boring you?"

Frances shook her head. "It's interesting—confusing, too."

"Yes, confusing," I said, meaning I wished I understood what they were talking about. "Life in the Sixteenth Arrondisement is life in a cocoon. No one talks about these things."

"What do they talk about?" asked Julian.

"My uncle is smart and fun. He works at the Bourse. But Mimi and her friends—all they talk about is what's important to *Le Monde*—who so-and-so hired to be the cook, what big shindig so-and-so was attending."

"*Le Monde?*" Alan said.

"My uncle's a count who can trace his lineage to 800 A.D. He doesn't take it seriously, because he teases his sister-in-law, a princess, a *nouveau-riche* one."

Our discussion turned to lighter fare, such as current films they'd seen and the jazz at the club Rose Rouge. Alan asked for the bill and paid and we agreed to meet again soon.

Walking to the Métro, I was aware of how little I understood politics, economics, and other worldly things. This was what Napo must have meant. Perhaps Mark had found me dull, too. I was glad to have met some intelligent Americans in Paris. Maybe if I spent time with them, I'd absorb something.

⇒ 5 ⇐

It was 2 p.m. when I got home, and my stomach was grumbling. The concierge waved envelopes from behind the glass door.

"*Pour vous, Mademoiselle.*" She handed me two letters. One was a light blue square envelope with Mark's straight-up-and-down handwriting. The other was airmail from my mother. I sat on the carpeted stairs and tore open Mark's, which bore a Buckinghamshire stamp mark.

> My dear fluffy American,
>
> I trust you are happily ensconced with your relatives. Are you learning French? I confess I hope they will not turn you into a French aristocrat, for your charm is, in great part, being American.
>
> Here all goes as well as can be expected. I must decide on a career path soon. My options are to ship off to Singapore or plunk myself back to The Old Ride. My father could use support. Not easy decisions. I envy you your year abroad with few responsibilities.
>
> I do hope this letter finds you well and happy.
>
> *A bientôt,* your
>
> Mark

I read the letter through three times, smelled the stiff blue sheet of paper and wondered what he meant by "fluffy American." Wasn't *fluffy* synonymous with *silly*? He thought of me like one might think of a puppy. How enraging! Inside the apartment I buzzed for Julie and asked for *quelque chose à manger.* "*Le déjuner est finis,*" she said. I requested tea *avec du pan,* to which Julie replied, "*Oui, Mademoiselle, tout de suite.*"

My mother's letter was newsy. They were experiencing rainstorms and the threat of flooding. She'd accompanied George to Petaluma, California's egg capital, to pick up grain. My mother seemed to think raising cattle was a step above being a chicken farmer. There was news about my two brothers, but it seemed such a long way from my current life that I tucked her letter into the pile of letters from home that I kept in a hand-carved Moroccan box on top of my desk. I read Mark's letter again before placing it in the box with his one postcard. A matchbox in the far corner caught my attention. I picked it up, remembering. On the reverse side in messy scrawl was "Igor Kuenetsov, U.S. Embassy; téléphone: 43 12 22 22." I could feel him pressing it into my palm as if no time had passed since that warm July evening five months ago. I had been both attracted to and afraid of my attraction.

Jolted awake as the floor-length metal shutters were clanked open, Raoul loomed over my bed in a white terry-cloth bathrobe for our morning routine.

"*Bonjour, ma bête.* Tell me three wonders of the world."

"The Pyramids, and . . . "

"No, no. You said that last time. Others."

"Okay, the Colosseum, right?"

"Good, and?"

"Roman Aqueducts."

Raoul moved around the room like an angry bear. As he tugged at my bed covers, which I struggled to hold on to, his size and energy seemed to swallow all the air.

"Do you know what they're for?"

"What?"

"Aqueducts."

"Water, right?"

"*Mon Dieu!*" He wiped one hand across a brow as if my answers were painful for him to hear. "A third!" he demanded, shaking the coverlet.

"*Crêpes avec du chocolat!*"

With a feigned disgusted huff, he left, but I knew this answer made him laugh. I hauled myself out of bed just as Julie entered with my breakfast tray. She set the tray down and left.

This morning there was something different in the air. Was it the scent of fresh coffee with chicory that wafted from the carafe? Perhaps it was the tangy strawberry jam and the sweet dollop of butter releasing their aromas from small white ramekins? I tasted the coffee, the bread, jam and butter and began to read the morning's news. On the front page were the large headlines "NATO Admits West Germany" and "Ministers Sign Pacts at Paris." To the left of that story was the following: "Bonn's Concessions Lead to Saar Accord."

While I wondered what the Saar Accords were, I skipped to page seven, the movie reviews, more my speed.

Today the Herald Tribune's movie critic reviewed *Le Rouge et le Noir* and *The High and the Mighty*. According to him, the former was terribly long and not as good as the novel. The latter was the story of a passenger plane's hazardous flight from Honolulu to San Francisco, starring John Wayne and Robert Stack.

"Who cares?" I thought and put the paper down. "Fat chance I'll get to see either one."

As I showered and dressed, a startling plan presented itself. I would somehow get rid of the loathsome virginity that had caused all the recent problems in my life. It's why I was sent away to boarding school. It's why Mark saw me as a "fluffy adolescent," not a woman. It must be why Arnaud dropped me and why Napo didn't know what to do with me. I wanted to be a mature, sensuous woman, one considered fascinating by the opposite sex. I was sick of being virgin goods. After losing my virginity, I'd be certain to exude womanly appeal and would join the status of other intriguing, sexually mature women, my rightful heritage. While the West was in a cold war with Russia, I was going to wage my own war with the mores of the '50s!

To launch my plan, I'd try to find the Russian who belonged to the matchbook cover. I wondered what he did at the U.S. Embassy or if he still worked there. What if he didn't even remember me? I decided to take the matchbook to jog his memory. I speak some French now, I figured, so we ought to be able to communicate basic things. Anyway, I didn't want to talk! I wanted him to get rid of my virginity.

The map showed the embassy being a few short blocks from the Concord Metro stop. Traveling Americans sometimes had mail sent c/o the U.S. Embassy, where they could claim it. If I lost my nerve, I'd just pretend I was checking for mail.

The Metro exit was on the north side of the Place de la Concorde next to the elegant Hotel Crillon. Dominating the Place de la Concorde was its *obélisque*, and beyond it was the Seine. The U.S. Embassy was easy to find, with its flag slapping back and forth in the November morning. Inside I asked where mail was held for American travelers. The woman pointed toward a window across the room.

"Can I help you?" a young woman at the window asked.

"I'm wondering if I have any mail." I gave her my name. While she looked for mail, I looked around the lobby. It was an elegant open space with upholstered chairs and sofas arranged in various groupings. There were reception-type offices on the perimeter with five-foot-high walls and openings much like windows in a hotel lobby.

"I'm sorry. There doesn't seem to be any mail here for you."

I asked her how or where I might find an Igor Kuznetsov who worked somewhere at the Embassy. She looked at the name, nodded and thumbed through a directory.

"In Records." She wrote his telephone extension on a scrap of paper, slid it to me, and pointed to a bank of interior telephones. I dialed extension 3506. After several rings, a voice announced, "Records. Silvia speaking." I asked for Igor Kuznetsov. I heard the receiver drop against a hard surface and bounce, mingling with muffled office noise.

"Kuznetsov."

"Hello, I'm in the lobby."

"*Excusez-moi?*"

"*Je suis ici.*"

"*Qui êtes vous?*"

"*Constance.*"

"*Vous êtes ici?*" asked Igor.

"*Oui.*" I looked down at my gray coat. "*Dans un manteau gris.*"

"*J'arrive.*"

I spotted four doors from which the Russian might appear. I settled in the main reception area and tried to look mysterious. Keeping my coat on, I picked up a magazine and leafed through it, scanning the room every thirty seconds. Three or four minutes passed. Many people came and went. Then I saw him, tall, lanky, thick light brown hair just as I remembered. He wore a dark suit with a white shirt, no tie, and his shirt was open at the neck.

I got up and walked toward him. He smiled. We shook hands and awkwardly walked to a more private area by a towering plant. I took the matchbook from my purse and handed it to him. He saw his writing, nodded. "*Oui, oui, je me souviens.*" I hopped from one foot to the other and sang "ta-ta-ta-ta-ta-*ta*" imitating the conga line step we'd danced in July. We laughed nervously. I pointed toward the main door and he nodded. Outside on the steps the air was bracing.

"*Café?*" I asked.

"*Oui.*" Igor led the way, and after walking several blocks we entered a bar/café and sat at a small table. The waiter took our orders. When the paper napkins and silverware arrived, I drew a map of the western part of the United States, showing California. I marked an X on the San Francisco Bay area. Igor didn't seem to comprehend. Our hot beverages arrived. I enlarged the drawing to include an outline of the entire U.S., and I marked New York City. I indicated the Atlantic Ocean with wavy lines and an arrow pointing eastward, over which I wrote *Europe.* His face suddenly lighted up.

"*Vous venez par là?*" he said, with his finger resting on California.

"*Oui.*"

We declined sumptuous-looking tarts and cakes from a waiter pushing a cart. It was liberating to be able to have a relationship conducted in French. Igor wasn't a count, thank goodness, and no snob. He worked in "Records" at the U.S. Embassy. So what? This wasn't about finding a suitable partner. It was about physical attraction.

I leaned toward him and asked where he lived. "*Où habitez-vous?*"

"*Dix minutes à pied.*"

"*Allons nous?*"

He rose quickly and called to the waiter. "*Garçon, l'addition toute suite.*"

We walked briskly down a wide boulevard, our arms linked. It was cold, and he had no overcoat. Three blocks later, he led me into a plain building and up five flights to an undistinguished hallway. Opening a door with his key, the cramped room was like a cell, with a single bed, a wooden chair, a bureau topped with junk, an ashtray and matches, a sink, one window, a small wardrobe, and a light bulb hanging from a cord in the middle of the ceiling. There were no books, no prints or photographs tacked to the walls or on the bureau. There was no sign that a person with memories or loved ones lived here. At one time, it must have been a servant's quarters.

Having second thoughts about everything, I nervously sat in the chair and fiddled with the buttons on my coat.

"*Je suis une vierge,*" I explained.

He looked down at me, walked over and unbuttoned my coat, sliding it off my shoulders. He knelt and unbuttoned my dress, running his hands down my arms. I stood up and let my dress drop to the floor. I slipped off my stockings and stepped out of my panties, and then got into the bed and pulled the covers over me. Igor took off his suit jacket and pants, folding them over the chair. As he removed his shirt, the sight of his masculine torso sent me into a swoon and a sudden spurt of wetness shot to my core.

When he joined me in bed, our warm bodies felt magical, electric, as we touched. I wanted what happened next, but I didn't know how to help other than to position myself under him with legs apart. From my supine position I noticed ceiling cracks, one in particular that looked like a big rabbit. He entered me slowly, and it hurt. A dry struggle ensued, and while I watched the rabbit on the ceiling, he thrust into me until reaching a crescendo. When he rolled off me, I felt a pool forming between my legs. Soon Igor was gently snoring.

Although I didn't know exactly what I'd expected, this was certainly not satisfying. I'd been more aroused necking in cars. I arose, noting the bloodstain on the sheet, dressed quietly, and closed his door softly. I hurriedly descended to the street before he could awaken or follow. All in all, I'd accomplished what I'd set out to do, but it was all pretty ho-hum.

At home I drew a bath and thoroughly washed myself. Was I ashamed? No. Scared? A little.

During supper, Raoul asked what I'd learned at the Alliance that day.

"We had a presentation by a Russian student," I said.

The next morning I joined Frances on the platform at the Trocadero Metro station.

"Where were you yesterday?" she asked

"I had a doctor's appointment," I lied. "I finally heard from Mark. He called me his 'fluffy American.'"

"English are a bit retarded."

"What?"

"I mean, can you imagine Alan or Julian calling either one of us a fluffy anything?" Frances said.

The train arrived. We boarded and sat together.

"Instead of retarded, don't you mean the English are socially inept with the opposite sex?" I probed.

"What's the difference?" she said.

"I'm socially inept, especially with the French," I confessed.

"French people love to make everyone else feel inferior," Frances said, "but the English are notoriously backward in the girl-guy department."

"I wonder why I like Mark so much."

"I bet he's the first educated male who's noticed you," Frances said. "Now there's Alan and Julian, so that makes three."

Our stop was next. We climbed from stale garlic-tinged air to a cold, bright November day on the Boulevard Raspail with bracing, sobering air.

"*A bientôt*," we cried to each other as we hurried toward separate classrooms.

⇒ 6 ⇐

The winter season accelerated in a flurry of activity. Raoul and Mimi took me to my first concert at the Champs Élysées Theatre to hear the National Orchestra play Weber's Euryanthe Overture and Brahms' Violin Concerto. How special I felt to accompany Raoul and Mimi, all of us in our finery, sitting in orchestra seats. During the intermission, we joined the throng in the lobby and sipped Champagne. In the second half of the program, a young American, Isaac Stern, was the featured violinist for the Brahms piece, and when the audience gave him a standing ovation, I felt proud to be an American.

During the taxi ride home, I privately reminisced about my life in New Canaan, Connecticut, while Dad was still alive. I'd had ballet and piano lessons, and our family always played charades on Saturday evenings. Had he not died, I was sure, the lessons would have continued and our lives would have included concerts and plays.

I asked Mimi's advice about helping Frances buy a new coat. Mimi directed us to the same department store where she'd bought my current wardrobe.

"Be sure to ask for Monique," she told me. "She is very, very smart about zees."

Monique brought a chestnut-brown coat that transformed Frances into a stylish, seemingly thinner young woman. Whereas before Frances had seemed short and squarish, the coat elongated her torso with smartly placed darts running from her bustline to below her waist, appearing to reduce her overall size. I was amazed by the power of the cut and style of cloth.

One day at Café Tournon while I was with Frances and a few students from both the Alliance and the Sorbonne, a young blond woman joined our table. She pulled off a Scandinavian-style knitted hat, revealing a cascading mane of shoulder-length hair. Next she peeled off her coat, revealing a curvaceous body in a tight-fitting purple leotard tucked into leather boots. Suddenly, every man in the café seemed to wake up. I could see the testosterone kick in as one guy after another suddenly called attention to himself. One raised his voice and slapped the tabletop for emphasis while speaking to his buddy. Another playfully punched a fellow in the solar plexus, showing off his muscular arms.

One guy turned toward her and, in a dignified voice, asked, "What brings you to Paris?"

She flirtatiously tossed her hair back from her face, combing it back with long fingers, then extended her other hand to him. "Nina Mueller, from Copenhagen."

I watched Nina smile at each man while refraining from making eye contact with me. She told us she'd spent the last year at UCLA. I watched with great interest the spell Nina cast on every single male in the room.

In the ensuing weeks, I made attempts to befriend Nina by offering to bring hot coffee to her hotel room before my French class. She fascinated me: gorgeous, independent, living on her own in a hotel, pursued by every male she met. So what if the hotel near the rue de Rivoli was run-down and she had to use a bathroom down the hall? Compared with mine, her life was exotic.

One morning when I arrived, I found her already dressed in a slip, carefully inspecting her makeup in a handheld mirror. A blue wool suit was carefully laid out on her bed. She seemed nervous and asked me to put her coffee on the dresser.

"Where are you going?"

"I've got a screen test with Erroll Flynn."

"No kidding! How did you meet *him*?"

"Crossing the rue de Rivoli. I can't be late," she said, turning toward the clothes lying on the bed.

"I'll telephone later." I left, cutting the visit short.

By mid-December I had gotten to know Nina well enough to learn that the screen test turned into an invitation from Erroll Flynn to remove all her clothes, at which point she left in tears. I invited her to come to rue Charles-Lamoureux to bathe in my oversize private bathroom. She immediately took me up on the offer. After bathing, she sat on my small balcony in the cold December afternoon air, toweling her blond tresses. This got back to the Faure household, and to Arnaud in particular, who telephoned one evening soon thereafter.

"I hear *le pin-up* is your friend."

"So what?"

"Don't hang up! Constance, how are you? I never see you anymore. I wonder how you are."

"Mmmmm."

"Don't you care how I am?"

"Sure."

"I'm very, very—how you say?—under stress."

"About?"

"Airplanes. Insurance. Everything. Listen, *ma petite cousine,* I hear you and *le pin-up* are friends. Is this true?"

"What if it is?"

"They say she's the mistress of a very rich Paris perfume-maker."

"So?"

"Constance, I detect a . . ."

"I'm hanging up."

"Wait! Tell your friend she is beautiful. Tell her I love her."

"Arnaud, you're pathetic."

Around this time, Frances and I met two young French men our age. Stanislaus Faure, a nephew of Uncle Jacques and Arnaud's cousin, lived in a different part of Paris with his father. His friend Paul Sirot lived in the 16ème. The two skied together and argued passionately in French about all sorts of things. Paul was masculine and self-assuredly attentive, displaying European manners. Stani, as he was called, was more introspective, adored film, and was more of an intellectual. We began doing things as a foursome on weekends.

One Saturday, Frances, Stani, Paul, and I went to the Normandie Cinema to see the newly released *On the Waterfront,* Elia Kazan's tale of gangs that rule the longshoremen's union in New York Harbor. Marlon Brando played the lead role of Terry Malloy, whose older brother is thick as thieves with the corrupt boss of the docks. Terry is torn between looking the other way and doing what he knows is right, which is the heart of the movie.

Afterward, the four of us sat at a café. Unlike the dockworkers in the film, we four came from privileged backgrounds.

"Could you identify with any of the film's characters?" I asked.

"*Bien sûr* if you mean 'question authority,'" said Stani. "It's a universal premise, no matter your socioeconomic status."

"Well," added Paul, "without the priest to constantly push them to organize against the union, they wouldn't have done it."

"What changes Terry is that he falls in love with Edie," I said. "In the scene where they kiss, he's changed. No. I mean they kiss *because* his love for Edie changes him."

"Love conquers all?" Stani said.

"It wasn't that clichéd," said Frances.

"Not at all," I said. "Terry cares more about Edie than about his own skin, and the priest nudges him to do what he knows is right, what takes courage. When they finally do the right thing, it's wonderful."

The characters' motivations are so artfully portrayed and the issues so clearly drawn in *On the Waterfront* that I knew Kazan was a director to watch.

After classes one day, Frances and I decided to visit the Louvre, on the Right Bank. Although within walking distance of the Alliance Francaise, because it was a cold winter day we took the Metro and got off just across from the Louvre.

The immense building has many architectural styles, each representative of the era in which that section was built. We entered on the ground floor and went to the department of Greek and Roman antiquities. The route led us through a long empty hallway and up some stairs leading to a landing on which presided a breathtaking statue, *The Winged Victory of Samothrace.*

Where did it come from? Who sculpted it? A nine-foot-tall marble goddess with wings, she appeared to be in midflight or just at the moment of alighting. Her body was thrust forward by giant outstretched wings, and the wind whipped her clothing revealingly about her body. I climbed the stairs to look closer. The head and forward-thrusting right foot of the statue were missing. A plaque read:

> The work was probably a Rhodian votive offering erected
> in Samothrace to celebrate a victory over Antiochos III of
> Syria.

It was created between 220 and 190 B.C. and found in 1863.

I tagged behind Frances in the adjacent room as she examined other Greek and Roman antiquities, but I was lost in a trance. *The Winged Victory of Samothrace* had ruined my appetite for other art. I was sated.

"Look!" cried Frances, "there's Byzantine, Coptic and later Christian stuff all together."

"My brain is on overload," I said and sat on a bench against a wall. I sleepily closed my eyes. Against my eyelids I saw the *Winged Victory*. How did the artist render such soft flesh and delicate folds of cloth out of cold, hard marble?

These thoughts led me from one venue to another, always lingering on the beautiful female form and questions about my own body. I played back my meeting with Igor. Pleased that I was technically no longer a virgin, I wished there were someone with whom I could talk about things. About the only sex education I'd had was a film shown to my sixth-grade class that depicted a graphic of a uterus, with a male voice-over explaining that the woman's ovaries released eggs once a month. These eggs travel down the fallopian tubes, where one lodges itself in the lining of the uterus. This lining accumulates blood until, once a month, blah, blah, blah.

Nobody in my circle of friends at that time was prone to discussing what goes on when a girl falls in love and marries. We wondered about it in the vaguest way, such as what our last names might become. This was far more interesting than the mechanics of sex. Living on a ranch, I had often observed animals mating, and it was no big deal.

Now, years later, I wondered how a person recognizes love. What's the difference between sexual attraction and love? How will I know which is which? I hadn't begun to grasp how my relationship with my father, stepfather, brothers, and mother would shape my future decisions. I felt a need for signposts pointing the way for me. Their absence—or my failure to recognize them—was not reassuring.

⇒7⇐

As winter progressed, my French slowly improved, although it still wasn't advanced enough to have conversations with Raoul and Mimi, whose English was impeccable. But sometimes I thought in French.

Mimi announced that I must give a dinner party *chez moi*. She'd help me plan the menu. She'd also compose the guest list. I asked if I might include Stani, Paul and Frances, but Mimi had already arranged to invite "*quelques* terribly nice young people" whom I'd never met. I dreaded *le dîner*.

Nonetheless, I halfheartedly chose from menu items Mimi had compiled on lined paper. *Entrecote du beuf à la bourguignon* sounded good. From two potato possibilities, I chose *pomme mousseline*, which Mimi explained are boiled potatoes put through a sieve and browned in a buttered casserole. I also loved how she described a vegetable called *bouchées à la julienne*. Julienne carrots, parsnips, leeks, and celery in cream are served individually on two-inch pastry rings. For dessert it was a toss-up between vanilla meringues with exotic fruit and *pear charlotte*, poached pears in custard on top of ladyfingers. I finally chose the vanilla meringues, which are made with mangos, kiwi, pineapple and passion fruit, mainly because I'd never eaten those fruits. I proved hopeless when it came to the wine selection, though, and Mimi excused me and rang the bell for Julie. Thank God I didn't have to cook.

As the day of my dinner approached, I learned my guests were four good friends and an acquaintance of one of them, all five close to my age. I couldn't remember any of their names. I was certain that since someone's "acquaintance" was invited, I wouldn't be the odd person out.

An intimate table setting had been arranged in an alcove in the hall, with a lace tablecloth, candles, and three sets of glasses at each place setting. It looked fetching. At 6:30, Mimi sent me to my room to change into my dark blue and black jacquard décolleté velvet dress, which I couldn't wait to wear. *Oh là là.*

At 7:30 the buzzer sounded. Gérôme, the butler, who had arrived from the country château, buzzed the outside door. As I waited for the antique elevator to ascend, I caught my pleasing reflection in a hall mirror. The decolleté framed my pale neck and shoulders and revealed the curves of my breasts above my small waist. *I like how I look—definitely a woman.* I joined Mimi in the living room.

The apartment doorbell chimed. Gérôme escorted our guests in.

"*Nous sommes ici,*" Mimi called from the living room, where we were seated. Each person greeted my aunt with, "*bonsoir, Madame la Comtesse,*" or a variation thereof. Mimi directed an outstretched arm toward me. *"Je vous présent my niece Americaine, Constance. Enchanté. Welcome!"* Coats and shawls were piled on Gérôme's arms, who moved them down the hall.

Mimi explained that she must leave shortly to join her husband for dinner downstairs at her mother-in-law's, and then she slipped out. With feigned assurance, I assumed the role of hostess and settled into a chair with a glass of Dubonnet, facing my guests while Gérôme served apéritifs and canapés.

Victoire was tall, dark-haired and had an alabaster complexion. She was wearing a glamorous red dress. Her nonchalance was conveyed in part by the relaxed manner in which she tossed her head from side to side, running a hand through her shoulder-length hair, unself-consciously crossing and uncrossing her legs, adjusting her bra strap under the red chiffon shoulder straps, and stretching her legs and wiggling her toes.

Her boyfriend, Alex, was well dressed and coifed. Light brown hair, medium-build. Nice suit, shirt, tie, shoes. Attentive manner. Smooth. Why did the word *lawyer* come to mind?

Marie-Claire was blond, petite, cherubic, curvaceous, with lacquered red fingernails. She was wearing a black dress with a lace collar and cuffs on the long sleeves. Her waist was tiny. Her boyfriend, Jacques, was extremely tall and thin and had enormous feet. His clothes didn't measure up to what Alex wore. His had a rumpled, lived-in look, implying he had more important things to worry about than a wardrobe. I found that masculine.

Last, I scrutinized Gérard. He was a friend of Jacques. I'm not sure how they knew one another. It was explained to me before that Gérard was the son of the proprietor of the well-known recital hall Salle Gaveau and of the Gaveau piano, which in France is as well known as Steinway and Baldwin are in America. Gérard was a little taller than I, with sandy-colored hair and a ruddy complexion. He had on a three-piece suit in dark charcoal with a thin sky-blue stripe and a red tie over a sky-blue shirt. He sat on the edge of the sofa near me, introduced himself with a strong handshake, and asked how long I'd been living in Paris at the de Lubersacs.

"Since August."

"Please explain how Mme. la Comtesse is your relative?"

"She's actually my first cousin once removed, but because she and Raoul are my parents' generation, I refer to them as aunt and uncle."

I inquired about his friendship with the others.

"Jacques and I are good friends. We study at the Institute de Science Politique, Sciences Po. I've met Marie-Claire, of course, but I only know Victoire and Alex in passing."

"Your English is impeccable."

"Thank you. Is that good? How is your French?"

"I'm struggling Alliance Française--every day. *Impeccable* means 'perfect.'"

Gérôme announced, *"Votre diner est servi."*

The six of us took our seats at the intimate candlelit table. Gérard sat opposite me at the other end of the table, Victoire to his left and Marie-Claire to his right. Damn! Why didn't Gérard sit near me? He was the only nice one who spoke to me before dinner.

Gérôme served each platter and poured red wine and water into glasses. The conversation picked up in French. The food was delicious, and I was glad they were having a good time—better than making small talk in English to be polite.

They spoke rapidly and used colloquialisms, so I couldn't understand what they said. Victoire led the animated conversation. Interjecting loudly was Jacques. Alex, on my left, was so engrossed that he leaned toward them and away from me.

I noticed that I'd drained two glasses of wine rather rapidly. Gérôme filled my glass a third time. Why couldn't they do more to include me? Didn't they understand that my French was minimal? Feeling bored and lonely, I checked my reflected image in the silver candlesticks in front of me, noting how my neck and cheek were broken up, duplicated.

By the time our main-course plates had been removed and dessert was served, others had remembered me as their hostess, but the attempts to bring me into the conversation were too late. They'd been inconsiderate and they knew it. I longed for this party to be over and wore a mask of polite coolness that hastened their exit.

A few weeks later as I arrived home, I ran into Mimi, also arriving with a lot of packages. We both entered the elevator. I smiled a friendly hello. She looked agitated. I asked, "How are you?"

She waved a wrist at me dismissively. "You don't really care how I am, so why pretend?"

Taken aback but not knowing what to say, I remained silent.

Mimi continued, "We do everything in our power to help you, to teach you, but you do not appreciate our efforts one tiny bit! I heard the dinner party was a disaster."

"They excluded me, spoke too fast, used colloquialisms, talked only to each other. I felt left out."

"Ungrateful! *C'est vrais.* And look what you are wearing!"

"What's wrong with what I've got on?"

"That stupid top does not go with the skirt. Your coat is passable, but look at your feet. Just look. Tennis shoes and white socks. *Alors! Mon Dieu!*"

"I walked miles today," I explained.

"Why is that? Why are you never home for a midday meal? Are you secretly meeting a man?"

I burst into tears and ran to my room, where I refused to come out for supper.

The dinner party left a bad taste in my mouth, and the disturbing and unpleasant episode in the elevator with Aunt Mimi cooled my feelings toward her. I began to spend as much time as possible away from No. 1 rue Charles-Lamoureux. Paul was a willing accomplice, meeting me at various cafes, joining me for screenings of movies, window shopping, or just walks around Paris. This had inherent problems, in that Paul tried everything in the book to get me into bed. Although I resisted, I never told him directly "no" but left the door of possibility open. I suppose this led him on, but I was so lonely I didn't want to lose him entirely. I was careful to get home in time for supper so as not to cause any more friction than already existed.

One evening when only Raoul and I were home, he indicated that Mimi was going through a difficult "female" time. "Don't take anything too seriously," he advised.

"But you didn't hear what she called me," I wailed, embarrassed by the sudden tears that flooded my eyes and the anguish that erupted from my throat.

Raoul pulled me to his chest, stroking my head.

"She hates me," I cried into his soft sweater.

"*Ma bete*, shush, shush," he whispered. We rocked like that until I managed a wan smile.

No more was said about the ugly incident, but things would never be all right between Mimi and me. It was a relief that Uncle Raoul didn't think our falling out was entirely my fault.

8

In mid-February there was a winter thaw, and the temperature climbed to sixty-five degrees. With this hint of spring, I began my campaign to join Frances and her friend and his friends—a bunch of American exchange students in Munich—for the spring break they were planning for an island off the coast of Spain.

At first, Raoul was adamant that I, a single young female, couldn't go. I dispatched several letters to my mother, asking permission to join the group. I made certain she knew I would be traveling with Frances Wister, the daughter of my mother's old friend, Billie Wister, and I was counting on that connection to secure her permission. Whatever exchange occurred between my mother and Raoul, I was pleased to learn that permission had been given for the March adventure to Mallorca, Spain.

The all-night train to Barcelona left from Paris' Austerlitz station at the Quai Austerlitz and Boulevard de L'Hopital. Aunt Constance's chauffeur deposited Frances and me and our luggage at the station an hour early. We were too independent to want to be seen with a uniformed chauffeur, so we sent him on his way and lugged our belongings through the station to the right track.

We had third-class tickets, but instead of trying to find the appropriate car, we threw our luggage onto the first car we came to, climbed on board, and collapsed on top of our bags at the end of the corridor. "Why did I bring my easel and paints?" I wondered as I surveyed what I was responsible for hauling through the Barcelona station, to a hotel room, and finally onto the boat bound for Mallorca.

The train started to move, gradually picking up speed. Passengers with luggage began to pass through the coaches. Each time the door opened, a cold blast of air jolted us. When the conductor arrived and asked for our tickets, motioning us toward the back of the train, we got up. Seven cars later, we took our seats and stowed luggage underneath and overhead.

Exhausted from the exertion, I immediately fell asleep, my head rolling against the cold window.

Twelve hours later, on a bright Barcelona morning, we caught a boat for the Balearic Islands. From the deck we watched Palma, the capital city, appear. In Palma, we took an electric train that rattled over the mountains before making its descent into Soller's station and on to Port de Soller, our final destination. At the small family hotel right on the bay, we met some of the German exchange students who selected this vacation spot. Willie Paulsen, short and athletic, knew Frances from their hometown, Short Hills, New Jersey. They hugged while Willie introduced us to others as they straggled in.

The Hotel Miramar faced a sandy beach on a horseshoe-shaped cove dotted with palms. Adjacent to the left of the lobby was an outdoor terrace and restaurant/bar shaded with hibiscus-covered trellises. Tables and chairs, covered in soft pastels, welcomed patrons. A young mother and her child sat at one of the tables. The child, in a high chair, was busy drawing with crayons on her tray, while her mother sipped a cool drink and nibbled at lunch.

I crossed the lobby and stepped outside. On the beach, gentle waves rolled in and out, and small boats bobbed up and down offshore. The combined sounds of gentle surf, seagulls, outboard motors, and human laughter formed a "relaxation symphony."

At dinner in the hotel's dining room, I met everyone all over again. We were six in all. Except for Willie and Frances, they knew one another as students in Munich. Although diminutive, Willie, from Yale, was the loudest and most aggressive of the four.

At 6-foot-3, Bob "Stretch" McDaniel was an engineering student from Yale. Fritz Dieter was a German friend who just wanted to come along, and John Chivers was from Wesleyan University in Connecticut. He seemed to be an outgoing, pleasant guy with dark brown eyes, light brown hair, and a nice smile.

Talk shifted to boats and waterskiing. I excused myself and went to my room to unpack and settle in.

The next day I was up early. Downstairs I found Frances having breakfast in a sunny corner of the dining room.

"They're planning a hike after breakfast," she said. "Want to come?"

"Thanks, but I'd rather paint," I replied.

She gave me a big smile, which to me meant that whatever I wanted to do was no problem. I smiled back.

By midmorning I had set up my easel, a folding chair, and tubes of paint under a palm tree facing the bay. I placed a small canvas on the easel, took a charcoal stick, and roughly sketched the curve of the bay, the horizon above, and a tree trunk in the foreground. Next I gathered the colors I was seeing. Cerulean blue, Naples yellow, ochre, Mediterranean blue. I poured a little turpentine into a small cup and a little oil medium into another. Starting with a large brush, I painted the canvas with a wash of diluted color.

"Constance."

Seeing no one, I stepped back from the easel a few feet. Then I saw a figure mostly hidden behind the palm tree. He stepped from behind the tree, and my shocked recognition must have registered, because Stani put a finger to his lips, indicating that I should keep quiet.

"What are you doing here?" I asked. "Why are you hiding?"

Shaking his head, he said, "It makes no sense. I'm asking myself."

"Why the secrecy?"

He shrugged. "Would you explain to Frances I'm here?"

"Of course, Stani. She went on a hike. I'll tell her as soon as I see her."

He looked somewhat relieved as he walked toward the parking lot.

"Where are you going?" I called after him.

"I'll walk around, but I'll be back."

I resumed work on my painting and reflected on Stani's sudden arrival. I had introduced them three months ago, and they'd been almost inseparable since. My guess was that Stani wanted to know Frances's world, which sounded serious. Stani looked so French: long hair, horizontal-striped French polo, loose pants, leather sandals, and small rucksack.

Around noon, I schlepped my equipment and chair to the hotel and wandered into the restaurant, where the menu featured a vast array of choices. After explaining to the waiter that I wanted something small, he suggested tapas, an assortment of hors d'oeuvres that included olives, prosciutto, and calamari, all of which I ended up enjoying.

In the afternoon, I put on a swimsuit, got a beach towel and some magazines, and plunked myself down on the sandy beach. I swam a short way out in the too-cold Mediterranean waters and then warmed under the sun. When I opened my eyes, the sun was no longer overhead but sliding down in the western sky.

Before dinner, I knocked on Frances's bedroom door. She told me to come in. I explained about Stani. She looked shocked but not unpleased.

"Where is he?" she asked.

I related what Stani had said. Frances gathered her things and hurried from the room.

I descended to the lobby. In the restaurant, others had gathered at our table. Presiding over the table was Willie, who announced he had rented a large Citroën and planned to drive around the island tomorrow morning. Noticing Frances' absence, Willie asked where she was.

"She'll be back," I mumbled.

"Where?" Willie repeated.

Just then Frances and Stani appeared. Frances introduced Stani to Willie and the others, while an extra chair was pulled up. Gradually, the animated conversation resumed through the evening meal. Frances and Stani decided not to go on the drive around the island, while the rest of us agreed to meet the following morning at 9.

The next day, five of us piled into the Citroën sedan and headed north to Port de Pollenca. Willie drove. Stretch, with his long legs, sat in the passenger seat. John, Fritz, and I sat in the back. The circuitous route north to Port de Pollenca wound along rugged headlands that dropped straight into the sea. From the port, we headed east to Arta, Mallorca's most famous hilltop fortress. We parked on the main square and, after a ten-minute climb, reached the fortress-church built on the site of an Arab castle. The views over the rooftops were spectacular. Seven kilometers southeast of Arta were the Coves d'Arta, thought to have inspired Jules Verne's 1864 novel, *Journey to the Centre of the Earth.* Being claustrophobic, I declined the tour but was happy to loll about in the sun. I bought snacks at the small concession stand and ate them at a picnic table decorated with pots of flowers.

From Cove d'Arta, we proceeded south over the winding narrow road that hugged the coastline. We fell behind a slow-moving vehicle. The longer we were stuck behind it, the more agitated Willie became, shouting insults in German. Suddenly, Willie pulled into the oncoming lane to pass. A blind dip in the road ahead obscured the view. Terrified, I pressed my face into John's neck, shutting both eyes. I heard the car accelerate as we passed and felt it swerve back into the right lane. I opened my eyes to see we were still alive.

"Wilheim, cool down," said Stretch. "We're in no rush. Want me to drive?"

"No! I can manage. The guy's a jerk. I can't stand jerks!" shouted Willie.

I wished Stretch *would* take over. What was the matter with Willie? Did he have a Napoleon complex?

We followed the interior through almond groves, apricot orchards, and small farms to bustling Palma. As the city receded in our rearview mirror, the traffic and humanity thinned.

Later, when I spotted John alone in the hotel lobby, I asked, "Why is Willie like that? I was scared. He could have gotten us all killed." John nodded as if to say, "What's new?"

When I tried to talk to Frances about Willie's aggressive driving, she changed the subject.

"I'm glad Stani came," she said. "He doesn't much like the others, though."

"He's so French," I exclaimed. "You only realize it when you see him next to a bunch of Americans."

The next two days were lazy ones for me. The guys had found a place to rent motorboats and gear for waterskiing. I pursued my oil painting at the same spot on the beach and watched dot-size humans flail about on water skis a long way off. Frances and Stani hung out together.

One afternoon, John invited me to join him for a walk. The trail followed coastal hills as they gradually climbed from the beach to overlook the horseshoe bay. We chatted about his family, mine, our siblings. I learned that he was a junior at Wesleyan University, in Connecticut. When he asked about my plans for when I was back in the states, I confessed that I felt confused and overwhelmed about what to do.

"I was so naïve before coming to Paris," I explained. "Life seemed so simple. Now I know how much I don't know, but I have no idea what to do or even if I *should* apply to college."

"I think you should," said John.

"Why?"

"I think you're perceptive, smart and cute, too."

I checked his expression as he watched me. Then he bent down and planted a soft kiss on my lips. No one had kissed me for a long time. I touched the place he'd kissed me. John tilted my chin up so our eyes met.

"If you go to college in the East, we can see each other next year," he said.

His smile was so welcoming and inviting that I thought about possibilities all the way back and for the rest of the afternoon.

John and I, Frances and Stani decided to sightsee in Palma on our last day in Mallorca. As we approached the city by tram, Palma seemed dwarfed by its Gothic cathedral, La Seu. As we walked its myriad streets, it felt like a big city, with chic restaurants and cafes, modern art, and shops selling local arts and crafts. Along the waterfront, palm trees lined a promenade that wound past a fishing port and a yacht club. It reminded me of the illustrations from the Barbar books.

For our last evening, I dressed with a decided effort to be *soigne*. In my limited wardrobe, I found crisp white pants and paired them with a beloved Guatemalan striped shirt, dangling earrings, and thong sandals. Downstairs, John escorted me to a chair and sat next to me, placing his left hand over my right. While he held the menu for us both to read, we made our choices, which he relayed to the waiter. He ordered a bottle of white wine.

Willie was holding court at his end of the table with loud remarks about their waterskiing adventures. Stretch made an attempt to include us by asking how we liked Palma, but Willie lobbed the conversation back to his court.

Looking at Stani, Willie said, "I guess the French are more interested in cooking than in sports, right?"

Stani shot back, "I was a contender for the Junior French Olympic Ski Team four years ago."

"What happened?" taunted Willie in a singsong voice.

Stani paused a moment, then said, "My mother got sick. She died. So I didn't go to the finals."

Our table was suddenly deadly quiet except for the waiter, who happily explained dessert selections. Conversation finally resumed to a more modified level.

After dinner, John and I wandered outside to the shoreline. The stars overhead and scattered lights from boats in the harbor and the surrounding villas created a luminous backdrop.

"I'll miss you," he said.

"I'd like to know you better," I said.

Abruptly, he kissed me as if he was dying of thirst and I was water. The urgency of our embrace made me wonder if I was still standing. We clung to each other, swaying in the sand. Hearing approaching voices, we pulled apart. Willie and Fritz were laughing. John took my hand and led me toward the hotel. As we crossed paths, Willie said something in German to John. Suddenly, John dropped my hand, swung around, and grabbed Willie's shirt from the back, turning him so they were facing. John swung with his right fist and hit Willie in the face. Fritz just stared, his mouth open. Willie raised his arms to shield his face. John then punched him in the stomach. When Willie dropped his arms protectively to his gut, John hit him again in the face. Willie dropped to the sand, hands covering his face.

"Fucking maniac," screamed Willie.

"Shut up, you cretin!" John yelled. "One more rotten word and I'll kill you!"

Fritz bent down to assist Willie.

"*Komm, Willie, lass uns gehen.*" They stood, and Willie hobbled with Fritz toward the hotel lobby. I stepped close to John, still not understanding what had prompted the sudden violence. John was breathing fast and massaging his right hand with his left. I took his right hand in both of mine and gently pressed it to my lips.

"You shouldn't have heard that," said John, shaking his head.

"I don't speak German."

"Good."

"What did he say?"

"Never mind."

"Because we were kissing?"

"Implying more, in dirty German slang." John put his arm around my shoulder as we went inside the lobby. He looked distracted as we said good night.

In the morning, Fritz and Willie appeared in the dining room. Willie's black eye was swollen shut. They sat at a table on the other side of the room from where John and I sat with Frances and Stani.

"My God," Frances said. "What happened to Willie?"

"There was a fight last night," I told her.

"Who? Why?" she asked.

"It was me," interjected John. "Willie was out of line. *Way* out."

Standing, John said he didn't want to travel back to Munich with the others and needed to make arrangements. Stretch came over to say goodbye. We agreed to meet in the lobby in an hour with our bags.

Packing, I wondered if or when I would ever see John again.

→ 9 ←

Paris was awakening to springtime. A fine rain permeated and washed the city. Colorful umbrellas floated above pedestrians wrapped in their mackintoshes. In the avenues, emerging pale green sprouts sprung from the pollarded trees, and a soft green canopy formed in the Bois de Boulogne, Paris's most beautiful park. When the sun came out, it dried park benches and pulled dandelions from the wet earth. Suddenly everything was in bloom.

One evening after dinner, I heard cries of "Oh, là, là" from the bathroom between my room and Raoul and Mimi's guest room.

Chantal called, "Consie, *viens ici.*"

I stood at the bathroom door. Perched on the toilet seat, with one bare foot braced on the bathtub, Chantal held a bottle of nail polish. Laughing, she swiped at her toes but couldn't reach over her enormous abdomen. I gladly painted them for her and listened to her chatter in French until she suddenly clutched her stomach and groaned from first signs of labor.

My God, I thought, is this really what a woman has to endure? Would her body ever resemble its former shape after the baby came out? I doubted it and vowed never to let anyone impregnate me.

When the contractions came faster, I felt so afraid that I retreated from the scene to my room. *Coward,* I thought of myself as I listened to the others getting her into a coat and heard the front door slam and the groan of the elevator as it descended and delivered them to the waiting taxi.

Over breakfast, we celebrated the birth of Raoul and Mimi's first grandchild with Champagne.

As Easter was still a major religious holiday in France, schools, banks, post offices and most business were closed from Good Friday through Easter Sunday. After Mass, the plan was to dine at home with Michel La Farge, a friend of Raoul and Mimi's who was involved in a consortium determined to build a tunnel under the English Channel, linking France and England.

Mimi was dressed elegantly for Mass. Her raspberry tweed Chanel suit was offset by a creamy wool felt beret, matching gloves, and a brown alligator purse and shoes. Raoul looked great in his yellow cashmere sweater over a French blue shirt under his tweed jacket, and gray wool slacks. A corner of a yellow silk handkerchief poked up from the jacket's breast pocket. I wore my ubiquitous tan raincoat, which made me feel like a common female mallard duck. Happily, the service ended sooner than I'd expected.

At No. 1 rue Charles-Lamoureux, we were served apéritifs in the living room. M. La Farge, a handsome, elegantly dressed man of medium height, spoke fluent American English with a decidedly East Coast accent. While Mimi offered him cheese and crackers, they enjoyed a playful repartee, which she punctuated with giggles. I got the sense that some non-verbal communication was going on between the two, especially when Raoul kept leaving the room and reappearing. Then he suddenly engaged me in conversation. "*Ma bete!*" he called, turning his back toward Mimi and Michel. "*Viens ici.*"

"Here I am," I said, sliding my arm through his and pressing my left side along the length of him.

"Are you going to write to us after you're home?"

I wondered where this was coming from, since I wasn't leaving for the states until June. "Of course I'll write," I answered. Could my tall, manly uncle be jealous of M. La Farge? When I caught Raoul throwing a furtive glance at Mimi and Michel, I knew that what I'd intuited was correct.

Julie announced *le diner*, and once we were seated at the table, everything seemed normal again, with Raoul assuming his usual role as host.

"Welcome, Michel." Raoul lifted his glass in Michel's direction.

We mock-clinked our glasses in a toast. I was glad that Raoul seemed to be back in charge, realizing how much I cared about him. Satisfied that nothing untoward had occurred, I turned my attention to the conversation at the table.

". . . three separate tunnels, one for ventilation and service," Michel said. "The other two will be designed for high-speed trains."

"Good God," said Mimi. "Who is going to pay for all that?"

"It's got to be a joint English and French venture. They'll have to sign a treaty," Michel replied. "It won't be built in my lifetime, I'm afraid," he said gloomily.

A week later during a rare telephone conversation with Arnaud, I learned that Michel La Farge and Mimi had been lovers during the war and, supposedly, afterward as well.

"*Tout le monde savait ça,*" said Arnaud.

Well, I, for one, didn't know, so there! If they were former lovers, why were they dining *en famille* as if it were the most regular thing? That must be why Raoul had felt threatened, I thought, pleased to learn that my female intuition had been dead-on. But I still wondered why Raoul had agreed to host such an invitation? *Oh well*, I thought, *c'est la vie Française.*

I booked passage on the *S.S. America,* which left Le Havre on June 6 and arrived four and a half days later in New York City, where Mom, George and Phil would meet me.

Now that my exit plans were set, I relaxed and enjoyed the final weeks in Paris and a few parties. Our class at the Alliance Française had a graduation potluck party in our classroom. While I brought a dozen stuffed eggs, others brought exotic Greek and Italian finger foods.

Mimi's niece, Marie, about my age, gave a fancy catered party at a boathouse with a band. I wore my favorite dress, the décolleté dark blue and black velvet jacquard. Not caring what people thought, I danced with whom I wished and turned others down.

I'd begun to think of seeing John Chivers again and of applying to colleges in New England. Hopefully, Mom would help me figure out how to put these puzzle pieces together. The week of my departure, I made the rounds of relatives to say a final goodbye. Aunt Constance invited me for a farewell tea downstairs in her flat.

"Consie, hello, my dear," she greeted me with a wide smile, framed by her lovely white hair. At six feet tall and thin, she reminded me of my mother. I followed her into the salon.

"Shall we sit by this window?" she suggested, lowering herself into one of a pair of peach-paisley-covered armchairs overlooking rue Charles-Lamoureux.

"It's so nice of you to invite me."

"Not at all, not at all," she said. "You young people have so much on your plates, I don't know how you manage."

"I'm sorry I wasn't what you and Mimi expected," I told her.

"Whatever do you mean?" she asked.

"I've let you all down," I said. "I'm afraid I can't be a proper French girl. It isn't in me."

She poured me another cup of tea. Perhaps it was due to the span in our ages, nineteen and eighty, that I never got to know her. I'd always felt intimidated by her legendary "unselfishness."

"Of course we don't expect you to be a French girl, only to learn French, my dear."

"I still have a long way to go to do that."

We continued chatting, and I promised to bring news of the entire Paris family to my mother.

The Faure household, with so many children of various ages and genders and dear Mlle. Bouchard, their governess, was jolly. Everyone hugged me goodbye. Cousin Arnaud arrived to say adieu, as if it was an inconvenience to appear at all. He certainly had put on airs since last summer. I didn't hug him.

Finally, I took leave of No. 1 rue Charles-Lamoureux in the bright light of morning. On the descent in the elevator, Uncle Raoul handed me a package, about 12 by 14 inches, wrapped in brown paper and taped shut.

"What's this?" I asked.

"It's my memoirs of the war and Buchenwald." When he handed it to me, he implored, "Do something with this, *ma bête*." With his fingers he urgently drummed on its cover.

"I'll try," I stammered, questioning my worthiness of even accepting such a document to transport it, much less "do something" with it. Somehow I knew this was a very important moment, and I couldn't control the tears that erupted and spilled down my cheeks.

On the sidewalk, we kissed and hugged and Raoul wiped my eyes with his handkerchief. Aunt Mimi waved from the balcony. As I climbed into Aunt Constance's chauffeured car that would take me to the boat train, I wondered if I would ever see him again.

It was a long drive from New York City to Rockland, Maine, where we would spend the night before taking the ferry to Vinalhaven Island. Apparently, I'd changed.

"It's not called *chemin duh* whatever. It's a plain old train," my brother Phil said to my comment as I watched a train snake through a tunnel under the mountain.

"I've lived in another country—culture, okay? That's what people speak there." God, I thought, fifteen-year-old boys are so juvenile.

"Well, you aren't there anymore."

"No kidding!"

Maybe his annoyance was about my having been in the spotlight from the moment I walked down the gangplank in New York.

The hotel in Rockland was old, right on the main street next to an Army-Navy store. Dry goods were cheaper on the mainland, so we stocked up on them and loaded them into the car. While it was my first trip here, our stepfather had spent every summer on the island in his youth. His family would pile furniture, pets and servants onto the boat that steamed up from Boston every summer.

We put our packed-to-the-ceiling car in line at the ferry terminal to be sure it would get on the first boat tomorrow.

The Vinalhaven ferry took about an hour and a half to reach Carver's Harbor in Penobscot Bay. Our small rental house was in the town of Carver's Harbor, a pretty little town on a harbor with lobster boats and shacks dotting the shoreline. We could walk from our house to the post office, grocery, or hardware store by crossing a bridge over tidal waters that flowed into and out of Carver's Pond. Getting the mail was a daily ritual that happily involved running into someone one knew, which usually led to chitchat and sometimes an invitation.

Days passed seamlessly. We swam in abandoned granite quarries; inland, we picked blueberries. At the Basin, a place where low tides left a four-foot granite ledge populated by hundreds of mussels, we pulled them free, threw them into buckets and scraped off their beards in a pail of water. We lived on lobster, mussels, clams, and corn.

We were often invited to the newly built home of Austin and Bodine Lamont, who owned ten acres on the northern point of the island. Dr. Lamont, a medical specialist from Philadelphia, had inherited great wealth. Bo, a distant cousin of George's, was much younger than her husband and enjoyed entertaining.

Mom arranged for me to hitch a ride to Boston with weekend guests of the Lamonts so I could spend time with my Uncle Francis and Aunt Camilla Richardson, who would escort me to prearranged interviews at Wellesley College, in Massachusetts, and Bennington College, in Vermont.

The young couple with whom I hitched a ride deposited me at Uncle Franny's door in Needham, Massachusetts, late on a Sunday afternoon. The minute I entered their house, I was transported back in time. The house had been featured in *House Beautiful* for its innovative architecture in the early

1940s. The window openings were finished in rounded plaster, without wood trim. Downstairs, the rough tile floor met expansive glass walls. The furnishings, including an English Refectory dining table on a Moroccan wool rug, and smells of wax and fireplace ashes all reminded me of my father's legacy.

Dad, like his famous grandfather, H.H. Richardson, had gone to L'Ecole des Beaux-Arts, in Paris, to study architecture after graduating from Harvard. That's when Uncle Raoul and Aunt Mimi had gotten to know them. My older brother, Arthur, was born in Paris in 1932 just before my parents returned to New York City, where Dad worked for McKim, Meade & White.

"Is that Consie?" boomed a male voice off the entrance hall. Uncle Franny came to hug me. "My, you look just like your father!" he exclaimed, scrutinizing me up and down. Uncle Franny stood about five foot ten inches and had thinning brown hair and a beer belly. He was the uncle who had brought Dad's ashes back from Tucson, where he had died in a freak accident.

Descending the staircase, Camilla, clad in shorts and holding a cigarette, gave a wave with her nonsmoking hand. "You made it!" she cried victoriously. "Let's have cocktails."

I followed them into the den off the entrance hall, where a fire burned in the rounded corner fireplace above a raised hearth.

"I'll get the ice," Camilla said, heading for the kitchen.

Franny opened two doors of a built-in cabinet that stood against a wall, exposing shelves stocked with bottles of liquor and various mixers. He pulled out a sliding tray. From above, he pulled down three highball glasses.

"Would you like whiskey?" he asked.

"Sure," I said.

"I'll make old-fashioneds."

Camilla returned with the ice bucket, which she placed on the tray.

We enjoyed cocktails by the fire, after which we had a stew with spices from Provence and a good red wine.

In bed that night, I replayed Uncle Franny's husky greeting and Camilla's smoky "hello," which reminded me that, unlike my stepfather, most of the Richardsons smoked and drank. My earliest memories were of walking through sawdust with Dad to inspect the progress of a number of buildings, and the sweet smells of newly sawn wood, the pungent whiff of turpentine and paint thinner. There's something about connecting with kin after a long separation, I thought, that's not unlike a salmon finding the stream it came from after a lifetime in the ocean. It evoked a calm knowing, a feeling of belonging that didn't need language. It just was.

I wasn't comfortable visiting the campus at Wellesley College, west of Boston, or meeting the director of admissions. I found the huge campus, with its gothic buildings and park-like setting, intimidating.

Bennington College, in North Bennington, Vermont, put me immediately at ease in its rural landscape with twelve clapboard houses facing a common. The campus was situated on a sizable amount of land on a slight plateau bordered by low New England stone walls. The feeling was relaxed and casual. Wearing a dark blue sheath dress and flat shoes, I made my way with Uncle Franny to the director of admissions' office in the barn-like administration building. The director welcomed us and took us on a tour. We learned that the student body was about 350, with a student-teacher ratio of twelve-to-one. He thought my year in France was a definite plus but wanted to give me additional tests, so we arranged to spend the night and return the following day.

Back on Vinalhaven Island, I anxiously waited to hear if I'd been accepted for the fall semester. When the official letter addressed to me arrived, I ripped it open and read, "We are pleased to inform you that you have been accepted in the Freshman Class for the 1955-56 academic year."

⇒ 10 ⇐

Uncle Franny took me to Needham, Massachusetts, to buy a new four-door 1954 Ford, paid for with money from the trust created when my father died. Not having known the trust existed, I learned that I would have authority over it when I turned twenty-one.

On the appointed day, I departed in my new bright blue car from Needham, bound for Bennington, Vermont, with all my belongings in the trunk and the back seat. How grown-up it felt to be behind the wheel of my first car, its new-car smell intoxicating. I imagined our journey as a shiny blue boat cutting west through an ocean of golden and russet fall foliage. The four-hour drive followed Route 2 to Williamstown, Massachusetts, where it intersected Vermont Route 7, and from there I turned north toward Bennington and then onto the winding college driveway framed by tall pine trees just east of the tiny town of North Bennington.

My room assignment was one half of a double suite, with a shared bathroom off the living room of Swan House, one of eight residence houses sprinkled around the common. Lucy Grier, my suite mate, from New York City, was short with wavy black hair and a big, friendly smile. My room faced east, away from the grassy tree-lined common, while Lucy's faced the road on the busy side toward it. The furniture, which consisted of a bed, a desk, a chair, and a bureau, was cutesy Colonial-style maple, a step down from the French Louis V and VI I'd gotten used to.

After organizing my stuff, I explored the Commons, the building where we would receive mail and eat most of our meals in the dining hall. As I passed through wearing my French gray wool skirt and white blouse, I noticed girls sitting in clusters and some alone. The uniform appeared to be leotards, bare feet, long hair, or anything exotic. No Peter Pan collars, no pleated skirts, nothing preppy in sight. "Well," I thought, "that's a relief. Jeans will be fine. This place is my cup of tea."

On my third morning at Bennington, I suddenly noticed people heading out the door early, carrying books. I asked a girl named Bobby where she was going.

"Lit 101," she replied.

Holy shit! I didn't have a clue where to go. I quickly made my way to the administration offices housed in what was called The Barn.

In Admissions, I asked a pleasant lady how to register for classes. She asked if I'd just arrived.

"No. I've been here three days, but no one told me I had to register," I explained.

She looked at me as if I were slightly retarded and stepped into another office and spoke to someone out of view.

"What's your name, dear?" the woman asked.

I told her. She and the other person conferred and then informed me that my academic adviser, Eugene Black, was the person I needed to see. They directed me to his office on the second floor. No one was there, but I learned from posted office hours that I might find him there later in the day. I left him a note.

What had I been doing for three days? Was I so out-of-it that I failed to notice what everyone else was doing? I had been driving around, reading, and, well, just enjoying my freedom. Until now, authority figures like Mom and Uncle Raoul had always told me what to do. Why hadn't anyone told me I needed to sign up for classes? What if all the classes were full? I began to worry that I had already ruined things before they started.

Feeling almost sick with worry, I was sitting on the floor outside Mr. Black's office at two o'clock, listening for approaching footsteps on the stairs. When he arrived, I scrambled to my feet and put out my hand to shake his. "Mr. Black, I'm so glad to meet you."

"What can I do for you?" He opened his office door and stepped inside, motioning for me to enter. As I explained my problem, he invited me to take a seat across from his desk.

"This is a self-directed kind of place, Constance. No one is going to tell you what to do or not do. In fact, it's pretty much the students who make the rules around here. If we, the faculty, didn't do our jobs or keep our commitments, we wouldn't be here. The students would make sure of that. Now, what do you hope to accomplish this semester? Let's start there."

"I'm not sure," I replied.

About an hour later, we had mapped out a course of study that would let me test the waters, so to speak, through a variety of courses, such as Language and Literature 101, Introduction to French Literature (conducted in French), Introduction to Visual Art, and Current World Tensions. Mr. Black guided me through the procedures I needed to pursue to assure official registration in each. Thus armed, I forged ahead.

By the time I attended my first meeting of Language and Literature 101, or Lit 101, held in Canfield, another residence's living room early one morning, I felt mildly confident, having successfully registered for all four classes, also managing to arrive on time.

Professor Howard Nemerov arrived. Tall and patrician, his accent was decidedly British. He lowered himself into an armchair and looked around the room at the small group.

"I'm not sure what any of you can do, so why don't you read *King Lear* and the book of Job and write a comparison of the two for next time?" He stood and left. *Paralyzed* isn't exactly the right word to describe the effect this assignment had on me; *terrified* is closer.

My other classes proved less intimidating, but all the students seemed better-prepared than I in almost every subject. French was an exception because I was by far the most accomplished student in Bernard Crowley's class. Introduction to Visual Art I could handle, but Current World Tensions was another challenge, involving complex political and historical issues. I hunkered down.

By November, Professor Nemerov had returned all my papers with comments such as "cliché" or "spell?" written in the margins. His policy was not to accept any paper with misspellings. Several times, I slept through my alarm clock on the mornings Lit 101 was held, staggering in without having had breakfast or a shower and I rarely spoke.

I bought a large dictionary and began to spend time in the library reading what others had to say about the subjects in question. He was right about spelling the English language correctly. Why was I so sloppy? Previous schools hadn't demanded more. Nemerov was demanding that I think, not just spew clichés or regurgitate views already expressed. As I clumsily attempted to do this, my respect for Professor Nemerov grew.

In Current World Tensions, I was writing a paper about Cyprus and Enosis, which involved learning about Turkey. I began to read *The New York Times'* Sunday edition. Joe Leibowitz, a Williams College student, often parked himself in the Swan House living room, and it was he who helped me understand political issues like those surrounding Cyprus, Turkey, and Enosis.

As the semester progressed, my self-confidence blossomed. My final assignment for Lit 101 before the December break was to read and write a book report on *Hadrian's Memoirs*, by Marguerite Yourcenar. I condensed my six-page rough draft, eliminating all but essentials, to barely two and a half pages before passing it in.

On an icy December morning as I climbed the stairs to retrieve my paper from the administrative offices, my legs trembled. I found it among others in the Lit 101 box attached to the door. Professor Nemerov had written: "Constance has performed a small miracle in her midterm report on *Hadrian's Memoirs*. HN." I'd never felt so proud of anything in my life.

Christmas 1955 on the ranch in northern California was wet. With a new storm headed toward flood-stricken southern Oregon and northern California on Christmas Eve, President Eisenhower declared the region a disaster zone. The Red Cross reported that 20,000 flood refugees had been taken into fifty-seven Red Cross shelters in northern California.

While most of the disaster area was farther north than Green Gulch Ranch, we spent all day sandbagging the dikes below each of the three ponds that lay above the house. If they didn't hold, the house would be under water.

Mercifully, they held. Christmas Day was mostly about not having to be evacuated. Exhausted, we ate the simple pot roast, potatoes, and carrots in relative silence, the only sounds the clinking of silverware on china. Everyone went to bed early, praying for the rain to stop.

I flew back to Vermont via Albany, N.Y., stopping at Bennington only to pack my car, and then proceeded to New York City to begin non-resident term, which would run through mid-March. Theoretically, it was implemented to give students a taste of the real work world, into which they would one day be expected to enter. Practically, it was instituted to save the college enormous heating bills during the coldest months.

I had arranged to live at the Barbizon Hotel for Women, on East 63rd Street, for $5.50 a day. I parked my car under the el a few blocks away and moved it every other day to avoid getting parking tickets. The only job I was able to get was as clerical assistant at Schroeder Trust Company, where I had a trust account. My room at the Barbizon Hotel was about twelve by fifteen feet and overheated. I spent as little time in it as possible.

The boring duties at Schroeder Trust involved transferring letters of credit from one department to another. I was a glorified "gofer" in a skirt, stockings, and heels.

The only break in this dismal routine was occasional dinner invitations to my elderly maternal grandparents' apartment on Park Avenue. Grandmère (Fanny) and Grandpère (Phil) Livermore lived in a sumptuous apartment and employed a cook and a live-in maid. They spent part of the winter in Palm Beach, and in the summer they retired to their large house in Jericho, Long Island.

Family gossip circulated that my grandfather, sibling to my Aunt Constance de Lubersac, married my grandmother for her money. At one time, Grandpère and J.P. Morgan were partners. There was some financial chicanery that caused the partnership legal problems. Grandpère left the country for France, where he waited out the storm, living under his stepmother Baroness Sellier's roof, while J.P. Morgan spent the ensuing years paying back the shareholders.

Grandpère adored my beautiful mother but was a dreadful father to Aunt Francesca, my mother's younger sister, and Uncle Pat, a paranoid schizophrenic committed to a mental institution in upstate New York. What precipitated Pat's breakdown was his father's parting remark when Pat left for Harvard College: "If you don't get into the Porcellian Club, don't bother to come home."

I arrived in the paneled foyer with a small bouquet of flowers, dropping my overcoat and gloves on the bench.

"In here," screeched Grandmère from the living room overlooking Park Avenue.

In a pretty room with overstuffed chairs, two matching sofas, and various small inlaid tables with marble tops, Grandmère was seated in a yellow silk upholstered chair wearing a soft gray shirtdress and a violet scarf. Her hair was dyed a soft brown and her makeup carefully applied. I crossed the room, bent down, planted a kiss on her left cheek, and handed her the flowers.

"Oh, you're cold," she said. "Would you like hot tea?"

"Offer her a drink," commanded Grandpère as he emerged from the hallway. He struggled with arthritic knees and now used a cane. Switching the cane to his left hand, he held out his right. "What would you like?"

"Sherry," I replied, taking his hand in mine.

A maid appeared. Grandpère asked her to bring three sherries.

"My, you've gotten good-looking," Grandpère said offhandedly.

"It's all that French grooming last year at the de Lubersacs," I modestly replied.

Over the next hour, we dined on a simple but excellent meal of lamb chops, mashed potatoes, string beans with almonds, and crème brulée. They wanted to know about the California floods and how my mother and George and my brothers were.

"We were afraid the sandbags wouldn't hold, but they did. It was exhausting," I said.

"Why didn't the fire department come?" asked Grandpere.

"On a ranch, you're on your own," I said, "except for neighbors, like the Pontis, who we've helped in a crisis."

"Why does your mother choose to live there?" asked Grandmere. "I've never understood that."

Realizing neither one had a clue about Mom's life on the ranch, I switched topics to the more amusing goings-on *chez* the de Lubersac and Faure families. Neither grandparent asked about my life or what I was doing in New York for three months. Around 8:30 I took my leave.

The rest of non-resident term passed in a haze of boredom and frustration at the complexity of learning how to navigate in an enormous city with little discretionary money and few friends. I was lonely, and my job at Schroeder's was dull, dull, triple dull. I couldn't wait for spring term to begin.

→ 11 ←

A fugue of gossip whipped around our small campus like dried dandelions in a gale.

"Did you hear Rachael was caught in Jack Riley's room at Dartmouth, and she's getting kicked out?"

"How can she get kicked out here by breaking rules there?"

"Don't ask me. They're in collusion maybe?"

"They'll let her graduate in absentia anyway. She's done a brilliant thesis."

"Says who?"

"Honest. She found some new origins of Old English in Spencer's *Fairie Queene.*"

"Origins, smorigins. Who cares? Spencer's about as fresh as embalming fluid. If she graduates, it's because her old man will *buy* her graduation, for Christ's sake."

"Whaddya mean?"

"He owns Bloomingdale's, dummy."

"Rachael's father *owns* Bloomingdale's?"

"Of course. Hey, Goy, where ya' been?"

The wind carried these tales to all corners of the college. Anyone with a survival instinct simply didn't get caught in a man's room off campus or get caught on her own campus with a man in her room. Men, that species we occasionally saw when the Dartmouth or Williams variety filtered through our campus, had to be out of student houses by 10 p.m. Period. There were campus cops who patrolled and manned the gates in all-night vigils.

While these rules were known and, for the most part, adhered to, I learned that it was perfectly okay to leave campus overnight as long as you signed a sheet indicating where you were. You didn't have to indicate with whom you were, only where you could be found. Why, I wondered, would anyone risk expulsion when she could legitimately sign out and spend the

70

whole night with whomever? It was just one of the conundrums of the 1950s.

Days were lengthening. The snows clung to muddy banks like torn rags on an army of survivors. The privet buds were emerging from their ice age. I was holding my own in all my spring-semester classes, which was progress after a weak first semester. Lit 101 was by far the most demanding course, but The Novella was also a challenge. I had thought writing a novella would be easy, but it wasn't, and the main reason was that I bored myself.

In Literature of Self Discovery, I was immersed in letters that Katherine Mansfield, the New Zealand writer, wrote to John M. Murray. Through them one could track her budding self-awareness and her fruition as an artist.

Sculpture Studio, taught by Simon Moselsio, was appealing because the sensuality of working with wet clay gave my overtaxed brain a break.

Current World Tensions was another challenging course in which I mostly floundered. Why? I appeared to be happily oblivious to anything that didn't directly affect me, such as, of course, national and international affairs.

My new friendship with Joe, a Williams undergraduate, was evolving into something a little more than casual. He invited me to dinner in Williamstown. I had to wear a dress, stockings, and heels. Oh my!

One afternoon, Lucy's friend Pinky Pinchot barged into my room and asked to borrow my car to get to the bank. My policy was not to lend it, period, which I told her. She pleaded, saying it would only take fifteen minutes. Again I said no. She was unrelenting. If she didn't make it to the bank in the next fifteen minutes, the world would blow up. Reluctantly, I handed her the keys.

Twenty minutes later, there was a loud knock on our suite door. Professor Paul Feeley stood in the doorway.

"There's been an accident involving your car. Don't panic. Pinky's alive. She's all right, but you need to come with me right away."

Somehow, the way he said this made me feel guilty *and* relieved. Guilty because it was *my* car, relieved that she wasn't killed in it. Was this his intent?

When Professor Feeley and I reached the scene, my blue car was lying on its roof in the middle of the two-lane road, its four wheels pointing skyward like a large dead insect. The police dispatch crackled from a black and white police cruiser, its driver door flung open. These sounds mingled with shouts from a man as he directed the tow-truck driver into position.

Pinky never even made it out of the driveway. At the long curve, she obviously lost control and probably overcorrected, flipping the car onto its roof. Paramedics had taken her to the hospital. I spoke to the police officer at the scene and signed papers for the tow-truck operator.

The accident put a wrench in my plans to drive across the United States that summer to see Mark, the elusive Englishman who'd stolen my heart two summers ago on the European tour. He'd written from Vancouver Island, British Colombia, where he said he was trying to figure out what direction his life should take. He hoped to see me while he was in the provinces. I really wanted to see him.

Because I didn't want to drive alone, Joe's friend Reggie Plesner decided to join me as far as Seattle, where his sister lived. Because Reggie's brother-in-law was incarcerated on drug charges, Reggie wanted to make sure his sister and her children were okay. I was relieved to have someone to share the costs and the driving, believing it was safer than driving the 3,000 miles alone.

Because the Ford was totaled and my insurance, less the $100 deductible, wasn't enough to buy a comparable automobile, I trolled for a used one. Thankfully, Joe and Reggie offered to help. The few used-car dealerships in Bennington yielded five possibilities in my price range. Joe and Reggie narrowed that list down to two choices that passed their mechanical inspections: a 1953 Pontiac with 20,000 miles and an older Ford with 53,000 miles. At their urging, I bought the red Pontiac.

Pinky waltzed into our suite one day and plunked a $50 bill on my bed.

"I won this at the track Sunday," she said flippantly. "It's to help with the deductible."

"Oh great, that *really* helps replace my car."

Pinky didn't appear to notice my sarcasm, nor did she communicate any remorse for totaling my car. Since it was well-known that she spent nearly every weekend and lots of money at the Sarasota racetrack, I'd developed a quick, palpable dislike of Pinky Pinchot, of the Social Register Pinchots.

Reggie and I set off early one June morning, the car packed with a tent, a stove, pots and pans, a cooler, sleeping bags, and tons of clothes. We drove west to Buffalo and Chicago, camping out in fields and national parks. West of Lake Michigan, we headed north to Spring Green, Wisconsin, to visit Frank Lloyd Wright's Taliesin East. There we camped in a nearby field next to a small pond.

Thoroughly grubby, I submerged myself in the pond with a bar of soap hanging from a soft rope I'd made. Emerging moments later and discovering leeches on my arms and legs, I screamed.

"Oh! Get it off!" I pulled at the black slug-like creature that clung to my midriff.

Reggie jumped up from his seat on the embankment and helped pull the creatures off. He wrapped a huge towel around my shaking body. I needed comfort and reluctantly accepted it from him. Reggie was a dolt, nice enough but slow. I was about as attracted to him as oil is to water.

The next day it was on to Minneapolis, then Fargo, Billings, Spokane, and finally Seattle, where I spent a night at his sister's before proceeding to Vancouver Island alone.

Mark's address was a country club in Maple Bay on Vancouver Island, where he was staying or had a job or both. His letter told me he would be there for the summer while trying to "sort out his life."

There were a number of ferry routes from various parts of Vancouver to various points on Vancouver Island. I studied the map and chose the northernmost ferry route, thinking it would be less crowded and therefore less confusing. From where it landed, I would drive south to Maple Bay. I decided to stay the night in Vancouver and embark early the next morning to catch the ferry. I hadn't spoken to Mark to confirm my arrival and suddenly wondered if he was really there. I looked up the telephone number of the country club in Maple Bay and dialed.

"Ocean Avenue Country Club. May I help you?"

"Mark Flynn, please."

I heard ringing. Nobody picked up.

"He must be out. Would you like to leave a message?" the lady asked.

At least he's really there. "Yes. Please tell Mr. Flynn that I'll be arriving tomorrow on the first ferry to Departure Bay."

"And your name is?"

"Constance Richardson."

Excited about seeing Mark, I also remembered how embarrassing it was when I revealed strong feelings for him that weren't reciprocated on the eve of my departure for France two summers ago. I resolved to be more reserved this time. If for some reason he wasn't there, I'd just sightsee, turn around, and go back to Seattle to collect Reggie.

The sky had a sharp, clear brightness with puffy white clouds and a stiff breeze. The Strait of Georgia was brilliant blue. The crossing was swift. I was rested and glad I'd taken the time off instead of rushing, only to have arrived in a wilted heap. As the ramp lowered onto the dock on Vancouver Island, I spotted Mark. Driving off the ramp, I pulled over to the side. He looked the same, light brown wavy hair, a robust complexion. He wore khakis and a short-sleeve shirt. He had a wonderful way of blending shyness with impeccable Queen's English.

"Follow me in the Austin." He gestured behind him to a light blue car.

At the Ocean Avenue Country Club, Mark escorted me to the terrace, where we collapsed into comfortable Victorian armchairs and ordered iced tea. I related highlights of the drive across the states, including the leech episode in the Wisconsin lake, and listened as Mark explained how he decided on this summer adventure in British Columbia.

"It's a test to see if I can survive in the ordinary world, not the world I was brought up in with a silver spoon," he explained.

"What do you do here?" I asked

"A little of this and that. I've waited on tables, and—"

"*You've* waited on tables?"

"Um, yes, although now they seem to find me more useful at the front desk or as a sommelier in the dining room."

"Testing you?"

"Sort of."

"How long will you be here?"

"The remainder of the summer."

"Mmm."

After a lull, I explained that I was short on money and asked if there was somewhere we could camp out for a couple of days rather than my incurring debt at a hotel. I still had all the camping gear in the Pontiac, including Reggie's sleeping bag, which Mark could use.

"Can you take a few days off?" I asked.

"I had planned on taking time off to spend with you. So, yes."

On the way to explore a remote section of the island where the population was almost nonexistent, we purchased food, bottled water, fuel for the Sterno stove, and mosquito spray. Veering off the paved highway onto a logging road, we emerged from a canopy of Douglas fir to a sunny knoll overlooking a horseshoe-shaped bay. Off the coast in the middle of a channel stood an island with a dock and boathouse. Inhaling a deep scent of pine and ozone from the sea and hearing the caws of seagulls, I wondered how the people who lived there got back and forth.

⇢ Swimming Upstream ⇠

We pitched the tent in the most level area and, after arranging our sleeping bags side by side, set about making dinner. The sterno stove did its job, and before long we were enjoying cheeseburgers and chips.

It had been a long day, so we climbed into the sleeping bags and chatted, holding hands in the dark. His smell and touch were still magic. I adored this person, but for now I kept this to myself.

The ground under me shook violently. A grinding engine in low gear nearby jolted me out of the sleeping bag and the tent and into the daylight. There, not fifteen feet away, was a large yellow earth-moving piece of equipment coming toward us. I shouted and waved my arms at the driver, who couldn't hear me over the noise of his machine or see me from his vantage point. Mark joined me in the logging road. We shouted and waved articles of clothing in the air above our heads. Finally the driver spotted us, threw the machine into idle, and opened his cab door.

"You can't camp here," he shouted. "This here is to be clear-cut. There's a logging crew just down the way."

"Much obliged," said Mark. "We'll be out of your hair."

We broke camp in record speed, grateful not to have been run over, and headed back to the country club.

"That didn't work out very well, did it?" I said.

"Um, no. What now?" Mark responded.

"Exactly. What now?" I glanced at his face and his eyes, which were focused on the road. He'd thrown the ball back into my court. I perused my options. Money was tight.

"I'll drive to Seattle, where I can stay tonight with friends. In the morning, I'll head home to Green Gulch," I told him.

"You only just got here," Mark said sadly, without offering any alternative.

I felt let down. He'd invited me to come and I'd driven three thousand miles. Couldn't he have arranged a place for me to stay?

⇥ 12 ⇤

After picking up Reggie in Seattle, we headed south on U.S. Route 5 through Washington. At Portland, Oregon, U.S. Route 5 turned inland a bit and then went straight south. By six o'clock we'd located a state park, and we camped for the night, having traveled 300 miles. The next day just north of Sacramento, we cut off southwest to pick up Highway 101 into Marin County. Taking turns driving the six hundred miles, with strategic stops for gas, bathrooms, and food, we reached Green Gulch Ranch late the second afternoon.

The fog-laden eucalyptus trees lining the half-mile-long dirt driveway emitted their pungent smells. At the U-turn at the bottom of the drive, the ranch jeep, driven by Art, the foreman, was heading up the drive. I pulled over to let him pass. He flashed me a big smile.

"Welcome home. How's the drive?"

"Long. Hi, Art." I introduced Art to Reggie.

"You have a visitor. English. Thick accent. Arrived this afternoon by cab. Name's Flynn."

"Mark? Where is he?"

"Knew you was coming, so I showed him a room in the house. Told him he'd have to fend for himself, fix his own meals. Your folks are gone. Cattle show in Denver. Be home day after tomorrow."

"Thanks, Art."

I felt mildly let down that they weren't here, but then, they'd had no idea when I'd arrive, only that it would be within two weeks. We continued down the driveway and parked below the upper pasture. I piloted Reggie past the outbuildings and down the concrete path to the kitchen, which was the hub of the house. A large black iron stove sat at one end of the remodeled space, with a living area at the other, dominated by a freestanding fireplace with built-in seating upholstered in brown Naugahyde. The counters were taller than standard to accommodate my mother's six foot one inch height. I spotted the residue of someone's meal on the counter, a dirty plate and utensils.

"Mark," I hollered.

"Hello."

Mark appeared from the hall to the downstairs bedroom, across from the laundry room. The three of us stood there, not knowing what to say. I tried to remember if I mentioned I had driven out with Reggie. "Ah, Mark, this is Reggie Plesner."

"Right." Mark extended his hand to Reggie.

Reggie looked momentarily stunned but gained enough composure to shake Mark's proffered hand. I fast-forwarded to my parents' arrival in two days and their likely reaction to my having two gentlemen here. I decided on the spot to put both men in the house and remove myself to the barn bunkhouse so there would be no perceived impropriety. I announced my decision and showed Reggie to his bedroom next to the back door.

I bade everyone good night and headed out to the barn with sheets and towels. I hadn't even had a chance to find out what had prompted Mark's impulsive journey from Vancouver Island, but I was excited that he came. At almost midnight, I turned out the lights and cradled my head in the pillow.

Breakfast. Reggie had figured out how to make coffee in the Chemex coffee pot, and Mark had located the tea bags. The icebox had plenty of eggs, milk, and orange juice. The freezer yielded frozen bread, which we thawed. Breakfast was a tango with three instead of two. We took efforts not to bump into one another. Body language, however, said something else. Reggie scowled at Mark, who asked him politely how he liked his toast.

"Toast is toast."

"As you say," replied Mark.

"Reggie, Mark was just trying to be polite."

"Well, he wasn't even invited here."

"Reggie. That's hostile. Mark is my friend. Say you're sorry."

"No need. It's true. Insanely spur-of-the-moment," Mark said.

"I'm glad," I said, beaming.

"I'm glad *you're* glad," said Mark.

"I'm sick of this!" snapped Reggie.

"*Mon Dieu, je suis désolé.*" Mark wiped a hand dramatically across his forehead.

"Butt out, Limey scum!" Reggie shook his fist at Mark.

Reggie was becoming more emotional and hostile toward Mark by the minute, and I wasn't sure what to do.

"Why don't we go for a hike after we clean up?" I suggested.

"Fine idea," Mark said. He rose from the table and took his dish to the sink.

Reggie didn't say anything, which I interpreted as benign. However, when we were ready to leave, he said he'd pass, so Mark and I headed off to Muir Beach, a mile away through the lower pastures. Mark explained that he'd taken the train to Oakland, then a cab here, which was expensive. I promised to drive him to Oakland when he left. Finally alone, I wanted to find out why he suddenly decided to come.

"When you left so suddenly, I, um, felt cheated, and—"

"Me, too, but I couldn't afford a hotel."

"Anyway, I wanted to see more of you and meet your folks. See where you grew up."

"Reggie is impossible, isn't he?" I apologized.

"He's behaving like a jealous lover," said Mark.

"Oh, I assure you, he's not one. We're strictly platonic. He wanted to visit his sister and nephews in Seattle. Her husband is in jail, and she's alone with two kids."

"Mmmm. How do you know him?"

"He goes to Williams College, near Bennington. He helped me buy the Pontiac after a girl totaled—wrecked my Ford. I don't know him well, but he's harmless."

"He's tiresome."

We reached Muir Beach, took off our shoes, and skipped in the icy Pacific shoreline from one end of the beach to the other. In front of a weathered log on the dry sand, we collapsed. A dog caught a Frisbee again and again as a young man threw it, and there were other dogs with their handlers. *Beach Theater* I thought. We talked about the last two years in our lives. For me, that encompassed a year in Paris and my first year at Bennington, which were diametrically opposite. For Mark, it was weighing the options of going to Singapore to forge a financial career or helping his father run The Old Ride boarding school in Buckinghamshire. When we felt more caught up, we headed back.

We arrived hungry for lunch. Reggie, it seems, had disappeared. I made tuna-salad sandwiches on dark rye bread for Mark and me. With my parents arriving tomorrow, I made a grocery list and told Mark we'd go to the market after lunch. I didn't want to be accused of using their ranch as a hotel for my friends and me.

Just then Reggie arrived looking hot and sweaty. I threw him a welcoming smile and asked if he'd like a tuna sandwich.

"Sure. Great."

"Where did you hike?" I asked.

"Top of the hill. You can see the Golden Gate Bridge and the whole bay."

I made Reggie his sandwich, poured him a glass of milk, and put his lunch in front of him.

"Thank you," Reggie said. "Where did you go?"

"Muir Beach," I answered. "It's wonderful to put your feet in the Pacific Ocean."

As Reggie ate his lunch, I explained that we needed to make a run to town to pick up groceries before my parents returned tomorrow. I asked if he'd like to come.

"I'll hang out here," he answered.

He couldn't say I hadn't tried to include him. "Reggie, what do you want for dinner? " I asked.

"Whatever you get is fine," he said.

Mark and I left for town, four miles away. I decided to make spaghetti sauce from my mother's recipe. At Mill Valley Market, where we'd shopped for a million years, I got all the ingredients for the sauce, along with fresh greens and French bread. Mark took the "replenish" list and found milk, orange juice, eggs, and dish detergent, although it took him forever. On the way home, Mark said he wanted to learn to make spaghetti sauce *à ma mère*.

I set Mark up with cloves of garlic, a cutting board and a sharp knife, instructing him to dice the cloves. As I peeled two onions, I watched Reggie walk toward the kitchen from the barn.

"Hi," I greeted him when he arrived.

"Domestic scene here," he said.

"We're making spaghetti sauce. Want to help?" I asked.

"Nah. I'm the third wheel," he responded dejectedly.

"Your rejecting *us* is more like it. Don't blame me!" I snapped, my voice escalating in anger. I turned my attention to chopping the onions, grabbed a skillet, tossed in olive oil and butter and sautéed the onions on "medium." My eyes began to tear up. Mark, who didn't know how to cook, thought it was Reggie who had made me cry.

"I rather think you're heavy-handed," Mark said to Reggie, pointing to me as I ran cold water and flushed my eyes, trying to stop the weeping.

Reggie looked at Mark. "You fruit!"

"Those are fighting words," Mark barked in the most pissed-off voice I'd heard out of his mouth.

The men scuffled toward one another like two bulls. I stepped between them.

"Listen. Stop it! No fighting." I turned to face Reggie. "I'm ashamed of you. You've been angling for a fight with Mark from the get-go. Not all right."

I heaved a big breath and then continued. "I drove out West with you because I didn't want to drive alone or pay all the gas. If you don't stop ruining my visit with Mark, you can find another way to get back East."

All conversation stopped. I resumed sautéing the onions and garlic. I pulled down the large glazed-iron casserole dish from over the big stove and assembled sauce ingredients.

The guys avoided each other. Reggie sat by the fireplace, thumbing through a magazine, while next to me Mark watched over my shoulder. Finally I put the top on the iron casserole.

"This will simmer on 'low.' The longer it cooks, the more blended the flavors will be. But we have to make sure it's not sticking to the bottom."

Dinner was delicious and, thankfully, almost pleasant. While we washed dishes and tidied up, Mark announced he had decided to return to Vancouver by train before my parents' arrival. I was certain his reason for leaving was because Reggie had ruined his visit, not because he wanted to avoid meeting my parents's. I accepted the news gracefully and offered to drive him to Oakland in the morning.

When I said good night to Reggie, I remarked, "I'm sure you're thrilled he's leaving!"

Reggie looked at me silently before dropping eye contact.

I walked to the bunkhouse feeling totally confused about Mark's feelings for me. Would he really leave if he were interested in me? Why would he have come all this way if he weren't? What a mess!

In the morning, we left early to make it to the Oakland railroad station with time to spare before his train departed. At least we would have that time without Reggie.

"It's best I get back to my job," Mark said.

"I'm sorry you have to leave. I'm sorry about Reggie. He's a jerk."

"He is rather, but that's not why I'm leaving."

"Why then?"

"I'm supposed to be working, not flitting around the states. We'll visit again. I want you to come to visit me in England, maybe next summer?"

"Really?"

"Yes. Could you manage that?"

"It's such a long way away. I don't know," I said.

"Think about it. We'll write. Time will fly as soon as you're back at Bennington. You'll see."

At the train station, we hugged, and he hurriedly kissed me on the cheek. Then he climbed aboard the train and found a seat facing the platform where I stood. I felt sad as the train inched away on the tracks and disappeared from view.

⇒13⇐

Mom and George arrived in the afternoon. I showed my mother the leftover spaghetti sauce from yesterday, and she seemed pleased about not having to figure out what to cook for dinner.

When I introduced Reggie, I explained that I dropped him off in Seattle at his sister's before proceeding to Vancouver to see Mark. I further explained that Mark had to get back to his job at the country club and was sorry not to meet them. I made it clear that I put the boys in the house and put myself in the bunkhouse. My mother seemed to be half-listening. On reflection, I thought she was distracted. Why didn't she ask anything about our long cross-country trip? Where were the hugs? In fact, why hadn't she asked about my driving partner *before* I left Vermont? Other mothers would. Why hadn't she?

I offered to set the table, heat up the spaghetti sauce, and boil more spaghetti for dinner.

"That's wonderful," she said, turning away.

When she came down for dinner, having freshened up, she was more relaxed. Our dinner was ready to serve on the big warm iron stove. George poured my mother a Jack Daniel's, while Reggie and I made our drinks and joined them around the fireplace.

"We didn't win a first prize, but one bull received an honorable mention," Mom said.

"That's great," Reggie said.

"Mom, I followed your recipe for the spaghetti sauce. Everyone said how good it was."

She smiled at the compliment, and I hoped things were going to turn out all right on this visit. Dinner was served and eaten, and Reggie and I offered to do the dishes so my parents could retire.

After cleaning up, I carried my stuff from the bunkhouse upstairs to my old bedroom and climbed into bed with a book but put it down and turned out the lights seconds later. As I lay there, I tried to envision Reggie's and my idea to earn some cash in the next few weeks. We had talked of sketching people's houses and selling them note cards. A friend of my parents' owned a small printing company in Sausalito. We'd call him in the morning and check out stationery and art-supply stores in the area.

I brought up these ideas over breakfast, and Reggie agreed it sounded promising. As we put our dishes in the dishwasher, Mom wished us luck.

Mr. Strawbridge was welcoming, showing us his old-fashioned printing press and the one-color offset printing process, suggesting we sell sets of at least one hundred cards and envelopes. He also recommended paper-supply stores in San Rafael.

By late afternoon, we had a much clearer idea of what to charge for each package, which would include our original drawing and one hundred folded personalized cards with matching envelopes on good-quality card stock. As we headed back to the ranch, I felt we had made a good start.

"Mr. Strawbridge was very helpful," I said to Mom in the kitchen. Expecting an enthusiastic reaction, I realized something was wrong because she avoided eye contact and her forehead creased in furrows.

"That's nice," she said unconvincingly. "I'd like to talk to you, Consie. Let's go upstairs."

"Sure." My stomach churned as I followed her to the living room.

"We've been hearing concern from Mrs. Ponti and other neighbors about you being here alone with two men." She motioned for me to sit on the matching sofa opposite where she sat. "It doesn't look right for a young woman when her parents aren't here."

Stunned at the implication of what she was saying, I blurted, "That's why I put the men in the house and why I slept in the bunkhouse."

"I know that's what you *said*."

"Are you calling me a liar? Don't you believe me?"

"Don't raise your voice."

"Do you even like Mrs. Ponti?" I asked.

My mother looked wounded, her mouth pinched, drawn, as if she was the one whose feelings had been hurt, not me. She would make her way downstairs to George, who would comfort and validate her martyrdom.

Why did I always let her down when I tried my best to be worthy? Even when I thought I'd been a gracious hostess to Mark and Reggie while anticipating and respecting my absent parents' wishes, I had apparently failed again.

Why did I yearn for my mother's love when it was so reluctantly given?

I ran to my room and sobbed into the chenille bedspread until sleep finally and mercifully enveloped me in its calming, restorative oblivion.

The rest of the week, I tried to bury hurt feelings and concentrate on working on our card business. We managed to sell five sets, all in the same neighborhood. Drawing was the most fun. We sat in the car and drew with pen and black ink. A small trick was to display the numerical address of each house on the curb in the bottom of the drawing or on a mailbox. We delivered our drawings to the printer and waited for the finished product.

Not wanting to hang around the ranch over the weekend, I suggested to Reggie that we drive to Santa Cruz and camp out. I didn't want to dwell on hurt feelings. When I told Mom where we were going, she noted it without objection. Did she care only about what neighbors thought?

The drive from San Jose over the descending, winding coastal Highway 17 to Santa Cruz was beautiful. Once there, my feelings unexpectedly erupted and I burst into tears.

"When I have children, I'll always believe them and give them the benefit of the doubt," I half-sobbed.

Reggie put his right hand over mine and squeezed. We were sitting in the car, parked at a campground, about to erect our tent under redwoods.

"It feels so awful when you always disappoint your own mother. My father loved me. I still remember how his face would light up when he saw me," I said, wiping my eyes and nose with a Kleenex.

"When did your father pass away?"

"Just after my tenth birthday."

"That's a shame. Was he sick?"

"It was an accident, carbon monoxide poisoning from a bad gas heater."

"How terrible."

We hauled the tent and tarpaulin from the trunk to a flat square of dirt, where we assembled it. Inside, we aligned our sleeping bags side by side with our pillows touching. We pulled folding chairs up to the cooler and set about making dinner of steak and beans on the Primus stove. We opened a bottle of red wine and poured it into metal cups.

We clinked our tin cups, a muffled salute, and savored the wine. Darkness closed in. Reggie built a fire and I pulled on a jacket. We had another bottle of the same wine, which we sipped in front of the fire.

"Reggie, *why* is my mother like that?" Emotionally devastated by Mom's lack of trust, I needed and wanted affection, validation. Scooting his chair closer to mine, he put an arm around my shoulders and pulled me toward him. I relaxed into the comforting warmth and began sobbing on his shoulder.

"I try to be a daughter she can be proud of," I said, sniffling.

Reggie stroked my hair and mumbled "Shush" in my ear.

"I'll die without her love. I miss Dot. I've lost everyone."

He gently lifted me into the tent, where we lay on top of the sleeping bags. Stroking me and softly kissing my eyelids only opened up more anguish.

"Why didn't Mom even ask me how I was doing at Bennington?" I cried. "I worked so hard there. Did she even ask?"

"Shhhh," he whispered, continuing his ministrations.

"She never asked me how I was getting across the country," I added. "I could have hitched a ride with an ax murderer!"

"I'm not a murderer," he whispered into my ear, his warm breath a tickle.

"Why do I always love the wrong people?" I sobbed. "Why?"

Caressing me, Reggie unzipped my jeans and pulled them and my panties off. He entered me and came so fast I almost didn't notice what was happening.

By morning light, it was a different matter. "Damn!" I muttered. It was July, but I wanted this summer to end. First, Mark's visit got screwed up. Now this. I couldn't drive across the country alone with Reggie, camping all the way. I'd have to find a third person so we could drive straight through. I'd put an ad in the newspaper at Berkeley, where there were lots of students. While I was pondering this, Reggie emerged from the tent dressed. Holding his socks and shoes, he sat next to me and began to put them on.

"We need to go back to the ranch," I said.

"Okay." Reggie tied his laces. "When?"

"Now. We can do more house drawings. We have to make more money for the trip back. And, Reggie, last night was a total mistake. Do you understand?"

"Speak for yourself."

"I do." I looked him directly in the eye to see if he got it.

"Okay." He held up both hands, palms toward me, signaling for me to stop.

Funneling my anger into a burst of energy, I took down the tent, rolled it up, and stuffed it into its duffel with the tarp. Reggie rolled up the sleeping bags and loaded everything into the car. We drove off silently. At a fast-food stop, we used the rest rooms and grabbed coffee and cinnamon rolls to go. It was a two-hour drive home.

"You need to move to the bunkhouse," I told Reggie. "We'll get groceries and keep them out there, make our meals there. That way Mom can't say we're a burden on her."

"Okay."

We stopped at the market in Mill Valley for groceries and pulled into the ranch driveway before noon. I told Mom my plan for Reggie to move to the barn and for us to take our meals out there to be less of a burden. She agreed, but her expression showed underlying emotions I wasn't able to decipher, except that they weren't happy.

"Can we use your washer and dryer, or should we use a commercial Laundromat?"

"Of course you can use them," she replied as if I thought she was a witch.

Reggie and I moved his stuff to the bunkhouse and put our food supplies on the shelves and in the small refrigerator. It was Sunday, so we couldn't sell our cards until tomorrow.

July slid by. The card business marched along quite well. Customers were pleased with the product, and we recouped enough cash for gas and food for a three-day return trip to the East Coast.

August arrived, but my period didn't. I was over a week late and growing concerned. Jane, my sister-in-law, gave me the name of her gynecologist, Dr. Tiller, whose office was in San Francisco. I made an appointment for later in the week but didn't tell anyone. I placed an ad in the Sunday *Berkeley Daily Planet* that read: *Rider to the East Coast wanted to share driving and costs. Leaving Bay Area mid-late August.*

Dr. Tiller was friendly. The visit consisted of shaking hands and my giving a urine sample. The next day I learned I was pregnant. I decided to deal with this when I got back to Bennington. If I confided in Mom, the roof would explode.

Toward Reggie I grew more and more hostile. I hadn't yet told him the sobering news, because I didn't trust what his reaction would be. I planned to tell him on the road.

A number of people responded to the *Berkeley Daily Planet* ad. One guy in particular sounded pretty normal and also wanted to drive straight through. We agreed to meet on the Marin County side of the San Rafael Richmond Bridge and I described my car and make.

Reggie and I parked overlooking the westbound exit lane of the bridge and waited. A young decently dressed man pulled up next to us.

"John?" I inquired

"That's me. Constance?"

I introduced Reggie. We explained that we'd meandered our way westward but wanted to get back quickly to save money. He was in complete agreement. We decided to travel Route 80 straight across, through Salt Lake, Chicago, Buffalo, and into New England. We set the date, exchanged telephone numbers, and shook hands.

Back at the ranch, I realized we had to ship the tent and our camping gear to make room for John. The next two weeks were spent winding up our little business, packing and shipping boxes, and getting the Pontiac serviced.

With all this activity, Mom suddenly realized I was leaving for another year of college. She suggested inviting my older brother, Turo, his wife, Jane, and their kids for a goodbye dinner. I said I'd love that.

Always leave on a high note, I thought.

⇒14⇐

The trip back east on U.S. Route 80, with sunrises in our eyes, coffee with No-Doz, and stops to fuel and use toilets, took almost four days. While one person drove, the one whose shift just ended, got to recline in the back seat for a few hours. Musical chairs all the way. Thank God the Pontiac held up.

We dropped John off at the train station in Albany, New York and continued east to Williamstown, Mass., where we pulled over outside Reggie's dorm. I left the engine running and turned to face Reggie, "I'm pregnant," I shouted.

I was furious—furious at Reggie, furious at myself, furious that I'd had to keep this nasty secret for weeks.

"What? I don't get it. Why didn't you tell me before?"

"I didn't trust how you would react around my parents. I don't want them to know. I found out before we left."

"My God." He slapped the side of his head like he had trouble believing the news.

"Tell me about it," I responded sarcastically. "You should have slapped your head like that before putting it in."

Reggie's eyes locked on mine. I hope he registered my distain.

"What are we going to do?"

"I'm the one who has to do something, not you.

"I'm sorry."

"Not as sorry as I am. I don't ever want to see you again, *capice?*"

I turned my head toward the windshield to indicate that the conversation was over, that I wanted to leave. I gunned the engine, emphasizing my words. Reggie leaned on the passenger side door, shaken. Then he closed the door and extracted his duffel bag from the trunk, all the while shaking his head in disbelief. As I drove off, I saw him in the rear view mirror standing there, looking after me.

I drove the last twenty miles to Bennington College, grateful that the summer was over and I was where I could hopefully get my "problem" taken care of.

My room assignment was in Canfield House, right across from Swan House. I was relieved to be in a different house this year where I would get to know new people. My room was on the ground floor facing the road, good for checking out the action.

As I registered for fall classes, I thought back to my unfavorable beginning at the same time the previous year, when I totally missed registration. In The Barn, I signed up for Traditions in English Literature, Prose Writing, and Sculpture Studio with Drawing. Over the weekend I'd deal with "personal business."

It was rumored that the best person to talk to was Bernard Crowley, the French literature professor, known for his prose translations of a major French poet. He had supposedly helped several girls in the same situation find doctors in New York City who would perform illegal abortions. I'd done well in his class last year and hoped he would be inclined to help. He lived on the other side of campus in an apartment beneath Bingham House, and it was to this location that I made my way to knock on his door.

A muffled voice said, "Yes, coming," while I stood nervously on the other side of the door. Professor Crowley was a man in his fifties of medium height with an almost-bald head ringed with wisps of gray above the ears.

"Come in, come in." He opened the door wide for me and I entered. "To what do I owe my good fortune?"

"I do wish it was for good news," I told him, relieved that he was glad to see me.

He motioned me to a chair in the living room. "I hope you're keeping up French and your interest in literature, Constance."

"I am." I listed the literature courses I was taking.

"Good, Good. Now what's this not-good news?'"

"It's embarrassing. I've gotten myself in a family way. I need an abortion." I dropped my chin to my chest.

"Oh, my dear. Unfortunate. Who is the gentleman, or is that not the correct *môt?*"

I stifled a laugh. "Actually, he's a platonic friend of a friend. It just happened once."

I checked out his reaction, which seemed concerned.

"We both drank too much wine on a camping trip. A moment's mistake. It's unfair. I'm scared and don't know who else to turn to. Can you help?"

"How far along are you?"

"Since August, about six weeks."

Speaking those words made my predicament real: in another thirty weeks I'd have a full-term baby.

"Mmm. Let me see. Give me a day or so to gather some information and get back to you. How's that?"

"How will you contact me?"

"Your mailbox in Commons. All right?"

I nodded, rose to leave and shook his hand. He put an arm around my shoulder and patted it. It was almost completely dark as I crunched across leaves under elms that lined the Common.

Five days later I found an envelope from Professor Crowley in my mailbox in Commons and tore it open. Inside on a plain sheet of paper were the names of two doctors and their New York City addresses and telephone numbers. Next to the first name was another name, Lisa Frank, the patient who supposedly referred me. There was no other information on the sheet. I hurried out with the paper clutched tightly in my fist and headed to the bank to get change so I could call from the privacy of a pay phone. I dialed the number for the first doctor listed and spoke to a receptionist. The first available appointment was two weeks away. I explained that I was calling from Vermont and it was an emergency. Didn't she have any openings sooner? I heard pages being flipped, and then I had to put more coins into the pay phone.

"Hello? Hello?" I said.

"I'm here," she returned. "Well, I could squeeze you in the day after tomorrow. Can you make that?"

"Of course," I answered. "Could you give me directions to your office?"

As she did, I was instructed to put more coins into the telephone or risk being cut off. A dime slipped through my fumbling fingers and rolled towards the curb. How impossible! Did I have enough change? How did you have a private conversation without having to stand in an uncomfortable public telephone booth, feeding an insatiable black object, surrounded by noisy traffic?

When I got back to Canfield, I checked my course schedule for Friday and learned I would miss Sculpture Studio and Drawing. I could make up that three-hour studio over the weekend if I got the assignment. I planned to drive down and back in the same day, which was eight hours of driving on top of the doctor's appointment. To arrive by 3, I planned to leave here by 10, allowing time to eat lunch and buy gas.

By the time Friday rolled around, I was so anxious to find a solution to the "growing problem" inside me that I was ready to go by nine o'clock. It was a gorgeous fall day, what the locals call the leaf-peeping time of year. The easiest way to get there was through Albany, N.Y., then south on Route 87 to Tarrytown, where I crossed the Hudson River and continued into Manhattan.

I found the offices of Philip Brownstone, M.D. OB/GYN Associates, parked across the street, put change in the meter, and entered an ordinary doctor's office. I was a half-hour early, which was good because I needed to fill out my medical history. I left the question *why I have made this appointment?* blank. I'd tell the doctor in person. I used the bathroom and brushed my hair. I wished I didn't feel so guilty or ashamed. Back in the waiting room, I flipped through magazines distractedly until my name was called. I followed an assistant to a cubicle with an examination table, where I removed my clothes and put on the gown that was lying on the table. Dr. Brownstone finally appeared and shook my hand. I told him that I didn't personally know Lisa Frank but that my professor at Bennington referred him as her doctor. I explained that my parents lived in California and that I discovered I was pregnant about three weeks ago just before I left California.

"I don't want the baby. Can you help?" I looked at him hopefully.

"Hop up here. Let's have a look," he said.

I climbed onto the examination table and put my feet into the cold metal stirrups. It was only the second time I'd had a pelvic exam, and it was still embarrassing. I felt the doctor easing the speculum into my vagina. His other hand examined my uterus from outside below my navel, pressing down.

"You appear consistent with someone in the first trimester of pregnancy. Did you know you have a tipped uterus, which presents problems?" He removed the speculum, turned from the table as he peeled off his rubber gloves, and stepped to the sink. "I can't help you," he told the metal cabinet over the sink that reflected his face while washing his hands. Wiping his hands on a paper towel, he turned to face me. "I'm sorry," he said.

"Why can't you?" I pleaded. Should I mention Lisa Frank again? Perhaps the assumption that he'd performed an abortion for Lisa Frank was wrong. Dr. Brownstone left me alone to wonder whether it was because of my tipped uterus or because abortions are illegal. Would anyone be able to help me? Feeling let down and more desperate, I dragged myself off the examination table, dressed and retraced the four-hour drive back.

On the way, I debated calling my mother for help. What if the second doctor, whose name and address I'd been given, wouldn't help either? The futility of making another round trip to New York City for another appointment and another disappointing outcome was foremost in my mind. Time was running out. At three months, abortion would be too dangerous to perform. That gave me only another six weeks. Maybe this was more than I could handle. If all else failed, I supposed I could have this baby and give it up for adoption, but I would have to drop out of school. Where would I go? I was feeling more and more vulnerable and miserable, not to mention the morning sickness I had begun to experience.

By the time I was safely in bed in my room in Canfield House, exhausted and depressed, I decided to call my mother in California and put myself at her mercy. Feelings of relief outweighed the dread I felt.

When I reached Mom, I said, "I'm pregnant." Silence screamed from the receiver of the pay phone for what seemed an eternity.

"Consie, I want you to call Aunt Emily tomorrow and prepare to be in New York next weekend."

"Will you be there?"

"Yes. I'll arrange a flight today. We'll meet at Emily's and figure out what to do. Do you have her address?"

"No. I'm calling from a pay phone outside a gas station in North Bennington."

"Write it down."

"Wait. I need to find paper." My right hand scrambled inside my purse for something on which to write. "Okay, I'm ready."

Mom read off the address, while I wrote it down on the crumpled piece of paper.

Relief washed over me. At least I was no longer facing this alone. I had the weekend to make up classes missed yesterday. Next week would be normal. I would leave for New York on Friday again.

I made up work for Mr. Moselsio's Studio Saturday afternoon. Unfortunately, I would miss the next Friday Studio, too, so I wrote him a note explaining that I had to meet my mother in New York City to deal with a family emergency. I spent time in the library and at the Laundromat on Sunday preparing for the week ahead. I also wrote to my adviser, saying that I had to miss some classes due to a family emergency, and I dropped the note into his box Sunday evening. Near-normalcy restored my equilibrium by Monday morning, but the weeklong activities still dragged by in slow motion.

From the Henry Hudson Parkway, I crossed town through Central Park to Lexington Avenue and 72nd on the East Side, where I found a parking space, locked the car, and rang Aunt Emily's bell. She lived on the fourth floor in a cozy three-bedroom apartment whose entry walls were painted barn red.

Aunt Emily was diminutive, five foot one and very Bostonian. I had to lean down to kiss her cheek. Her hair was swept up to fluffy sprays and held in place with tortoiseshell combs on top of her head, giving her an inch or two more in height. Aunt Emily worked at the Museum of Modern Art, though I didn't know in what capacity. Mom, towering over us, gave me a hug and an encouraging smile. Aunt Emily showed me to my bedroom and instructed me to join them for a drink. After I freshened up, I followed their laughter to a cozy den with a bar and a scattering of unmatched chairs. They were old friends going back to Paris days, and it was fun to hear them catching up. I was thankful not to be grilled about my predicament. I made myself a drink and sat.

"Consie, tell us how far along you are," said my mother offhandedly, as if my condition were perfectly natural.

"I found out just before leaving California," I said. "So now I'm about five or six weeks along." I paused. "I drove here last Friday to see a doctor recommended by a professor. I've got a tipped uterus. He said he couldn't help me."

"A very good doctor who still practices and lives in the city, and is an old friend, wants to know how pregnant you are. Or we could go to Puerto Rico where it's legal. Let's sleep on all this tonight, okay?"

"And let's have a delicious dinner, shall we?" suggested a cheerful Aunt Emily.

Relieved, I nodded. I wondered how Mom and Aunt Emily could be so *laiser faire* about my situation, but I didn't want to rock the boat by asking.

I was up before Mom in the morning and found Aunt Emily reading the paper at the table in the kitchen with a mug of coffee in front of her.

"Smells wonderful!" I found the coffee pot and opened a cabinet looking for a mug.

"On the right," said Aunt Emily without turning around.

I poured myself a cup and sleepily wandered into the den, where, to distract myself, I peered out a window at the activity on Lexington Avenue below. A brown dog led its owner, dressed in a plaid shirt and Levis, across 72nd Street. A yellow cab pulled to the curb, a door opened, and out climbed a woman and a young child clutching a stuffed toy.

I turned my attention inside. Nicely stained mahogany bookcases crossed an entire wall, with a cutout work area housing a sleek modern desk and chair, with room above for a bulletin board. I peered at notices on the bulletin board. There was an invitation to a MoMA event where Aunt Emily worked. Another was to a Valentino fashion show at Bergdorf Goodman. The last was to someone's wedding in November. Too bad that wasn't what we were planning. I wandered back to the kitchen just as Mom appeared in her bathrobe and slippers.

"Did you sleep well?" I kissed her.

"Yes, thanks," she replied.

I offered to make scrambled eggs for the three of us. Aunt Emily told me where the frying pan was and where to find a mixing bowl, a wire whisk, and bread for the toaster. It was a relief to be useful. I slid slices of bread into the toaster and scrambled the egg-and-milk mixture. Dividing the eggs and toast among three plates, I called everyone to the table.

It was strange to realize that now that I'd really screwed up big time, Mom hadn't made me feel worse than I already felt. In the past, when I had tried diligently to be worthy of her love and something went wrong, she always assumed I deliberately caused it. Those rejections hurt terribly. Now it felt like I was being rewarded for having screwed up. Crazy.

After breakfast we left to shower and dress in our rooms. Mom needed to speak to the doctor in privacy, so Aunt Emily said she would stay off the line for the next hour.

A plan was put into action. "He will take care of you," said Mom in the hallway outside her bedroom. We'd need to follow his instructions to the letter. At noon Mom and I took a taxicab to the Hotel Luxor, on the west side off Amsterdam Avenue. We placed $1,000 in cash in Aunt Emily's St. James version of the Bible and were instructed to leave it on the back seat. As our cab pulled in front of Hotel Luxor, I noticed a man in a dark trench coat and a fedora, one hand raised for our taxicab, the other gripping a small suitcase. It felt like we were in a bad movie. We got out of the cab, and I saw a flicker of recognition pass between Mom and the man.

→ Swimming Upstream ←

I went straight into the shabby lobby of the Hotel Luxor and registered as Shirley Booth. I concocted a fictional address, paid $7 for the room, and got a key to Room 24.

It was a large room with a double bed, bedside table, a three-drawer bureau, a larger table, and a chair. There was a bathroom. I undressed to my slip and crawled under the covers.

Soon there was a knock on the door. I went to the door to listen.

"Consie?" a low voice whispered.

"Yes," I answered softly as I unlocked and opened the door.

It was the same man in the trench coat and the fedora with a suitcase. He closed and locked the door, removed his coat and hat, and opened the suitcase on the table under the window. Inside were medical instruments, vials, syringes, and bandages of all sorts. Middle-aged and of slight build, he swiveled to look around the room, then walked to the bureau and grabbed its sides. He began dragging it across the floor, where he positioned it facing the table. Eschewing any bedside manner, he prepared a syringe and plunged it into my arm.

"You'll begin to feel sleepy," he said.

He guided me onto the table, where he had me brace my legs against the bureau. He clamped a spotlight to an edge of a bureau drawer, and then he inserted an instrument inside my vagina. He began to scrape and it hurt. Time somehow stretched, or was it shorter than it should be? I couldn't tell because it was so elastic, and I tried to imagine a blue sky and a field of green, not this place, but then I heard my voice cry out, asking him to please stop because it hurt so much, but he kept scraping and scraping; I wanted to go back to the green field with the tree and the blue sky, but I heard a sound, a plop, like something hitting a metal container and asked what it was, and he said that it was out and almost over but he had to get every single bit of the placenta out so I won't hemorrhage, and then I would soon be able to sleep.

Yes, I thought, sleep, and I tried to go back to my field under a blue sky lying on the grass looking up through the branches, but when he scraped, I was still stuck in the room, stuck with hurt. I couldn't leave. I pleaded for him to stop, and finally he said I could lower my legs to the floor and get off the table, but I felt so wobbly he had to lead me to the bed and I just collapsed.

I didn't remember his leaving; I just went to sleep, and when I came to my mother was helping me dress and leading me out of that awful room.

⇒15⇐

Back at Bennington, I needed to pick up the pace to stay afloat in my literature courses. I'd caught up on my female torso in clay for Studio Sculpture.
Molding clay was relaxing and meditative, whereas I needed to focus in
literature, which I hadn't been able to do under the recent pressures. So I
threw myself into reading and writing for two course assignments.

Days were shortening in our southern corner of Vermont, where early
one evening in Commons I ran into Professor Crowley. He signaled me over
and I plopped down my bundle of books and mail on the table to join him.

"How are you?" he asked.

"Everything is fine now," I said.

"Good, good. We'll say no more."

I let him think he was the one who helped solve my problem. There was
no point in going into the miserable details of my unproductive visit to Dr.
Brownstone or of my subsequent trip to New York City and the Hotel Luxor.

"I've been working long hours to catch up." I nodded toward the bundle
of books.

"Of course! Good for you," he said.

"Well, I'm off." I rose, shook his hand, picked up my bundle and
headed out the door.

Over the weekend, Carol Friedman and I went to see the Oscar-win-
ning movie *Marty*, starring Ernest Borgnine. It was a touching film even
though its star played a lonely, overweight and homely butcher. After the
movie, we grabbed hamburgers, fries, and Cokes at the Brown Hen on
Route 7.

The Brown Hen was mostly filled with local middle-aged couples, the
women sporting tight gray curls sprayed on like helmets and the men in
slacks and nicely pressed shirts without ties. It was their Saturday-night-out
spot. We came here, away from all the big ears of the Bennington community, because I wanted to confide in Carol about what I'd recently gone
through. She listened intently and promised not to repeat it to anyone.

"You hear these stories, but you never think you actually know someone who has gone through it," she said.

"Well, now you do," I said.

We took our checks to the register to pay. On the short drive home, I told her how good it felt to have a friend I could confide in. Now I needed to put it all behind me so I could be my old self again.

"What about Reggie?" Carol asked.

"I never want to see him again." I said.

"What about Joe?" she asked.

"What about him?"

"Don't you think Reggie will tell Joe?" Carol asked.

"My God, you're right. He will. Do I have to explain all this to Joe? It's not like he and I are going together, but maybe I need to tell Joe my side so he won't think I'm a slut."

"Why not say Reggie doped you?" Carol suggested.

"Because Reggie's too dumb to think of that," I said, breaking into peals of laughter.

Saturday I met Joe, whom I hadn't seen since before summer. We drove in his car and parked at a spot overlooking the small lake in North Bennington. As I explained the entire sordid episode, including the abortion at the Hotel Luxor, Joe's right hand was a fist that he slammed into his left.

"Does Reggie know?"

"He knows he got me pregnant. No, he doesn't know what I've just gone through."

I hoped Joe believed that it was a one-time mistake with Reggie. Then he shocked me by confiding his own terrible secret of stealing things, an expensive camera, someone's leather briefcase. He was ashamed, but shame didn't stop him. He felt compelled to steal. Joe could never afford Williams College tuition without a scholarship. He thought it had something to do with watching his father, once a successful attorney, suffer a debilitating stroke two years before that left him an immobilized invalid. I advised Joe to seek the college's counseling services and arrange a way to return the stolen items anonymously.

"How would I return a camera?" he asked.

"You could put a notice in the college newsletter that such and such had been found and is awaiting its rightful owner."

"They could trace it to me."

"You could get the counselor to call in the notice to keep it anonymous."

"I'll think about it." He stroked his chin as if he had a beard. "What are your plans this Thanksgiving?"

"Gee, I don't have any. California's too far and too expensive."

"Would you like to come home with me for Thanksgiving?"

"Joe, that's sweet! In New York City, right?" Joe nodded. "I'd love to."

We anchored our friendship with a hug and then got out of the car and walked around the lake, crunching fallen crimson and yellow oak leaves. Joe told me a little about his older sister, Beth, who worked in the film business in New York. Joe, his mother and sister would visit his father in an assisted-living facility, but I wouldn't have to go.

I felt closer to Joe, who seemed relieved to have confided his secrets. I was certain that if he didn't believe that my one night with Reggie was an aberration, it would have destroyed our friendship. Although I was now terrified of any physicality with a guy or letting down my guard as I had with Reggie, it felt good to solidify our friendship on this level.

When the first snow fell the week before Thanksgiving, it was about eight inches of beautiful, pure white on the flat terrain and more than twice that in drifts. I watched a snowplow work at clearing the one-lane road between Canfield and Swan while muffled shapes in snowsuits, hats, and gloves shoveled walkways to the front entry of each dorm and all major paths to the Commons and The Barn. The resident houses were overheated. Their antiquated steam heaters banged a furious response to winter's demands in earsplitting *pings* and *pongs* that ricocheted around the walls. The air was permeated with the smell of wet wool from mittens, scarves, and hats draped over chairs near the radiators. Boots stood in rows emitting wet-leather smells.

I plodded through the snow to the sculpture studio to check on the plaster cast of my clay torso that I made with Mr. Moselsio. It sat in the same place, a two-foot-tall lump of hard white plaster, its front and back separated by a line of tin that ran vertically up over the neck and arms and down again to the base. The following Friday, Mr. Moselsio would show me how to separate the two halves of the mold and pour plaster into the onetime mold.

Thanksgiving weekend with Joe's pretty mother and friendly sister, Beth, a single woman with a series of freelance jobs on documentary films, was lighthearted. Seeing the way Beth teased Joe, I was able to see Joe as the "baby" of the family.

After putting the turkey in the oven, Joe's mom and sister left to visit Mr. Leibowitz in the nursing home. Joe and I were put in charge of basting the turkey, peeling potatoes, and setting the table, after which we played 78s on the turntable in the living room.

A roomy apartment with three bedrooms and two baths in a modest neighborhood, the view was toward the Hudson River, which you could faintly see in the distance. The quality of the living accommodations was directly related to the lack of income the family had had since Mr. Leibowitz's stroke, which may have shed light on what was behind Joe's kleptomania. Can you steal affluence? Joe's paradoxical need to try to and shame at having done so seemed to say no.

After the meal, I helped the women clean dishes and put leftovers away while Joe went to visit his father. Later, all four of us sipped aperitifs in the living room and listened to the radio. A weather advisory predicted that a major winter storm would set in early Saturday all along the East Coast, so Joe and I decided to return to college before it hit. Mrs. Leibowitz was sad we couldn't stay longer but understood the severity of a New England nor'easter.

There was hardly enough time between Thanksgiving and Christmas to wind things up and execute plans for non-resident term. Planning for NRT began in September, but it was still a rush to complete course requirements for the semester and tend to the last-minute details of packing one's belongings and moving into temporary housing in the city. My plan was to study sculpture at Columbia University, for which I had secured my adviser's permission. I planned to move into a suite at the Gramercy Park Hotel with a telephone and a tiny kitchen. Added to this mix was the element of weather and more than twenty inches of snow dumped by Thanksgiving's nor'easter, all ingredients for character-building.

I registered for the class uptown at Columbia, which meant standing in a long line in the cold until we moved indoors. Eventually I found my way to the sculpture studio, which was in a huge two-story room, where I presented my registration receipt to Professor Alessandro Borgia. He looked at it, then at me and smiled.

"Welcome, Constance."

I had brought a snapshot of my clay torso, which I showed him. "This is the only thing I've done in sculpture," I said.

"Where did you do this?"

"Bennington."

"Very nice. Yes. Well, what do you want to work on here?"

I wasn't sure and said so. I was eyeing an enormous sculpture in a corner of the ceiling and asked him about it. He explained that it was an enlarged copy of an eye on Michelangelo's *David*. The student wanted to learn how to make an armature for a large sculpture, so he picked that project. I spent the next hour looking at works in progress all around the studio before leaving for the day

On the way home via subway, I bought a rotisserie chicken from a vendor, still warm in its cardboard box. My apartment was plain but so much better than the one room I lived in the year before at the Barbizon Hotel. This one consisted of a living room, a tiny kitchen, including dishes, pots and pans, and a bedroom with bath. I put the chicken into the oven, prepared a cup of rice and turned the gas burner to "medium." While waiting for the water to boil, I took off my coat and hung it in the closet. No mail. I fixed a small salad, poured a glass of red wine and waited for the rice to cook.

I mused over what was realistic to accomplish at Columbia in the ten-week time period. Lately, I had begun to question why I was majoring in sculpture when I naturally seemed to gravitate to literature. My mother had always told me how artistic I was, and taking my artistic talent for granted over the years, I'd never questioned it. Could that be because I wanted to fulfill her expectations and wanted her love? Did I know myself better? These nascent musings were percolating just under the surface.

The following week brought a surprise in the form of a visit from Frances Wister, my friend from Paris, whom I hadn't seen for two years and who was currently living in New York City and working at the Cloisters Museum. She said someone told her I was in town. We made a date to dine *chez moi* that weekend.

When the evening arrived, I was astounded to find a much more subdued Frances than the person I remembered. When I asked about the status quo with Stanislaus, she meekly said he was fulfilling his French military obligations. When I asked, "When will you see him again?" she dejectedly told me there were no plans.

"But he's your big love, isn't he?"

"Yes," she responded without emotion.

"For God's sake, call and tell him!" I said.

"Really?" A light in her eyes ignited.

I handed her the telephone and disappeared into the tiny kitchen, where I prepared our dinner while listening as Frances was transferred from one operator to another. When she finally reached Stani, I went into the bathroom to give them privacy.

"Well?" I said after emerging from the bathroom. Frances held the black telephone in her lap, a satisfied smile on her face.

"It was the middle of the night over there," she said wistfully.

"How is he?"

"Sleepy."

"I mean, you know. Did you tell him you love him?"

"Yes."

"And?"

"He loves me, too."

"So, what are you going to do?"

"I'm not sure. Listen, about the phone bill."

"I'll let you know when it comes in. Don't worry. Let's eat."

We carried our plates into the living room and chatted about day-to-day life in New York City. After dinner, Frances called for a taxicab. I accompanied her to the front door to wait for the cab and hugged her goodbye.

That was the last time I would see Frances. Later, I heard that she'd moved to France. I like to think I gave her the push out of inertia to call Stani, which, in turn, led to their eventual marriage.

I slogged through non-resident term in a haze of mediocrity. Lacking real inspiration, I nonetheless began work on a bas-relief on a plywood board with chicken wire nailed onto it for the raised portions. The board measured three by two and a half feet. I began to apply clay on top of the wire and roughed-in imaginary figures in a landscaped background that I wanted to recede in the distance. I envisioned the figures reclining, drinking wine and eating grapes.

When Professor Borgia saw it taking shape, he asked, "Is that from a Caravaggio painting?"

Knowing zero about Caravaggio and hiding my ignorance, I simply replied "No."

Raising his eyebrows like a question mark, he mumbled under his breath each time he walked by. I looked up Caravaggio in the library. He was a sixteenth century Italian Baroque painter who appeared in the art world out of nowhere, painted his way into brilliance, and died young, leaving only sixty or so paintings. Most of his paintings were interiors with dramatic one-source lighting rather than flat lighting from a sun overhead. I couldn't find one painting that looked anything like my bas-relief. What was the professor thinking? His implications were that I had somehow plagiarized.

Days became weeks, and weeks eventually rolled into months. It was more difficult than I thought to make the background recede and to distinguish each figure without getting too detailed.

The weekends were gloomy, with no parties or friends. I called Frances twice, but she seemed preoccupied with her roommates and her job, and she never called me. It was lonely to be plunked down in the middle of an enormous city with few contacts and not enough events or social situations in which to make new friends. I was genuinely glad when spring semester at Bennington began and I could leave my unfinished bas-relief, my hotel suite, and the lonely city behind.

⇒ 16 ⇐

Mud season in Vermont and spring semester at Bennington were synonymous. I sloshed through melting snow and mud in my boots to enroll in Graphic Arts Studio, Prose Writing, Sculpture Studio, and The Art of Western Tradition.

In some ways, Bennington was remiss in its lack of structure. The college didn't require me to fulfill a set of ready-made requirements. Instead, it challenged me to discover my own intellectual identity and design a curriculum that would help turn me into the person I hoped to become. Its practice of providing written comments rather than assigning grades could leave a student like me in a perpetual state of anxiety. What did this professor's comments mean? Was my work substandard? Mediocre? Good? How did my work compare with that of my peers? I didn't know.

I was surprised how much I liked Graphic Arts Studio, in which we were introduced to lithography and etching.

Because the renowned literature faculty scared me, Prose Writing was the only literature course I took.

In Sculpture Studio, I realized how glad I was that there was time to complete the sculpture correctly and not in a rush. I had made sure my plaster wouldn't be mistaken for junk, and there it stood still covered in plastic with a *DO NOT TOUCH* sign attached with masking tape and *Property of C. RICHARDSON* with a skull and crossbones.

I opened the mold and removed the now-dried-out clay. Mr. Moselsio showed me how to prepare a slip, which I painted on the inside to keep the plaster from adhering to the mold. I watched as he prepared the plaster by sifting dry plaster into a bucket half-filled with water, much like sowing seeds. Its consistency was that of pancake batter. He poured some plaster into half the mold with a ladle and, blowing through a straw, moved the thin plaster into hard-to-reach nooks. I followed this technique. It was important to work quickly, because plaster dried fast. Finally we joined the two halves. When completely dried, I'd learn how to break the mold to reveal the plaster statue inside.

The Carriage Barn sat on the northern boundary of the campus and was used for staging plays and concerts. Getting there on foot involved a walk through the orchard and past the pond and Jennings, an enormous mansion that was home to the music department. The Carriage Barn was a two-story building with a wrap-around gallery on the second floor that overlooked the first floor. Student productions were staged there. On weekend nights, there was usually a dance performance or a recital by a trio of musicians or a play rehearsal in progress.

This evening as I sat on the gallery floor with legs dangling through the spokes in the railing and a bird's-eye view of the proceedings below, I was struck by how "out there" we students were and by the risks we were willing to take. A senior was choreographing an ensemble dance piece with two men and two women while a drummer beat out the rhythm on kettle drums. They repeated the moves again and again until the choreographer finally said, "That's it."

Spring in southern Vermont took one step forward and three back. One day, icicles were melting into puddles of vanishing snow. The next, I awakened to the muffled blanket of a fresh white layer over everything. Out came the boots, gloves, hats, and scarves. My tires spun on the ice-filled ruts in the dirt road, and the clean white snow turned to muddy mocha mixed with salt and sprinkled with soot. Then one day, all the mess was gone and buds emerged.

This Easter was April 21st. I would stay put during spring break to save money. By the time Canfield House emptied out for the break, only a handful of us remained: my neighbor Rajansee, from Bombay, India; Perfect Pat, so named for her stash of twenty-five perfect button-down Oxford shirts; and me.

I was spring-cleaning my room on a pleasant Saturday afternoon. As I pushed a broom into Canfield's vestibule, hoping to sweep the dirt into the dustpan and out the front door, I saw a guy sitting on the stairway strumming a guitar. Our eyes met. He was blond and handsome. Surprise overcame shyness.

"What's your name?"

"Constantin," he responded in a foreign accent.

"It can't be. That's *my* name."

"What? You are Constantin?" he asked.

"No. My name is Constance."

"Oh." He laughed. "I'm from Dartmouth. I'm going to Florida."

"Alone?"

"No. We are four."

More strumming.

"Are you on spring break?" I asked.

"Yes."

"That's a lot of driving. Why don't you stay here with me? I'm not going anywhere."

He looked directly at me and grinned. "I will see," he said and then got up and went out, presumably to find his companions. I finished cleaning and noticed with relief that I was wearing white pants and a clean shirt. Thank goodness I wasn't in sloppy sweats. He came back inside Canfield and called my name.

"Yes," I answered.

"Ah, it's me, Constantin."

We were in the vestibule.

"I will not to go to Florida. They will go in another car. I will stay, all right?"

"You can't actually *stay* here, for the night, I mean. But we can go to Dartmouth, or do stuff around here. We can, for instance, go to Stateline."

"What's Stateline?"

"It's a club just over the border in New York. Not far. You dance. They have food. They serve liquor."

"Let's go," he suggested.

"It's too early. I'll show you around here first."

I gave him the cook's tour of Bennington's grounds and walked him through Commons. I learned that his father was president and CEO of AEG, Germany's General Electric. It was his father's idea to send him to Dartmouth, because his father didn't see a promising future for postwar Germany. From me he learned that my stepfather and Edwin Land invented Polaroid in the 1930s, that we lived on a ranch in Northern California, and that I was named after Great-Aunt Constance, who'd married a French count.

At Stateline, we sat side by side in a half-circle booth and ordered Budweiser beer. The jukebox lowered a record onto the turntable. Fats Domino began to sing *Blueberry Hill*.

"I found my thrill on blueberry hill . . .

On blueberry hill, when I found you."

We began to slow-dance under the dimmed lights on the dance floor. He nuzzled my right earlobe. When the song ended, he took my hand and led me back to our booth, where we ordered more beer and two chicken-fried steaks with fries.

"When I came in September, I know no English except how to read," he said.

"Wow. You learn fast."

"I have four years Latin and Greek. That helps."

"It took me a whole year before I dreamt in French," I told him.

"What?"

The waitress placed our steaks and French fries on the table along with two steak knives. She got a bottle of catsup from another table and asked if there was anything else we needed.

"No, thank you," said Constantin.

"Where was I?" I asked.

"You were dreaming in French. Why?"

"Because I spent the year before last in Paris," I said.

"Oh?"

"Yes. It was amazing."

He looked up, eyes alert with interest, while chewing a piece of steak, so I continued. "In the first place, they are incredibly rich. They own châteaux, plural, in the country, *and* the four-story building where we lived in Paris. They're called Madame La Comtesse and Monsieur Le Comte by the servants," I explained. "They burned my blue jeans. First I was upset. Then Aunt Mimi bought me a proper wardrobe, and I *adore* it." I looked down at my clothes. "Not this," I indicated, pinching my white pants between a thumb and forefinger.

"You look nice to me," he said.

"I have a Christian Dior suit." He didn't look impressed in the least. Perhaps he didn't know who Dior is. Why was I trying to impress him? That his father was a big German industrialist was intriguing. It was the same world in which I'd become a recent participant. I wasn't a California girl. I never *had* been a California girl, because I was always shipped off to one place or another. France definitely polished my rough edges. I acknowledged feeling comfortably at home with Constantin.

Every weekend in May and June, Constantin and I were inseparable. Either we camped out on the Bennington campus or stayed at the Hanover Inn in

Hanover, N.H. Because I was still so traumatized and fearful about getting pregnant, we agreed to keep it platonic—barely.

I was called in to meet with Dean Haskel in early June. Having failed to declare my major, my choice now was to take a leave of absence or declare a major by next week. This ultimatum left me confused and immobilized. Why hadn't my adviser warned me? Put on the spot and feeling undone, I stormed out of the dean's office. I spotted Alan Arkin, one of three token male students, who rose from his chair to go in as I left.

I waited for Alan on the lawn outside The Barn and tried to process what had just happened. It was a blow to be asked to take a leave of absence. Afraid I wasn't good enough to succeed in literature with Bennington's renowned faculty, I had buried literary aspirations and taken a safe path in sculpture.

When Alan emerged from The Barn, I asked, "Not that it's any of my business, but why were you seeing the dean?"

"I'm leaving this place."

"Me, too," I said.

While Alan looked resolved, even glad, I felt like a failure. It never occurred to me that it was just a procedural point, that I could choose a major and change it later.

Constantin completed a four-year curriculum at Dartmouth in two years and would soon graduate. Eugene and Mariesa Garbatti, old German friends of his parents, drove from Connecticut for his graduation ceremony. I took a photograph of Constantin unwrapping the Garbattis' graduation gift, an enormous unabridged English dictionary.

My plan that summer was to visit Mark Flynn, who had indicated more than once that I should come so he could show me England. Constantin and I decided to take the same boat from Montreal to Southampton, England, where Constantin went on to Frankfurt to visit his sisters and parents.

In London, I spent a long, lonely weekend looking for a place to stay. Although I realized my sudden decision to make this trip was precipitated by my demise at Bennington, I still expected Mark to take me under his wing. Instead, after a brief hello, he was conspicuously absent. I realized that I thought of him as a father figure, someone I missed and needed, and those needs were beginning to feel overwhelming.

After two weeks by myself in London, having barely seen Mark, I called Constantin in Germany.

"It's terrible here. I'm so lonely I feel invisible."

"Don't go anywhere. I'm coming. Tomorrow."

I was so relieved to see him that when he announced he would escort me home to the United States, I didn't object. With Constantin by my side, I went to say farewell to Mark. The three of us stood outside his apartment.

"If you care about me, stop me from leaving," I told Mark.

"I won't stop you."

In humiliation, I dropped my eyes and let Constantin lead me away. I knew I would never see Mark again.

Constantin's plan was to ride his motorcycle from New York City and take the Pan American highway to South America. We became engaged to be married before he left. He surprised me by buying a sidecar for his motorcycle, but I was too afraid to join him on such a long trip. Aunt Emily and I sent him off on Lexington Avenue outside Emily's apartment before I boarded an airplane at La Guardia that carried me to San Francisco.

As my part of the conditions of living at home, I had agreed to get a job and see a counselor. Why my parents insisted I undertake counseling, I had no idea, but it hadn't escaped me that everything with them boiled down to Jungian psychobabble.

I secured a job at Leo Diner Films, on Golden Gate Avenue in the city. George bought me a red dix-chevaux Citroën that looked like a cross between an insect and a Volkswagen. Its top speed was thirty-five miles per hour with a tailwind, but I loved its funkiness. To get to work by 8:30 a.m., I had to leave the ranch no later than 7:30.

My job was to receive film from any cameraman who dropped it off, give it to the lab guy to process, and have it ready for that same person in the afternoon. Diner Films processed most of the film shot for news stations in San Francisco. Leo Diner taught me how to mix the developer and thread the film into the machine that pulled it through the developing baths. I usually got home after 7 p.m.

By November it was obvious that my mother wasn't happy about my being there. One morning I asked if she could pick me up a tube of toothpaste when she went shopping.

"You're taking advantage of me," she replied.

"What's the big deal? I'll reimburse you," I said, but she looked cornered and angry.

It came to a head Thanksgiving weekend when she announced, "Two women can't live in the same house."

Furiously backing my car right onto the lawn outside the second-floor door near my bedroom, I began throwing belongings into it without knowing where to spend the night. My mother was so unbelievably hurtful I couldn't stay a moment longer. I'd fulfilled our contractual agreement by getting a job and being willing to see a therapist; she'd broken our contract!

Mom came to stand where I was loading the car, noticed a striped shower-curtain remnant, and said, "You can't take that." It was a piece I'd cut off from the too-long shower curtain that *I* purchased.

"It's only what I *had* to cut off so the curtain I bought would fit," I said with contempt. I'd never hated my mother so much or delighted so much in trying to make her feel small.

I got a room at a nearby motel for the night. In the morning, I drove to Kentfield, where my stepbrother, Mike, lived in an apartment. In the manager's office, I signed a lease agreement and paid a one-month security deposit and one month's rent for the smallest unit. The manager handed me my keys, and I dragged in all my belongings from the car.

By the middle of the week, I had settled into the apartment and bought some pots and pans, a few dishes, and some cutlery. Mike was ten doors down, but we saw each other only sporadically. He was enrolled in classes at Marin Junior College by day and building a rowboat in the evenings. I was tired after dinner and went to bed early.

Mom wanted to see my apartment, so we set a time on a Saturday after-noon. She came bearing a houseplant as a housewarming gift, for which I mumbled a thank-you. The visit was stiff but polite. After drinking a cup of coffee and acting as if nothing was wrong between us, she left.

I decided to lose fifteen pounds and was also working on a tan with the recent purchase of a sun lamp. One night I fell asleep while lying on the floor with my back to the sun lamp reading a book propped in front of me. I woke up in the middle of the night and turned the bedside light on but couldn't see. I felt a sudden wave of panic, using my hands to feel my way to the toilet, then to the telephone. I found zero on the dial and dialed the operator.

"Hello, can you help me?"

"What's wrong?" the operator asked.

"I woke up and can't see anything, not the numbers on the dial. Can you dial my parents?" I asked.

Mom and George took me to the emergency room in Marin General Hospital at 5 a.m., where we learned I'd burned the corneas in both eyes. The white pages of the book I was reading had reflected the damaging rays into my eyes, almost as if I were looking straight into the lamp. I was given ointment to put in both eyes every four hours and black patches to cover them and told to see an eye specialist in two days.

After assuring my parents that I was fine in my apartment alone, I called in sick to Leo Diner Films. In the follow-up appointment with the doctor, he said I was lucky not to be blind. I still wore dark glasses during the day to allow my eyes to continue to heal.

At work one day, I met Sandy Zane, a reporter for *The San Francisco Chronicle* who came in with a cameraman to drop off film. Sandy got my telephone number and the following week invited me out.

Sandy was tall and skinny with sandy hair and freckles. His shirts sometimes were missing buttons, and his shoes needed a shine, but always the natty dresser, he wore a bow tie and jacket. He played jazz piano anywhere there was a piano. It was fun to be with a known man about town in the snazzy bar circuit of San Francisco.

At the end of Hyde Street facing the bay, the Buena Vista Café was where celebrities from Pacific Heights hung out and where Sandy and I sometimes met after work. Sandy was adept at pointing out any juicy tidbits he knew from working at the newspaper.

Another place Sandy took me was The Cellar, *the* hangout for the Beat Generation. Dark and filled with smoke, we sat at tables facing a center stage on the same level, and a guy named Allen Ginsberg stepped up to the mike and read a long poem called *Howl*.

Correspondence between Constantin and me was hit and miss. His letters weren't frequent, but when one arrived, it was informative. In one, I learned he'd had to sell the original motorcycle because it was too heavy to take apart and ford across streams and rivers on the Pan American Highway.

I sent letters c/o General Delivery in cities and countries where I expected he would be at the ETA. I learned whether my calculations were correct when I'd receive responses to specific letters. When the last letter, mailed in mid-December, said I was arriving in Bogota on January 9th, I received an excited reply that said, "Am ready and willing for everything. Love, Constantin."

I had lost over fifteen pounds, so I spent money from my trust fund on a clean white linen sheath and a pair of silk pajamas in blush color.

I notified Leo Diner Films and my parents about plans to visit my fiancé. Leo Diner said he was sorry I was leaving and hoped I would come back. When I told Sandy Zane that I was flying to Bogota to see my fiancé, he looked forlorn. Saying our goodbyes, he handed me a thick ream of typewritten pages to take along. It was the first draft of a novel in progress. When I packed, I tossed it in my luggage, thinking that if things didn't work out with Constantin, at least I'd have something original to read.

Great-Aunt Constance's marriage to Comte Odon de Lubersac, 1904

Corbeil-Cerf, Great-Aunt Constance's chateau

Mark Flynn

Comte Raoul de Lubersac

Bennington College buildings.

1958

THE BOSTON HERALD

Social Chatter

By Alison Arnold

MRS. BODEN

TO LIVE IN BOGOTA, Colombia, after a wedding trip to Germany, are Mr. and Mrs. Constantin Boden, who were married Jan. 14, at St. Andrew's Episcopal Church, in Cocoli, Canal Zone. The bride is the former Constance Richardson, daughter of Mrs. George William Wheelwright, 3d, of Sausalito, Calif., and the late Arthur Welland Richardson of Boston. She's the granddaughter of Frederick L. W. Richardson of Boston and of Mr. and Mrs. Philip W. Livermore of New York, and a great-granddaughter of the late H. H. Richardson, famous architect, and of the late C. Oliver Iselin, banker and yachtsman. A graduate of the Santa Cruz Valley School in Arizona, Constance attended the Sorbonne in Paris for a year and also studied at Bennington College. The bridegroom is the son of Dr. and Mrs. Hans Constantin Boden of Berlin and a grandson of His Excellency Robert Von Boden and Karl Gutheinz of Germany. A graduate of the Frankfurt Gymnasium in 1954, he received a degree in Economics from Dartmouth College last June.

Wedding announcement

Consie & Nina

Constantin & Hans Boden

Constantin & Uncle Raoul

Mr & Mrs Boden with Hans & Nina

Nina Boden

Hans Boden

Vinalhaven ferry & my dix-chevaux

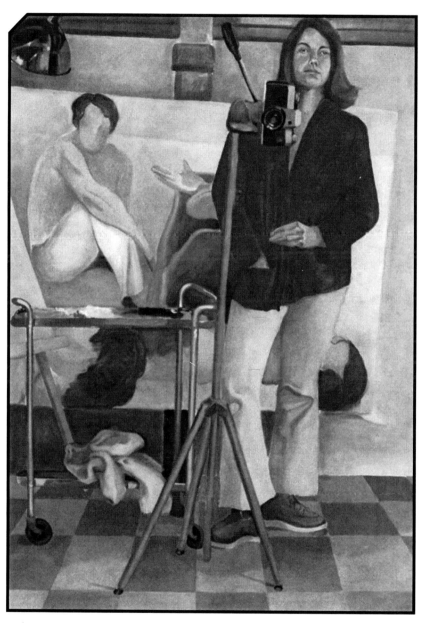

Self portrait in oils 4' X 5'

My Bennington College graduation picture in newspaper

⇒17⇐

The Pan American World Airways flight from San Francisco to Bogota took sixteen hours, with a change of planes in Panama City. Through the long night hours, I reflected on my parents' parting words, "Be sure to telegraph or call before you get married." At first, I was insulted that they ignored my serious mission of flying all the way to South America because I questioned my intended marriage to Constantin. Then I wondered whether my parents knew me better than I knew myself and whether this trip would result in our marriage. I recalled the time Mom and George had suggested that if I were to elope, they'd reward me with a new car. Wasn't I worth planning for and paying for a wedding? Didn't parents regard a daughter's marriage sacred? They had hurt my feelings. While thus musing, I fell asleep, and when I awoke it was light outside and we had arrived in Panama City.

The short flight from Panama City to Bogota through the Andes Mountains in an old DC-3 wasn't short enough. A flight attendant passed out chewing gum and cotton for our ears, and the airplane shook and rumbled through air turbulence before its descent to Bogota's 10,000-foot-high plateau. We taxied to Aeropuerto Internacional El Dorado. Constantin was waiting for me just beyond customs. His blond head towered above all the others, and when his eyes caught mine, a huge smile cleaved his face in two. We ran into each other's arms.

Our room in the modest hotel was clean but had only one bed. Not prepared for all the implications of this, I decided to play it by ear. We left our suitcases side by side and explored the city on foot. It was obvious we were gringos, because the local population parted to let us pass. At 5 foot 10 and 6 foot 1, we towered over most Colombians. The smells of Bogota were pungent and varied: a wood smell, unlike cedar but as aromatic; strong coffee, called *tinto negro*; lots of exhaust, mostly from a flotilla of broken-down, patched-together aging American and English automobiles; clean lemony smells from the sudden rain that dumped sheets of water and then stopped just as suddenly. Music pouring forth from every storefront and café. Bogota's buildings were dirty and its sidewalks uneven. Several men made kissing sounds as their eyes caressed my body while I clutched Constantin closer.

After eating a good meal, we retired to the hotel room. I was feeling exhausted from the combination of the trip and the 10,000-foot elevation. We showered separately and reemerged in nightclothes. In bed I was playful but resistant about going all the way before marriage. Constantin didn't push it. We made out. We smoked. We made out some more. He opened a bottle of scotch, and we sipped from the same glass.

He talked about how he ended up trading the original motorcycle for the lighter Triumph so that he could take it apart and carry parts across rivers where the Pan American Highway didn't exist. He showed me his rear end as evidence. It was covered in calluses and hard as a rock from the pounding it had taken.

I related the saga of my parents' not keeping their word after I had met their conditions for living on the ranch.

"Mom's conditions were that I find a job and start to see a therapist. Well, I got a job at Leo Diner Films in the city. Three weeks into the job, Mom wanted to have this little talk. She said two women couldn't live in the same house. I asked if she really wanted me to move out. She did. I went ballistic. What a traitor! I threw all my belongings into my car. I had no idea where I would sleep that night."

"Where did you?"

"In a motel." I explained how I had found the apartment in Kentfield. "I'll never forgive her."

He comforted me until we fell asleep in each other's arms.

The next day, we rode the motorcycle to the old part of Bogota, Plaza de Bolivar. The climate was surprisingly mild, about 65 degrees, so a light jacket was enough. The Capitolio Nacional, or Congress, was on one side, the Palacio de Justicia on the opposite. The Catedral Primada sat on the east side of the plaza. After lunch, we rode out to the east side of town and took the cable car to Cerro de Monserrate, a shrine overlooking the city. A statue of El Señor Caido, the fallen Christ, sat atop, and miracles were rumored to have occurred nearby.

I hadn't once mentioned my cold feet about our engagement; in fact, I was wearing the ring. I tried to explain that it wasn't about him. "I'm just terrified of getting married. Irrational as that is, I think all marriages end in divorce like my father's and mother's." I needed time and an English-speaking minister with whom I could talk about my fears.

He pooh-poohed this. He was, after all, a man of action, not one to equivocate. He wanted to marry me. I should marry him. That's that. Typical German.

For the moment, I dropped the subject. My return flight to San Francisco was scheduled for January 12, three days away. When I thought of leaving him or being separated, it hurt, so I tried not to think and enjoy the present.

One day we visited the world-famous Museo del Oro, which housed the world's largest collection of pre-Colombian gold. The next, we rode to the upscale residential area near the country club. It reminded me of similar wealthy areas in the states. We dined at a wonderful restaurant, El Son de los Grillos.

On the morning of my departure, Constantin accompanied me in the taxicab to the airport to see me off. At the gate for my departing flight, I turned to kiss him goodbye, but with his hand in the small of my back, he nudged me onto the tarmac, up the stairway, and into the aircraft. He sat in the seat next to me.

"What are you doing?"

"What does it look like?"

"How can you leave with only your jeans and T-shirt?" I stupidly asked.

"Watch."

He explained to the flight attendant that at the last minute, he had decided to join me on the flight to Panama City. She looked at me to check my response. I smiled affirmatively.

"Young love." She sighed and walked toward the front of the cabin.

The door was closed and the flight taxied away from the terminal. I couldn't believe he was sitting right next to me on the flight to Panama. What next?

At Tocumen International Airport, in Panama City, we canceled my connecting flight to San Francisco, reserved a room at the Hilton Hotel and hired a taxicab to take us there. At the front desk, I explained that I needed charge privileges until I could access money from my bank in New York City. I called my broker at Schroeder's Bank and arranged for money to be sent.

Checking into a room, we agreed to share the facilities, but I insisted that Constantin not sleep in the bed with me. We needed to figure out what we were going to do.

In the telephone book under "Episcopal Churches" were several listings. I dialed the number for Saint Francis Episcopal Church and spoke to a pleasant-sounding woman, asking if it was possible to receive pre-marriage counseling with a minister.

"Of course. That would be with Father Baldwin. Would you like to speak with him?"

When he picked up the telephone, I said, "Father, my name is Constance. My fiancé and I just arrived from Bogota. We're staying at the Hilton. You see, he just got on the flight from Bogota without a ticket. I was on my way home to San Francisco. Oh, it's hard to explain everything over the phone."

"Would you like to explain in person this afternoon?"

"Yes. Very much."

We arranged to meet at his parish at 2 p.m. and I got directions. I wanted to talk to Father Baldwin by myself, so Constantin agreed to hang out at the hotel. I still had enough cash to take a cab to his address in Coclé.

Father Baldwin was a kindly looking man with a big smile and a large girth. His study was paneled in dark wood. One wall held shelves filled with books, while his desk was heaped with paper stacks, writing implements, a toy French horn, and other paraphernalia. I sat in one of the two upholstered chairs facing him, while he sat in a swivel chair, his back to a window that framed a banana plant.

I began to explain my irrational fears about marriage turning into divorce or death, stemming from what had happened with my parents. He listened without interrupting.

"How long have you known your fiancé?"

"Almost a year. He's from Germany. We met last spring, and he just graduated from Dartmouth."

"I see. What were you doing in Bogota?"

"Constantin rode a motorcycle all the way from New York City and a United Fruit boat to Colombia. I flew down to see him."

"And you live in San Francisco?"

"Yes."

"And you say that he just got on the plane without a ticket this morning?"

"Yes."

"I deduce he's a very persuasive, take-charge guy. Am I right?"

"Yes. I love him, but I'm afraid of marriage, Father."

"The Holy Ghost is present in you, child. You mustn't be afraid."

It was a tremendous relief to share my concerns with such a comforting person. I confided that we were penniless, charging everything until funds arrived from my bank in New York City.

"May I, we, come again, Father?"

"Of course. I look forward to meeting your fiancé." He checked his appointment schedule, and we set up a meeting for the next day at the same time.

Constantin looked spiffy in a new tropical-weight suit, white shirt, and tie that he charged at the chic men's shop off the lobby. He was cleanly shaven, thanks to the drugstore that sold razors and shaving cream. His sneakers, however, stood out, and I couldn't help staring at them. Following my eyes, he explained, "There's no shoe store here."

At the pool, I told him about the meeting with Father Baldwin and about the next day's meeting. We recognized George Hamilton, the movie star, tanning in a chaise on the other side of the pool and wondered if he was there to shoot a film.

The next day we arrived at St. Francis Parish, with Constantin in his new pants and shirt with the sleeves rolled up. Father Baldwin greeted us warmly and ushered us into his study. I intuited that Constantin liked Father Baldwin by the way he smiled and the relaxed look around his eyes.

"I hope she makes up her mind soon, because it's not very comfortable sleeping in the referee's chair on the tennis court," he told Father Baldwin.

"Oh my goodness," I exclaimed. "I'm so sorry. I never asked you where you slept last night."

He looked righteously injured for a moment and then laughed.

"Speaking of practical matters," interrupted Father Baldwin, "I understand that you're living on credit at the Hilton, charging things, like your meals, clothing, and the like. Is that right?"

"Only until money from New York arrives," I said.

"Still," said Father Baldwin, "I'd rather see you not incurring debt. I've got an idea. If you both decide to go ahead and marry, I'll perform the ceremony here in this church. Afterwards, we own a camp up the coast, where we hold church retreats. You could honeymoon there for free."

"That's wonderful," Constantin said enthusiastically.

"When would it be available?" I asked.

"Now. And for the next few weeks," said Father Baldwin.

"Why wait? What about tomorrow?" asked Constantin.

"Tomorrow is good," said Father Baldwin.

Feeling pressured and unsure, I said I needed to think things over.

After we'd returned to the Hilton, loud sirens filled the air and smoke blackened the sky, and we saw that entire rows of three-story houses were aflame on both sides of the street. Water hoses crisscrossed in tangles, their streams a dismal trickle into the conflagration. Inhabitants were throwing belongings out windows to the pavement below. One man dropped a large mattress from the third-story window. Sirens screamed the approach of more fire trucks. The heat of the fire made me involuntarily cover my face with both hands. Acrid smoke invaded my lungs. Coughing, I tried to back away, but Constantin pulled me through a labyrinth of hoses. The deafening slap of helicopter blades directly overhead almost drowned other sounds.

"*¡Hola, par aqíi!,*" yelled a man to another holding a hose.

"*¡No es bastante!*" he shouted back.

"*¡Agua agua!*" demanded a third.

Constantin dragged me closer until, panicking, I tore my hand out of his and retreated. It was a relief to turn away from the heat. At a safe distance, I turned to search for Constantin. He was in the middle of the action, smiling almost as if he was enjoying the excitement, whereas I was convinced that people would die here.

Later at the hotel, we learned that firefighters were planning to bomb a gas station in an effort to contain the fire. The next morning it was a front-page story with frightening photographs. A twelve-block area of Panama City had been destroyed.

Constantin was in a foul mood. He was tired of sleeping on the tennis court and weary of my resistance. I kissed him lightly and began to rub his shoulders. He took both my hands down and spun me around so I was facing him. With a stern face and a determined voice, he said, "If you don't marry me, I'll never see you again."

I felt torn between two alternatives, one of which I wasn't ready for and the other too painful to consider. My stomach lurched; the coffee I'd drunk threatened to come up. Tears rolled down my cheeks as I sank to the bed. Constantin softened momentarily. He sat next to me, turned my face toward his, and in the calmest voice said, "Marry me. You'll see. It's all going to work out. I promise."

Smiling through tears, I acquiesced. Constantin called the Baldwins to arrange our wedding for that afternoon, which was mercifully short and private. The Baldwins decorated each pew with a small spray of fresh flowers. I wore my navy-blue dress with white piping and a lace headscarf, and Constantin wore his new suit. My arms and hands shook so uncontrollably throughout the ceremony that it was a relief when it was over.

An enormous basket of fruit and chocolate wrapped in cellophane and with a congratulatory card sat on a table in our hotel room next to a bottle of warm Champagne and two flute glasses. Constantin trotted off for ice while I phoned Mom and George with the news. They offered to fly down.

"It's done. No point now. We'll see you when we get there in a week or so." I needed to terminate my lease on the Ross apartment and pack my belongings or put them in storage. Constantin telephoned Germany, sounding agitated, the way all German sounded to me. His mother cried and his father sent congratulations and wanted us to visit.

We made arrangements to pay our bill and check out of the Hilton early the next morning. Father Baldwin would drive us to the parish retreat at Bahia de Parita.

Coclé Province was beautiful. White-sand beaches and abrupt mountains, lush with forests, revealed themselves as the old sedan chugged along.

"Our caretaker will deliver ice," Father Baldwin said, our eyes meeting in the rearview mirror. "He'll also make sure the electricity is working."

We turned off the main highway onto a one-lane dirt road south toward the ocean and passed a tiny store where Father Baldwin said we could buy most of our provisions. The retreat was an old, large weathered two-story house right on the beach. There was no refrigerator per se, only a deep chest with a block of ice slowly melting inside.

"You'll be fine," said Father Baldwin as he turned the car around and waved goodbye. "I'll pick you up in four days." The white car was swallowed by dust.

Roaming around the place, we discovered a sleeping porch with about twenty cots lined up in two rows. We pushed two cots together and arranged our toiletries on a board in the primitive bathroom and then decided to change into shorts and amble to the store for provisions.

The store displayed items behind the counter, on shelves, and in bins. When I asked for meat or chicken, the proprietor asked me, "*Pollo?*"

"*Sí*," I answered.

He disappeared through a door to his yard. We heard loud clucking noises and then silence. He reemerged holding a headless chicken by its feet and passed it to me. I shrank back, forcing Constantin to take it. I purchased some potatoes, lettuce and tomatoes, a loaf of bread, and a half-dozen eggs, all wrapped in old newspapers.

We dumped the chicken right on top of the ice block, feathers and all, and nestled the other items around the perimeter.

After donning bathing suits, we headed to the beach. The ocean temperature was perfect. Small crabs scuttled from their holes along the wet sand, and seagulls called and swooped. A light breeze kept the hot afternoon sun manageable. We lay on towels on our stomachs, facing one another, holding hands.

"We're married," I said.

"Mmmm."

"On U.S. soil. I mean, this *is* the Canal Zone, so it's legal."

We decided to deal with the dead chicken while there was still daylight. I was familiar with the mechanics of plucking a chicken, because on the ranch we had a machine with a wheel covered with rubber nodes. I had watched as a chicken carcass was held against the wheel, knocking off the feathers. Then a blowtorch was passed over it to remove the fine pinfeathers.

Constantin brought the carcass to the beach, and we started to pull out the feathers. A half-hour later, our naked chicken was a sorry sight, its skin torn and jagged; the once-pristine beach was covered in white chicken feathers blowing back and forth with the breeze. How could one chicken have so many feathers?

Feeling chilled after the sunset turned the sky to a deepening lavender, and having lost any appetite for chicken, we dumped the carcass into the ice chest and made toast and eggs for supper.

It was a luxury to spend all night in each other's arms and not worry about the whole sex-outside-marriage issue. But I still didn't "get" the big deal about sex. Once again it was over before it began, maybe because we were amateur lovers.

Our honeymoon passed in a haze of sun, sand, gentle waves, walks along the dusty road to the store, reading mystery stories, and playful exploration of one another's bodies. The gentle rhythm of the moon and tides dictated our days and nights. All too soon, it was over.

There was a whirlwind of activity as we arrived in California for a wedding reception at the ranch. I picked out wedding presents in the city and began to disassemble my Kentfield apartment.

At the ranch, Mom took me aside one morning and said, "It's bad luck for a wife to have more money than her husband. It's emasculating, and I'm sure you don't want to start off on the wrong foot, Consie."

"No, I don't. What should I do?" I asked.

"Well, you could give some to Turo. He, Jane, and all the children really need a house, and they just found a perfect one in Mill Valley," she suggested.

"What about all *his* money? He inherited the same amount I did."

"They spent it all in New Orleans and Vermont. I'm afraid there's none left." She looked shyly down. "It's only a suggestion."

In less than five minutes, I'd been conned into giving my older brother a sizable chunk of my inheritance so that I wouldn't emasculate my new husband, which, of course I didn't want to do.

That same day I called Turo to tell him I was giving him money for the house.

"It's an outright gift. You don't owe it back."

Then I made arrangements with Schroeder Trust Co. to cut him a check.

Constantin helped me pack up the Kentfield apartment. We filled and marked a trunk of things to be shipped to Bogota and put what was left into my suitcase for a two-week visit with the Bodens in Frankfurt.

We flew from San Francisco to Los Angeles, where we changed planes. Boarding our L.A. flight to Copenhagen, we noticed a couple standing on the mobile stairway, surrounded by flashing bulbs, and wondered who they were.

In Gandor, where we deplaned for a refuelling, Constantin met the gentleman in the men's room, asked and was told he was Ray Bolger, the actor who had played the Scarecrow in *The Wizard of Oz*. He was traveling with his wife, Gwendolyn.

In Copenhagen we bumped into them again at our hotel, and they invited us to dinner.

"We were just married in the Canal Zone—Panama," I told them.

"We're going to Frankfurt to see my family." Constantin said. "Then on to Bogota."

They ordered Champagne to toast us. Gwen told me she and Ray were high school sweethearts who'd been married for twenty-eight years.

Maybe we'll be taking a newly married couple to dinner twenty-eight years from now, I thought.

Our arrival in Frankfurt and the ride in a chauffeur-driven Mercedes to the house on Eschesheimer Land Strasse was swift. Set back from a handsome wrought-iron fence, the house was three stories tall, sitting on two park-like acres. We were deposited at the front door, me in my Christian Dior suit to make a good impression.

A uniformed servant opened the door. My mother-in-law appeared, looked at me, and burst into tears. Constantin ushered me into the foyer. Servants dealt with the luggage. His mother disappeared up a staircase to the second floor, dabbing her eyes with a handkerchief. The atmosphere was a bit stiff.

Constantin's sister, Monika, a tall blonde, her hair twisted into a chignon, led me to an alcove off the foyer, "the breakfast room," she said in good English. Dorothy, Constantin's twin sister, a medium-tall and slender brunette, shook my hand softly and smiled in a shy but friendly way. Rehlein, the middle sister, a blonde with strong features, noisily joined us. A maid placed a tray of glasses and several large bottles of apple cider and soda water on the table. We chatted amiably about the flight over the Arctic from San Francisco, but I was concentrating on their body language. Was it friendly? Would I be accepted?

"Hello, hello, welcome!" Hans Boden called out as he descended the staircase. Constantin's father stood over six feet tall and wore a dark blue sport jacket, gray trousers, and a silk ascot.

Constantin hugged his father while I rose to shake his hand. Mr. Boden handed me a small carved inlaid box saying, "I found this charming sixteenth century box with a secret compartment in Vienna last week. Please accept it as a token of my admiration."

"Thank you." I held it high for everyone to see.

"See if you can find its secret," suggested Mr. Boden.

Constantin and his father retreated to the library while Constantin's sisters and I tried to unravel the box's secret. Its exterior was inlaid with ivory, ebony, rosewood, mahogany, and silver. All the joints were dovetailed. I uncovered two obvious compartments, while Monika discovered another. Then Dorothy examined the box, turning it over. She fiddled with two ebony legs on either side in the middle. Suddenly, she was pulling the legs out, revealing four-inch long vertical "beams" with carved footrests. Now Dorothy was able to slide a panel off that was held in place by the ebony beams. Under it was the very secret compartment.

"I found it!" she exclaimed.

We all bent over to look at the tiny compartment.

"How charming!" I said.

Constantin and I climbed the stairs to his old bedroom on the second floor. His mother had redone the furnishings, he unhappily told me, gesturing toward the single bed with a fitted covering with box pleats and matching pillows. His suitcase sat on a hard-backed chair.

"Honey, where is mine?"

"I'll find out," he replied before he left. Moments later, he angrily said, "My mother sent your suitcase to the third floor."

We climbed another flight of stairs and found my suitcase and carry-on bag in one of the third-floor bedrooms.

When we gathered at 7 in the dining room for dinner, his mother appeared to have recovered, smiling benevolently. The duck with orange sauce, tiny white potatoes, and string beans were delicious, as was the wine from Mr. Boden's cellar. Everyone's English was better than good; they were all bilingual. I was asked to call Mrs. Boden "Mummi" and Mr. Boden "Pappi."

We four, Mummi, Pappi, Constantin and I, were to visit Bayreuth and Baroque churches along the way, leaving the next day. This was announced as a fait accompli, without any query such as "would you like to?"

After dinner, I was invited to play bridge, but I declined and went upstairs early. I hoped we could both fit into the single bed and get some sleep.

On the drive to Bayreuth, Pappi sat in the passenger seat next to his chauffeur. Constantin, Mummi, and I sat in the back as we headed east through towns like Aschaffenburg and Wurzburg, then along the Rhine River. We stopped to look inside several Baroque churches and lunched in a charming roadside restaurant.

Back in the car, Mummi leaned toward me and asked in a low whisper, "Are you with child?"

"No, I'm not," I replied, offended by her question. Did she think that ours was a shotgun wedding or that I entrapped her son into marriage? How insulting! I tried not to show my feelings but found myself leaning closer to the door, my face plastered to the window.

For the rest of the trip, I avoided my mother-in-law, leaning forward to join in conversations with my husband and father-in-law. I learned about Bayreuth, Wagner's stronghold, which hosted the famous Wagner Music Festival every summer.

Back in Frankfurt, we fell into the everyday routine of the household. Pappi was driven to his office in the morning and picked up at 6 in time for dinner. Monica was working on her Ph.D. and would soon return to Basel, Switzerland. Dorothy was preparing to take the examination to enter Germany's Foreign Service. Rehlein was engaged to Bruno.

One day I learned how to make German potato salad from the cook, who spoke only German. It was easy to follow what she did. Another day I learned to make red cabbage, a delicious aromatic vegetable, which we ate for lunch with hot dogs, mustard, and bread. While the women busied themselves with domestic duties of food shopping and preparation, Constantin visited his father at AEG headquarters and saw some of his old friends.

All of a sudden our prolonged honeymoon was over, and it was time to leave for Bogota. On the day of our departure, everything was smoothly taken care of. With our luggage loaded into the Mercedes, we kissed goodbye, and the Bodens waved from the front porch as the car rolled down the gravel driveway to Eschesheimer Land Strasse and to the airport.

⇶18⇷

My father-in-law had given us the name of a German couple at AEG who planned to visit Germany and whose house near the country club in Bogota was available for two months. We immediately got in touch with them and were invited for an interview.

Their house was in a desirable neighborhood north of downtown on a quiet, tree-lined street. It was fully furnished and had three bedrooms upstairs, a large living room with a piano, and a dining room, and it came with a part-time maid.

All discussion was conducted in German, but I understood nonetheless that they wanted to size us up in the flesh. Although we had arrived on a motorcycle, we obviously passed scrutiny, because when we shook hands the man handed Constantin a set of house keys.

Having a base of operation made the transition to married life a lot easier, although I wondered what we would do to generate income. Constantin didn't worry much. He spent at least an hour every day playing the piano, in particular practicing the Minute Waltz, by Mozart.

Unfortunately, there was a correlation between the Minute Waltz and our sex life. I didn't bring up my frustration, probably because I thought it was *my* failure to climax. Our lack of communication compounded my frustration, but never having discussed sex with anyone or read any relevant practical literature, I was too timid to broach the subject. I buried my disappointment and frustration.

It was decided I would fly to Cartagena to inspect and claim our belongings at customs. A short flight from Bogota, the coastal city of Cartagena was founded in 1533 by a Spanish conquistador and had been a hub of the Spanish Empire, a major shipping port for New World riches, a slave market, and an Inquisition center. I took a taxicab to a hotel in Old Town, not far from the pretty Parque de San Diego.

Cartagena had a different feel from Bogota. Its lush bougainvillea, abundant tropical birds, and towering palm trees complemented the Old Town architecture, and the turquoise Caribbean Sea lapped languorously along the northwestern shore. I felt the weight of sea-level atmosphere as it wrapped its warmth around my body.

My room on the second story overlooked a patio surrounded by lush grounds, citrus trees, and exotic plantings. The blue of a swimming pool peeked between dense green foliage. After changing into shorts and a T-shirt, I asked at the front desk for directions to customs and was advised to take a taxi.

The docks weren't far. Inside a cavernous building, I was directed to a fenced-off area with a waist-high counter where I produced the bill of lading to an official-looking man. A footlocker sealed with a padlock and a piece of wire through the U-shaped latch was hoisted onto the counter. I produced a key to the padlock. A customs official cut the secondary wire barrier and opened the padlock with my key. Inside the footlocker, buried under towels and sheets, was our wedding silverware in a handsome wood box. Opening its lid to inspect the Gump's setting for twelve, I counted it all there. I was given a form to sign, which was officially stamped three times. The box was put back in the trunk, the padlock closed, and another wire placed through the U-shaped latch and sealed. I arranged to have the footlocker trucked to Bogota and left customs happy that our belongings had arrived safely.

On my way back to the hotel, I learned about and decided to join a tour aboard a *chiva*, a brightly painted open-air bus that went all the way to a convent located at the city's highest point and on to the Castillo, the famous fort built by the Spaniards centuries ago.

Before dinner, I decided on a swim in the hotel's pool. A good-looking older man, around thirty, and I were the only people there. As I swam its length twice, I noticed he was preoccupied with catching something at the shallow end. As I passed him, he held up a frog.

"Oh, my," I exclaimed, hoping he would release it away from the pool area. Instead, he treaded water and moved closer to me with the frog at chest level.

"Look! He's handsome, is he not?" He thrust the frog toward my face and laughed.

I retreated to the deep end, lifting my elbows behind me onto the pool edge, and surveyed the situation. He was tall with dark wavy hair and light skin, and because his American English was so good, he probably belonged to Colombia's upper class.

"What brings you to Cartagena?" he asked.

"Customs," I replied.

"Where do you come from?"

"We moved here from California and Germany. Bogota," I clarified.

He stared at the cleavage revealed by my black bathing suit, made eye contact, and smiled. He was flirting with me!

"If you like, I'll accompany you to customs," he offered.

"No thanks. I already went this morning."

"How about an aperitif before dinner?" he persisted.

"All right." I kicked off from the deep end and crawled to the shallow end, made an underwater turn, and crawled back, hoisting myself out of the water. I grabbed a towel and pulled off my bathing cap, shaking and toweling my hair. He watched me from the pool, which made me flush. I'm not supposed to pay attention to strange men. What's going on?

"My name is Manuel Restrepo," he said as he got out of the pool. "Let's meet in, say, an hour?"

"All right." I turned and headed indoors without telling him my name.

I dressed in the royal blue sheath I'd worn on the plane from Bogota without its matching jacket. I was looking forward to cocktails with Manuel, which would probably lead to dinner, I thought, as I adjusted a string of pearls that accentuated my rosy complexion. What would happen after dinner?

Manuel was sitting facing the bank of elevators and the stairs when I descended to the lobby. He rose to greet me and placed his right hand under my elbow to direct me toward the adjacent bar. We sat in a horseshoe-shaped booth with a small marble table. I ordered a daiquiri and he ordered a margarita.

"So, you are?" He looked at me questioningly.

"Constance," I replied. "Boden."

"Señora?"

"Yes, señora. My husband is in Bogota on business," I added to make us sound more settled.

Our drinks arrived. He clicked his glass against mine, *"Por la señora bonita."*

I clicked mine against his. "To the very dashing gentleman, who never *was* a frog."

He looked blank.

"Haven't you heard of the kind princess who kisses the frog, and the frog turns into a handsome prince?"

"*Sí, sí,* ahh, what do you call that?"

"A fairy story."

We sipped our drinks. He reached a hand across the table and stroked my arm. I pulled my arm off the table.

"That is intimate," I said, looking directly into his brown eyes and trying not to show that I liked it.

"I can't *not* touch you," he whispered.

All my life I'd heard what great lovers Latin men make, but I'd dismissed it as a cliché or thought it meant they viewed making love to a woman as a sport and went on to conquer a new female. Don Juans. This felt different. This is what I had been missing. I didn't want to resist him.

"Would you like another daiquiri?" he asked.

Confused, I resolved *not* to have another drink and to act standoffish.

"Thank you, no. Thanks for the drink. See you." I rose from the banquette, waved with a tiny flick of my wrist, and marched blindly off. He also stood, whipped out his wallet, and signaled for the waiter. He followed me into the wait staff's vestibule, into which I had accidentally stumbled.

"Here, this way." He took my elbow and guided me out of the vestibule and into the dining room. Manuel said something in Spanish to the mâitre d', and we were seated in a quiet corner away from the main dining area. I liked the way he took over.

I looked at Manuel's left hand and asked, "And you—are you married?"

"Yes."

"Do you have children?"

"Yes, two beautiful girls."

"Why are you in Cartagena?"

"I represent a shipping company that's headquartered here."

Menus were presented. A waiter brought glasses of water with lemon slices.

"In what capacity do you represent the company?"

"I'm one of their attorneys."

"Your American English is good."

"I went to law school at Georgetown University."

"Oh." I was wondering if he came from a terribly wealthy Colombian family.

"What will you have?" he asked.

"I'm dying for steak. Which one do you recommend?"

The waiter reappeared. Manuel ordered in Spanish. Presently, our salad arrived. Then wine was served.

I raised my glass of red wine and saluted him.

"To my mystery man. I got married last month, and now I'm wondering if I should have." I smiled.

"That's obvious."

"What's obvious?" I asked.

"That you're not happy."

"You can tell?"

"Body language. A woman who is well loved looks satisfied. You don't."

Shocked that my dissatisfaction was so transparent, I was mute. Dinner arrived. My steak was served with potatoes and root vegetables. His salmon and peas with squash in a pastry shell looked appealing.

"You're beautiful. Your husband should see this. Since he doesn't, let me honor your feminine beauty. Let me make love to you." He reached across the table and took my hand in his.

I almost choked on a mouthful. Withdrawing my hand and lowering my eyes, I tried to concentrate on the food on my plate. I *did* need whatever he was offering, and accepting felt like the most natural thing I could possibly do at this moment in time. But wouldn't I feel dreadful afterward? And what about his being married? What kind of a man sleeps with a woman he's just met? What kind of a woman does? Maybe I should get up now and leave without looking back. Check out of this hotel. Find another one near the airport. No. He might follow me. Why hadn't I taken the elevator to my room after the cocktail, locked the door, and stayed there until tomorrow?

"Constance."

I realized he was speaking to me.

"Where are you?" He waved a hand across my face to see if my eyes registered. "On another planet?"

"Oh. Sorry. I was just wondering where the bathrooms are," I said, looking toward the opposite wall, the way we came in. I stood, dropped my napkin by my plate and headed toward the right side of the restaurant. "Be right back," I said.

When I found the ladies room, I backed up, turned the other way, and found myself approaching the lobby. I headed for the elevator, pushed the "up" button, got inside, hit the Level 2 button, and prayed for the doors to close. They did. When the doors opened, I ran down the hall to my room. Fumbling with the key, I managed to open the door, closed and bolted it from inside, and collapsed onto the bed.

The footlocker arrived in Bogota a few days later, and when we unpacked our belongings, we found all the silverware gone and the box filled with rocks. Customs had stolen it! This was the first experience that would ultimately stack the deck against my ever living in a Third World country. Customs in the United States was, for the most part, still accountable. Not so here.

To see more of Colombia, we decided to take the local Flota Magdalena to Cali. The trip in a rickety old bus took sixteen hours and crossed two mountain ranges with valleys in the middle. The two-lane road curved along frightening drops into deep ravines. Before the road was built in the 1930s, all travel and transportation was conducted on horse and mule.

In addition to human passengers, there was all manner of cargo aboard, including two chickens, dry goods, plumbing and welding supplies, and a kitchen sink. Out my window, I spotted a corrugated roofed shack with a few animals standing about a dirt yard. A young girl, maybe twelve years old, stood with legs apart, urinating.

Twice the bus came to a stop on the shoulder of the road, where official-looking Colombians bearing side arms in holsters pulled the men outside. Conversation among those left in the bus came to a standstill. In the eerie silence, we watched the men being frisked before being let back onto the bus.

As we descended into the Cauca Valley from the north, Cali was spread out in front of us like a green-jeweled necklace. It was a large city located between the west coast of the Cauca River and the east slope of the Western Mountain Range. All around the city were rural areas planted with sugar cane and dotted with what looked like industrial plants to process the sugar from cane.

We walked from the bus station to the main square, which had a Gothic church at one end facing a pretty park with trees and dotted with benches. We sat on one and watched people go by. It was a balmy 74 degrees. Children in dark blue uniforms, carrying books strapped together, passed us on their way home from school. It was almost 6, and we needed to find a hotel for the night and a place to eat. The church bells chimed as we wandered across the park to a bank of small shops across from the church. From one of them, we were directed to a restaurant not far away and a hotel that was also close by. We checked into the hotel and then found our way to the tiny restaurant, where we were the only foreigners. Our waiter told us that Cali wasn't far from the ocean at Buenaventura.

After dinner, we sat in the park enjoying the cool evening air. After sixteen hours of captivity in the Flota Magdalena, we couldn't bear the thought of a return trip via the bus, so we decided to fly. I noticed a scuttling underfoot and lifted my sandaled feet off the ground while Constantin flashed his Zippo lighter. Huge cockroaches scuttled in all directions. I screamed, jumped up, and ran across the street to stand under a streetlight where I could see my feet. We retired to our room in the boutique hotel and fell into a deep sleep.

Shortly after arriving back in Bogota, we began looking in earnest for a more permanent place to live. The German couple who sub-rented to us would be returning in two weeks.

Constantin surprised me one morning by telling me to look out the bedroom window to the driveway below. I did. There stood an old gray English car.

"Whose car is it?" I asked

"Yours." His smile was a mile wide.

I ran downstairs and hopped into the driver's seat. It smelled musty.

"It's a little old but cute, don't you think?" he said. "It is a 1953 Austin."

"It's wonderful," I said excitedly.

Early one morning, we were awakened by the loud sounds of airplanes over the neighborhood. Constantin immediately rolled off the bed and under it, while I ran to the window, where I watched a fighter plane as it swooped low over the roofs in the next block, then another.

"My God, it's an invasion," I cried, running to the radio on the chest of drawers, where I dialed frantically for a news station. Finally I located an announcer, who said *Attention!* in Spanish. Constantin, whose instincts had been shaped by living in Berlin during World War II, rolled out from under the bed as we tried to decipher the news bulletin.

When it was all over, we read that Rojas Pinilla, former President and dictator, had staged a revolt to take back the country from the ruling junta. The air strikes in our neighborhood were aimed to take out two members of the junta, but the attempted coup failed within six hours. In the following day's *El Tempo* newspaper, a tank and other armed vehicles were pictured in the Zocalo downtown.

With calm restored, we looked for lodging in the midcity area of *calles* that ran east-west and *carreteras* that ran north/south, which was a more affordable area than the tony neighborhood we'd been living in. We found a house for rent on *calle* 44. It was a typical South American urban house with a courtyard surrounded by a kitchen, a formal dining and living room, and a staircase to the second floor, which had two bedrooms and one bath. It had no closets and ugly dark-stained chair railings in the living and dining room, but it was affordable. We rented it and moved in.

Items I'd taken for granted in the states, such as cabinets and shelving for storing dishes and cutlery, were nonexistent. There was a rudimentary gas stove with oven, a sink, and one low wood cabinet with one drawer. There was no storage on the top half of the ten-by-twelve-foot kitchen and absolutely no counter space. Where, for instance, was one supposed to chop an onion? The house had no refrigerator, which we learned was considered a luxury.

Unable to imagine living without one, we bought a used yellow *naverra* and had it placed in the dining portion of the living/dining room, where it stood like a sentinel. Another solution was to purchase a dining-room table that functioned as a kitchen prep area as well. Since the refrigerator was already in the dining room, this space seemed logical. The drawback of this arrangement was that one prepared the food in the dining room and then had to pass through the outdoor patio to reach the stove, even when it was raining.

Life began to develop a routine. Constantin found work at a language school teaching English and departed most mornings at 8 on his motorcycle. I made food lists and went on rounds gathering greens at the green grocer, meat at the butchers, and so on.

One day we bought a puppy from a street vendor and named her Violetta. She was black and white and very affectionate, which partially filled the chasm growing between Constantin and me.

A month after moving in, my stepbrother, George Wheelwright, and his new bride, Caroline, came to visit for a few days. They had planned a trip down the Amazon before George began working for the Heifer Project in Chile, part of AID and the World Bank. The few days extended into a week, then another and another until they seemed to be part of our family.

George's domestic task was to boil and store the water that we drank. On a number of occasions when we left the house to go somewhere, George would suddenly remember he'd left water boiling on the stove, so we would have to turn around.

We four occasionally went to local bullfights. Caroline was a drop-dead gorgeous blonde who, when we entered the stadium at the bullring, elicited shouts of *"olé"* from every male watching. She took it all in stride, but it seemed to irritate George.

There was a growing hostility between my husband and George because George kept appropriating Constantin's desk without asking. Constantin vented his anger to me, while I tried to mediate by explaining how Constantin felt to Caroline, who diplomatically tried to get George to stop. Despite his wife's remonstrations, George continued to barge in and take over Constantin's study.

Caroline and I embarked on finding a worker to build closets in the bedrooms. We commandeered a man from the street and communicated by gesticulating and showing him a sketch of two upright boards topped by a horizontal board and a round dowel running the width from which to hang clothes.

"Sí, sí," said Pedro, nodding convincingly. We shook hands and advanced him pesos for the lumber and other materials. Off he went. Two days later, we looked at an exact replica of our drawing, except that this structure listed at a 45-degree angle to the right. When we pushed, it righted itself and went to the left 45 degrees. It obviously needed cross bracing. On our drawing we added cross braces to the corners and showed it to Pedro.

"Sí, sí." He nodded and took some measurements with a tape measure, extended his hand for more money, and left, presumably to buy lumber for cross bracing. We never saw Pedro again.

Caroline and George's prolonged visit provided diversion and company, but I noticed that I'd buried my longings for erotic closeness and fulfillment with my husband. When we did make love, it was like two stars crossing paths in an immense, ever-expanding universe. It was never long enough for me, and Constantin didn't ask what I wanted or needed.

I felt the need to disappear by myself for a day in my little Austin so I wouldn't have to pretend anything. As Violetta and I headed north from the city, my plan was to stop at the small organic farm where we bought vegetables and then explore farther north. I pulled into the farm, run by a large middle-aged German woman, parked the car and strolled with Violetta on her leash through the planted rows of lettuce, carrots, and beets. There were several workers weeding and mulching. I bought two oranges and a bag of walnuts at the stand and sat on a bench in the sun, peeling an orange into sections. I thought about how I'd ended up in Colombia. Remembering Constantin's "I'll never see you again unless you marry me" ultimatum, followed by our marriage in Coclé, Canal Zone, and our globe-trotting honeymoon, it was all pretty confusing. I naively thought everything would be somehow wonderful once we were married. Instead, our love life was a non-event, leaving me sexually frustrated and disappointed. Why did I automatically think it was *my* fault, my failure, not *our* ignorance or inexperience?

I wished I could erase the seven months since I'd flown here in January. This realization produced a flood of tears. I popped a shelled walnut into my mouth and then a section of orange. The combined flavors were like music to me, and when I ran my tongue over my upper lip, I tasted salt from my tears. It felt good to be in touch with my feelings, even sad ones. I hugged Violetta.

After a while, we got back in the car and drove farther north through a fertile valley with scattered farms. Because I was nervous about running out of gas with the untrustworthy gas gauge, I turned around and headed home. On the outskirts, I could see Bogota's pollution hanging like a shroud over the city. Once in it, however, it became an invisible veil, common in any large industrial city. Violetta wagged her tail and made excited little yelps as we pulled in front of our house. I'm glad one of us was excited about arriving home.

By August, Caroline and George had gone, and Constantin and I joined others on horseback to Lake Guatavita, into which the Incas supposedly dumped a fortune of gold before retreating from the Spaniards. We rode for a half a day to reach a pristine lake surrounded by cliffs. Another group, headed by an American named George Bass, was trying to recover the buried gold using sonar, inflatable boats, and other equipment. We were spending only one night, while George Bass' expedition was extended. I wondered who was paying his tab.

We hobbled the horses, set up tents, and cooked a simple meal over wood fires. After the sun set, it was quite cold, so I burrowed inside our sleeping bag and welcomed Constantin's warmth when he joined me.

In the morning, I decided that camping wasn't my thing. My hair felt yucky, there was no running water nearby, and I just wanted to go home, take a shower, and brush my teeth. I somehow had the sense that we had conceived a child the previous night, because I felt I'd ovulated.

Almost immediately I experienced morning sickness, unable to keep anything down for breakfast. When my period failed to arrive, I scheduled an appointment for a pregnancy test, which came back positive. Our baby was due in May. Constantin was thrilled, while I was apprehensive about delivering a baby in a foreign country.

Constantin, who became friends with George Bass and his group, began talking about growing roses for the perfume industry. Recent graduates from the Harvard Business School, George and the others were entrepreneurs with big ideas; Constantin had caught the Big Idea bug.

"George says there's a *finca* for sale that's a perfect place to grow roses. In fact, all the neighboring *fincas* grow roses," said Constantin excitedly.

"But we don't have any capital to invest. And you don't really know George Bass or his track record."

The thought of being pregnant on a *finca* on the savanna in Colombia scared me to death. I tried to steer Constantin back to the states by urging him to apply to Dartmouth's graduate business school.

"Honey, let's get an application for Dartmouth. They already know you. If you're accepted, and I bet you will be, I can give birth safely in the states."

As an afterthought I added, "All those guys have MBAs from Harvard. I bet they've also got money or know where to find investment money. We have zilch."

He didn't agree, but he didn't disagree. We requested application materials from Dartmouth. By October, we had filled out and mailed the completed application materials and had begun another application process to the Harvard Business School, which was reputed to be the best business school in the country.

"All my father's family live in Boston. Uncles Francis, Julian, Joe, Fred, and David. Everyone but David is married. I've got tons of cousins there," I added.

With notification of his acceptance into Dartmouth, we hurriedly completed the Harvard application and mailed it, crossing our fingers.

It was more than a month before we heard from Harvard. Constantin accepted the admission notification from Harvard via telegram. That evening, we celebrated with a bottle of Champagne. It was a big relief to know we'd be returning home to the states in my fourth month of pregnancy.

I notified Boston and West Coast relatives of the news and our plan to arrive in Boston by Christmas. I asked if anyone could put us up temporarily.

We happily began to dismantle our lives in Bogota. I made arrangements to have a sale of our belongings, including wedding presents, the yellow refrigerator, the car, and most of our clothes. The businesswoman I contacted made all the arrangements, including advertising, pricing, and security, and would be paid a percentage of the gross sales. The sale was scheduled for early in December at 6 in the morning.

American friends agreed to keep Violetta and ship her to Boston after we were settled. We planned to spend the last two nights with another friend. All that remained to be done was to secure our exit visas, buy our airfare, and board the Pan American flight home.

⇒19⇐

The tarmac at Logan International Airport was a freezing twenty-five degrees. Under my light wool coat, I shivered at the blast of frigid air that slapped my face awake. Although the ground was without snow, my sneaker-clad feet had shriveled into numb appendages. Inside the terminal building, I searched the crowd on the other side of a glass wall for a familiar face, hoping my aunt and uncle had come to meet us. At four months pregnant, I was just beginning to show. I spotted Uncle Joe and Aunt Peggy waving. We moved aside from the flow of arriving passengers and embraced.

"We've been traveling since yesterday morning," I explained. "Customs in New York took forever." I introduced them to Constantin.

"Let's get your luggage," said Joe, turning toward the stairs to baggage claim.

"It's so good to see you!" I said to Aunt Peggy.

"It's wonderful you're here," she said.

In the car, Peggy turned toward us in the back seat.

"I've got a lovely secret, Consie." She locked her eyes on mine. "I'm pregnant, too, due in May."

"Oh, my God. So is ours," I exclaimed, laughter filling the car.

Aunt Peggy and Uncle Joe already had five children, and Peggy must have been over forty, so I was guessing this was an accidental baby.

I'd heard that Aunt Peggy wasn't educated in the conventional sense. Mr. Stevenson, Peggy's father, had had her chauffeured to the racetrack, where she learned to bet on the horses. She was given a lavish coming out party as a New York debutante, at which she met Uncle Joe. My favorite of Dad's five brothers, Uncle Joe was senior partner and director in the architectural firm Shepley, Bulfinch, Richardson & Abbott, Inc. His blustery, terse manner belied his generosity: Every year since our father died twelve years prior, he'd given Turo, Phil and me a Christmas check.

Their house on Clyde Street was a three-story wood-frame Victorian with a cobblestone drive, sitting on half an acre across from The Brookline

Country Club. Joe Jr., age sixteen, greeted us. In the kitchen, we met the twins, Alison and Emily, age six, Annie, ten, and Stevie, eleven. Annie showed us to a pretty guest room on the third floor with a private bath. We hauled our belongings up, but too tired and wired to sleep, we came back down to the kitchen to find everyone eating leftovers. Uncle Joe fixed us drinks.

The next day when we woke up it was past 10, and everyone had gone either to school or to work. We breakfasted, showered, and dressed. Constantin planned to contact someone his father knew high in rank at First National Bank of Boston about a job. The telephone was our lifeline. After Peggy returned with groceries at noon and we had helped her unload the car and put the supplies away, we brought her up to date on our progress. Peggy wrote down the name of her OB/GYN in Brookline, and I made an appointment for later that week.

Another uncle, Francis, offered us the use of his 1952 pickup, which Constantin gladly accepted. I'd learned not to trust Uncle Francis, who had a misogynistic history. I vowed never to drive it, explaining why to Constantin.

Over the next couple of months and as Constantin racked up parking tickets, my fears proved justified when I learned that Francis was spreading a lie: "Consie is causing me to get hundreds of parking tickets."

"Please tell Uncle Francis you are the one driving his car, not me," I told Constantin.

"All right," he said.

He never did.

Dr. Langert was a well-known OB/GYN, practicing at Boston Lying-In Hospital, part of Harvard Medical School, with offices on Beacon Street.

"Everything appears normal," he said, "but since you've lived outside the states, let's get blood and stool tests."

I went back to learn the results. Stool samples revealed a parasite called amebiasis, which attacks the colon and is a familiar malady in South America and Southeast Asia. I was given a prescription for medication and told to eat well and come for follow-up tests in a month.

Aware that we might be overstaying our welcome at Aunt Peggy and Uncle Joe's, we started to look for an apartment within walking distance of First National Bank, where Constantin had landed an entry-level job.

On Mt. Vernon Street, in the back of No. 1 Louisberg Square, was a tiny L-shaped apartment with its own entrance. Mrs. Diamond, who owned and lived in the upper townhouse, rented it to us for $125 a month. She generously agreed to furnish it and met us at Jordan Marsh one afternoon, where we picked out a red sofa bed and matching chair for the living/sleeping room. She also bought floor-to-ceiling curtains. We bought a crib and a changing table for the tiny bedroom.

It was exciting to have our own place on Beacon Hill, just steps from the State House, historic downtown and the waterfront, even though money was tight. After bills were paid, we argued over whether to buy beer or wash clothes at the Laundromat. Still, I scraped money from Constantin's paycheck and hid it to fly Violetta to Boston from Bogota. Having wired money to our Bogota friends, we awaited notification from the freight carrier.

In late February I received a telephone call from the freight office at Logan International Airport.

"We have a dog just in from South America," said the male voice. I heard barking in the background.

I asked if they were open after 5.

"Here until midnight."

I wrote down the address.

When Constantin got off work, we retrieved Uncle Franny's pickup in a friend's two-car garage. The freight offices were easy to find, and parking right outside, we immediately heard Violetta's bark.

"*Violetta*," I called. Excited squeals and yips announced she'd recognized my voice.

Inside the office sat an amateur-made wooden crate about three by three feet made of pine with a reinforced wire-mesh door. Inside the crate, surrounded by the remnants of several cans of spaghetti and meatballs, squirmed an excited Violetta, who had tipped over the water bowl. We unlatched the door and clipped on her collar and leash. Outside, she immediately did her business before we signed papers, left the crate, and headed home. After parking Uncle Franny's pickup, we walked the length of Mt. Vernon Street from below Charles Street, Violetta straining at the leash. The next day we'd let her run next to the Charles River on the Esplanade.

I saw Dr. Langert once a month during my pregnancy. My tropical-parasite problem was gone, but I struggled to follow his advice to eat "plenty of steak." We didn't have the money. All my maternity clothes were hand-me-downs from the wife of a stepcousin, and purchases were on an emergency-only basis.

Spring was a slow but steady thaw that revealed emerging buds on magnolias and privets. Tulips and daffodils decorated the paths in the Public Garden, and a soft green sheen lay underfoot on the Esplanade.

Uncle Joe was in the middle of an extensive landscaping project on the Clyde Street house. One Saturday I noticed vehicle tracks ripped across the lawn and a fresh mountain of earth piled near where the grade sloped at least ten feet on the kitchen side of the house. The operator of a backhoe loader and excavator was shoveling earth and dumping each shovelful into the hollow, the machine beeping each time it was put in reverse, groaning when it moved forward.

Inside the kitchen, Joe explained, "There'll be a door here and a deck with stairs down. I've got to build up the height of the yard so the height of stairs down from the deck is reasonable." He gestured through the kitchen window.

"When will the builders begin?" asked Constantin.

"Peggy wants it done yesterday," he grumbled. "I want to wait until the kids are out of school and they can all go to Narragansett." He added, "How can they remodel the kitchen with us using it?"

He sidled over to the built-in bar and began making himself a Bloody Mary. Remembering us, he turned and asked sheepishly, "Oh, would you both like one?"

We accepted and I got two glasses and put them next to the ice bucket on the counter.

"When's Peggy's due date?" I asked.

"I can't keep track," he answered. "There's too many kids, dogs, you name it. Know what I mean?"

As if on cue, a parade of children tromped into the kitchen, followed by Violetta and, too close behind her, Turkey, their golden Lab.

"Take the dogs down to the basement," Joe said to the group.

Noticing that Turkey was extraordinarily interested in Violetta and was in fact attempting to mount her right there in the kitchen, I yelled, "Hey, Constantin, give me a hand! I bet she's in heat."

I wondered if we were too late. I guess we'd find out.

As my May due date approached, Violetta and I walked up Mt. Vernon Street with increased difficulty. Violetta was obviously pregnant, her belly swooping lower each day. I wondered who would go into labor first. Peggy, me or Violetta. *Uncomfortable* was my middle name: My feet and ankles were swollen, my bladder needed to be emptied every other minute, and I couldn't sleep comfortably in any position.

At 5 one morning I awoke awash in water as if my boat had developed a leak. Constantin called a taxi while I dressed in the most comfortable clothes I owned. We were in the back of the cab when the first labor pain hit. I watched as my uterus performed the most amazing involuntary roller-coaster maneuver, visible through the fabric over my abdomen. It felt as if hands were squeezing the fetus sideways.

"Ohhh, God, it hurts," I yelled.

"What is it, lady?" the driver caught my eye in the rearview mirror.

"She's having a baby," said Constantin.

The driver stepped on the accelerator as we careened up Beacon Street, and I gripped the handhold with my right hand and clutched Constantin's hand with my left.

"Don't kill us!" commanded Constantin.

"Oh, it hurts!" I moaned.

At the hospital, I was put into a wheelchair and rolled into the lobby. An elevator deposited me on the labor-and-delivery floor, where I was eventually wheeled to a cubicle in a room filled with women in various stages of labor. Here I spent the next sixteen hours learning how to time my contractions using the wall clock and reporting their frequency to a team of nurses and student interns. When I was weakened to the point of exhaustion and the fetal heartbeat plunged to less than ninety, the decision was made to use forceps delivery.

I awoke in a cubicle made private by flapping white curtains. A nurse was standing over me.

"You delivered a beautiful baby girl. Would you like to see her?"

"Oh, please, yes."

I registered two bouquets of flowers, one on the floor and another on the bedside table, and wondered how long I'd been there. The nurse returned and placed a tightly wrapped bundle into my arms, and I looked into my daughter's solemn oval face with her perfectly curved mouth and wide-spaced eyes. I unwrapped the blanket to examine her marvelous tiny hands and feet. I'd never seen anything so beautiful.

"You'll want to put her on the breast as soon as you can," the nurse said.

"Already?"

"That's what they're for," she answered as both eyes shot to my bosom.

I put her on my left breast and tried to stuff the nipple into her mouth, but she appeared to be sleepy and uninterested. We lay there for quite a while. I wondered where Constantin was and who'd sent the flowers. From a hospital volunteer I learned that it was 8 in the morning, May 16.

The same nurse returned. "Any luck nursing?" she asked.

"She's too sleepy," I explained.

She stood over the baby, took her thumb and third finger, and snapped it hard against the baby's cheek. "Wake up!"

The baby cried.

"Don't hurt my baby!" I exclaimed.

Paying no attention to me, the nurse shoved the crying baby's mouth onto my nipple. "Lady, she needs to wake up and nurse."

I watched as the baby began to suck my breast. "Do you know when she was born?"

She picked up my chart on the end of my bed and read, "3 a.m. today by forceps."

She said she'd come back in thirty minutes and left us alone.

I must have dozed off, for when I opened my eyes, Constantin was there, holding a red rose out to me, a cigar poking out of his shirt pocket.

I took the rose, smiling. "Did you stay until she was born?" I asked.

"Yup. I saw her through the nursery window. Then I got some sleep."

I rang for the nurse.

"We have to give her a name," I said. "Do you still like Nina?"

"Yes, it's the same in German."

"I'd like her to have a family middle name. Livermore," I suggested.

"Nina Livermore Boden it is, then."

When the nurse arrived, I asked her to bring our baby. While we were waiting, I pulled aside a corner of the curtain surrounding my cubicle, revealing an identical one with a woman in a bed just like mine.

"Excuse me," I said to the woman, letting the curtain drop.

"There's a whole row of these," said Constantin. "It's the bargain-basement baby factory."

"Very funny," I murmured. "If you're poor, this is how it is. We could be worse off—in Bogota, for instance. Did you know the doctor had to use forceps?"

He didn't ask why. The nurse handed our baby to Constantin, who took her gingerly in his arms and gazed into her face. He laid her on his thighs and examined her toes and fingers.

"She's perfect," he said.

Checking out of the hospital, I was shocked to learn from the bill that I'd had a blood transfusion. Was Nina nearly stillborn? At my next appointment with Dr. Langert, he assured me that neither my baby's life nor mine had been in jeopardy.

"I would have performed a C-section if things hadn't straightened out," he told me. He also explained why I had no recollection of the actual birth. "We use a wonder drug here that mimics anesthesia without actually putting you out." This explained why I had no memory of the process, including an episiotomy.

At home on Louisberg Square, I was ashamed to find myself so jittery. What if I didn't have enough milk? Why was Nina crying? Was she hungry or wet? Was something else the matter? How would I know? I'd never done this before and had no idea how to take care of a newborn.

Compounding the problem was that we were such new transplants in Boston that I didn't have female friends to whom I might have turned for help. Aunt Peggy had her hands full with that busy household, not to mention her own imminent labor and delivery. Adding to my postpartum decline was the ongoing discomfort of my episiotomy, a raw open wound. I was supposed to sit in a basin of warm water several times a day to soak the stitches.

If I had known what a brutal, bloody, exhausting physical ordeal birthing actually was, I might have taken precautions never to get pregnant.

When Nina and I arrived for our first appointment with the pediatrician, Dr. Reuchlin, I had many questions that revealed my insecurities.

"Your baby is fine. Good weight, alert," she said as she examined Nina.

"Then why does she cry when I put her down *after* nursing?" I asked.

The doctor paused, turned to look at me and, thoughtfully, without sarcasm, said, "Although she's only a little more than a week old, your baby is smarter than you are. She knows if she cries, she'll get picked up."

"Oh."

After outlining a reasonable nursing schedule to follow and advising me to keep her dry and clean, Dr. Reuchlin said it was up to me to teach Nina that I, not Nina, was in charge. I made another appointment for the following month and left her office feeling hopeful.

151

Each day as our bonding progressed, my confidence as a mother grew. When I was certain she was full, clean, and dry, I put her in her crib and let her cry without rushing over to pick her up. Eventually she fell asleep, and I realized the doctor was right: It was up to me to set boundaries.

Not convinced that I was producing enough milk, I decided to switch to formula. Although it was somewhat of a production to sterilize the bottles, nipples, and screw tops, I could measure and document how much formula Nina drank. Constantin could now help with the feeding schedule, letting me catch up on sleep.

Mid-June brought my mother and stepfather to visit. When they called from the Ritz, Mom offered to baby-sit one-month-old Nina and told me to plan something fun for myself "to get out of the house," a wonderful offer, because I hadn't been anywhere by myself for a month.

We met them at the Ritz the next day and ordered lunch from room service in a handsome room overlooking the Public Garden. I proudly passed Nina to Mom and searched her face for approval. My mother beamed at her granddaughter.

"Just look at you, look at you," she sang to Nina.

Nina cooed back.

Watching them, I felt as if this was the first *right* thing I'd accomplished in my mother's eyes in all my twenty-three years.

Lunch arrived on rolling carts. The waiter set a round table with a white tablecloth and napkins and served from covered serving dishes. He uncorked a bottle of Champagne, and we toasted the newest member of the family. My mother made a date to baby-sit the next morning, saying she'd telephone when she was about to leave the hotel.

I was dressed and ready to leave when her call came.

"I will just put the key over the door on the doorjamb and you can let yourself in."

"You're going to leave the baby *alone* in the apartment?" she asked.

"Oh, my God!" I said. "I completely forgot."

We both burst out laughing.

One night not long after my parents' visit, I was preparing the living/bedroom for the night, which involved pulling out the sofa bed and moving the chair out of the way. Constantin was taking a shower. I saw a face watching me through a space in the drapes covering the picture window.

"Constantin!" I screamed.

He came flying out of the bathroom, a towel wrapped around his middle.

"Somebody is in our garden." I pointed at the window.

He ran to the front door and threw it open. Violetta let out a vicious growl and chased a dark shape as it hauled itself over the six-foot-high garden wall, but she wasn't fast enough.

From that moment on, I didn't feel safe on our ground-floor apartment and began a quest for an affordable apartment with two bedrooms nearer the Harvard Business School.

Violetta had five puppies in our small closet in a box I'd cobbled together with cedar shavings. The puppies looked more retriever than Colombian mutt. As soon as they were weaned, we gave them away. Aunt Peggy's family took one. We gave the four remaining puppies to Angel Memorial Veterinary Hospital for adoption.

After signing a lease for a year at 109 St. Paul Street in Brookline, we set off one Saturday to buy a bed and other basics. In Roxbury, a decidedly African-American district, we found streets advertising pawnshops, bargain clothing, and cheap furniture. In one, we bought a queen-size bed from a salesman who gave us an extra 15 percent off the price when we also purchased two bedside tables. Next door, we found a used metal bed frame with wheels, a decent sofa, and a wood coffee table. We hauled it all to St. Paul Street in the pickup, and Constantin paid some guys on the street to help carry the stuff to the fourth floor.

As we slowly settled into the new apartment, I explored our new corner of the world. It was a three-block walk to Cleveland Circle, where the trolley cars stopped. With Violetta on a leash, I pushed Nina in a pram there every day to buy groceries, pick up cleaning, and do other errands. In the Howard Johnson on one corner, it was fun to sit with a cup of coffee and watch people go by.

Constantin was immersed in business-school activities and classes and seemed happy. He'd been assigned to a small group, within which we were making acquaintances: Virginia and Roger Hall from Colorado, Maris and Jed Goldfedder from California, Luther and Dot Hodges, son and daughter-in-law of the current governor of North Carolina.

In addition to Constantin's classes, we attended potluck dinners and football games, all low-key and pleasant. I was aware that many of his classmates had a lot more money than we did. The Goldfedders, for example, had bought a house in a desirable neighborhood in Lexington. I heard that Goldfedder's father was a major honcho at the Heinz Company in Southern California.

I spent most of my energy and time taking care of Nina, preparing meals and keeping a tidy apartment. This traditional role felt comfortable and secure. Constantin had definite ideas of how I should take care of his clothes and the bedding. I was to air his suits, not send them to the cleaners, which he claimed broke down wool fibers. I was thankful that he ate what I prepared, for I was just learning to cook.

For our first potluck dinner with the Harvard crowd, I was asked to bring potato salad. The recipe in my only cookbook took hours to make. It wasn't until after I explained how I'd made it to the other women that one of them told me, "You made mayonnaise from scratch."

Fall slipped quickly into winter, our second one in Boston. The first snowfall deposited a silent white carpet over dirty, tired macadam and sidewalks. Sunlight and moonlight reflected its sparkling crystals before an army of plows and vehicles with rotating yellow lights atop that spread sand or salt converged on the city. By day's end, the streets were passable for vehicles, while the snowdrifts, punctured by parking meters, presented a formidable challenge to humans and canines.

Christmas 1959 came and went without much fanfare. One afternoon we attended a post-Christmas party at ancient Great-Aunt Julia's house in Chestnut Hill. The Christmas tree must have been at least nine feet tall. Under it were marvelous antique toys, including an iron train, a horse and carriage and a monkey bank from another era. Uncle Joe and Aunt Peggy, their six-month old, Marjory, and the other five children were all there enjoying eggnog and hot cider. There were other relatives, most of whom I knew only by name, but I felt as if I belonged to part of an important, large New England family.

I was surprised when Constantin gave me a gold bracelet for our first anniversary in January, because to say my husband wasn't demonstrative or affectionate was an understatement.

At nine months, Nina could wave, clap her hands, and emit a variety of sounds, such as *ma-ma-ma* and *da-da-da-da*. She was eating all sorts of solid baby foods and had two pearly new teeth, which came with plenty of crying and tears. Every night our ritual was to read *Goodnight Moon*. On our tiny balcony, we then said goodnight to the stars and the moon before I put her down to sleep.

Routine was a comfort. Daily, Constantin rode his bicycle to the B School, as it was known, and home again. School papers were due every Saturday, which occupied all Friday afternoon and much of the night. I was a full-time Mom to Nina and an as-needed housekeeper, meaning I cleaned and bought and prepared food because no one else did. I was slowly learning to cook.

We bought a used VW one weekend and finally returned the pickup to Uncle Francis. I followed Constantin in the VW to Franny's house but refused to go inside. We were no longer beholden to Francis in any way.

Over spring break we went to the Ski Club Hochgebirge, a co-op ski club in New Hampshire, and were the only couple with an infant. Everyone else was on the slopes after breakfast until darkness struck by 4:30. That day I pulled Nina on a sled at Canon Mountain, Violetta running alongside. Evening was fun, with everyone participating in the preparation of communal meals in the big kitchen at two long tables in front of a roaring fire.

I realized that I was different from the other women there. Neither a young single professional nor a middle-aged wife of a WASP, I didn't fit into any category and didn't ski. I was discovering that just being Mrs. Boden didn't answer the nagging questions after all: Who was I? What was my purpose? What would I accomplish in my life?

⇒ 20 ⇐

Violetta was lost during a weekend outing at Blue Hills Reservation, in Milton. For more than an hour we called repeatedly, but she had vanished. That evening, I called in a lost-dog notice at Angel Memorial Animal Hospital and by Tuesday had put up posters with a black-and-white photo and our phone number on telephone poles in the Blue Hills area. Not one person called. My heart had to let go of my good four-legged Colombian friend.

In August, we joined my parents for a week at our summer house on Vinalhaven Island, Maine, an hour's ferry ride east of Rockland in Penobscot Bay. Mom and George had bought the property the summer before, sight unseen.

Vinalhaven was studded with Douglas fir, spruce, and aspen, interspersed with grassy meadows sloping to miles of granite shoreline. The air was clear, cool in the evenings and warm in the day. The house and barn sat on more than an acre facing Arey's Cove, a small south-facing inlet. The furniture, which came with the house, was turn-of-the-century funky, including an organ with foot pedals, a wood-carved serpentine upholstered sofa, and an ancient black wood-burning stove.

Alta Coombs, our caretaker, brought us a berry pie and homemade bread on our first day. We ate lobster, corn on the cob, mussels that we picked at low tide, and blueberries that grew all over the island. One evening we joined an old-fashioned clambake on the beach with friends of my parents. Over the weekend there was a summer concert and an art show. We swam daily in an old granite quarry filled with spring water. I didn't want to leave this paradise.

There was another reason I didn't want to leave. I was becoming increasingly aware of how nicely George treated my mother, which was in stark contrast with how Constantin treated me. For example, after breakfast, George asked my mother, "Would you like to go over to the Lamonts' for a walk?"

"Darling, I've got to make a run for groceries first. But after that, yes, let's go."

"Right. I'll just give Bo a jingle."

It wasn't that my husband was rude or outwardly mean; more that this sort of thoughtful inquiry wasn't part of his repertoire. He did what *he* wanted when *he* wanted to. If I wanted to come along, fine. If not, fine. I realized I was longing for the sort intimacy practiced by my parents.

On the long drive back to Brookline from Rockland, I felt depressed about leaving the island and saying goodbye to my parents. I hugged Nina, who dozed in my lap. As usual, Constantin drove at least twenty miles over the speed limit and toyed with the radio knob to locate any clear station, stopping in Freeport at L.L. Bean's for a meal and to use the restrooms. It was dark when we pulled up at No. 109 St. Paul Street, parked the car, and climbed the stairs to our apartment.

Second year at Harvard Business School was in full swing. Constantin's schedule resembled last year's, only more intense. I was left on my own much of the time. I loved taking Nina to the local park with its swings and sandbox, where we met other mothers with children, and for a while our children played happily together. Every day brought new faces and children of different ages—all preschool—to the park. I often wondered what I'd do when Nina started school. Nagging at the corners of my consciousness was the awareness that I'd have to discover who I was, what it was I was put on this earth to do, and not rely solely on being Nina's mother and Constantin's wife.

Fall in New England was a kaleidoscopic canopy of leaves, once green, turning to cadmium yellow, crimson, burnt sienna, lemon yellow. Eventually, all fluttered colorfully to the ground like multicolored confetti thrown by a giant's hand. The dark winter months followed. On the shortest days, daylight ended at 4:30 and the streetlights came on.

The presidential election this year was thrilling because it was my first as a voter, and our Massachusetts senator, John F. Kennedy, was running against Vice President Nixon. Constantin and I, with opposing views, avoided all political discussions and the ensuing arguments. I was thrilled when Kennedy was elected to be our 35th president.

In mid-February, Nina got really sick. She vomited and had diarrhea. Dr. Reuchlin told us that if she couldn't keep liquids down, we should insert small amounts of water with an eyedropper into her rectum, which we did for forty-eight hours. Exhausted, the third night we drove her to the emergency room at Children's' Hospital. When at last a nurse called our name, I stepped into an examination room holding Nina on my hip. The nurse handed Nina an orange lollipop, which she immediately began to suck. With no fever, she seemed miraculously cured. As we recounted our forty-eight-hour nightmare, the nurse listened, smiled, and told us, "You both did just the right things. Her fever broke."

We three went home to sleep.

A new series of colds hit all three of us, lingering well into March. So sick of the winter that I wanted to scream, I decided to take Nina to someplace warm like Florida. I researched and discovered Sanibel Island off the coast of Fort Myers, a world-famous spot for collecting shells. Virginia Hall, wife of business-school colleague Roger Hall, decided to come with us. We rented a small fully furnished house right on the beach.

Virginia, Nina, and I flew to Fort Myers, where, after catching a taxi, we were deposited on the sand near the ferry slip. Sanibel Island lay four miles off the coast. The short ferry ride was over before it began. From the dock we taxied to our condo twenty steps from the gentle surf. It was perfect: a flat-roofed two-bedroom unit with a generous living room facing the surf. The next unit was at least thirty feet away, affording us privacy.

Besides being known for its pristine shorelines and abundance of shells, Sanibel was also brought to fame by Anne Morrow Lindberg's book *Gift From the Sea*. Virginia, Nina and I swam in the gentle surf and collected shells by the hundreds. These we boiled, stacking them to dry in the sun, while Nina played alongside. When they had dried, we fished out the dead inhabitants and washed the shells with clean water from our garden hose.

Our week came to a close and three rested, happy people arrived in Boston with hundreds of shells.

Constantin's commencement ceremony took place in Harvard Yard on a hot June morning in 1961. The undergraduate student body and all the graduate-school candidates assembled, by school, filling the quadrangle outside Memorial Chapel. The university marshal, the president, and other dignitaries filed onto the podium while guests filled chairs facing it. Nina and I sat fairly near the front, but I had to lift Nina so she could watch the proceedings. Commencement was a solemn yet colorful and joyous pageant, with robes of different colors and mortarboards sporting various-colored tassels that represented disciplines particular to each graduate school. By noon, two-year old Nina and I were wilting. There was another ceremony at the business school proper in the afternoon to which Constantin had to go but which I elected to skip. Uncle Joe and Aunt Peggy would be there. Nina and I took a cab home to collapse on our respective beds with fans whirring on high speed.

I fell asleep, and when I awoke the bedside clock showed 4 p.m. I woke Nina to give her a bath in tepid water, then dressed her in diapers and a T-shirt.

As a graduation gift, my folks had given us the Maine house on Vinalhaven for a whole week, starting tomorrow. They wouldn't be coming East this summer, because my mother, who had been diagnosed with breast cancer, was dealing with postsurgery, radiation, and, in six weeks, a round of chemotherapy.

Constantin was taking the week off before starting a new job at First National Bank of Boston.

The only way to guarantee getting your car on the ferry in Rockland, Maine, was to put it in line early. That meant sometimes having to get there three hours before the ferry was scheduled to leave. There were only three ferry trips a day from Rockland to Carver's Harbor. Aiming for the midday crossing, we departed Boston early after I'd packed supplies and cleaned out the icebox.

Somewhere north of Kittery, Constantin said, "We've been invited by the Watsons to go sailing."

"Who are the Watsons?"

"Thomas Watson Jr. He's the CEO of IBM. Pappi and he are friends— he asked me to give him a call."

"My God! When did he call you?"

"I called him. Last week sometime," he said as if it was the most ordinary thing in the world.

"I wish you'd told me. I would have packed something decent to wear." Bermuda shorts, a sleeveless white blouse, sweater, and top siders—I pictured the preppy uniform even though I didn't own anything like it.

"Actually, Pappi gave me Tom's private number. They have a place on North Haven. I told him we'd be on Vinalhaven this week."

"You call him Tom, not Mr. Watson?"

He nodded.

I just hoped that the Watsons would be casual, because all I brought to wear were faded jeans and overwashed T shirts.

At the ferry terminal, I noted with satisfaction that our VW was twelfth in line, which meant it was highly likely we'd get on the 1:30 crossing. Needing to stretch our legs after such a long drive, we wandered from the terminal to the main hotel in the center of town, whose lobby featured Louise Nevelson's collages and sculptures, stunning constructions of wood, metal, paper, and paint. What a surprise to find such contemporary art in this seemingly out-of-the-way place. On our way back to the car, we picked up grocery staples because they were much cheaper there than on the island.

The Vinalhaven ferry arrived and disgorged its passengers and cars, and we slowly inched down the ramp onto the boat in two lines facing the stern. Leaving Rockland, presided over by Owl's Head lighthouse, the ferry headed due east for an hour until entering the narrow passageway between a string of smaller islands. Here we turned and headed southeast for about twenty minutes, gliding close to small islands on either side. Finally we turned east into Carver's Harbor, filled with boats of all sorts, and pulled into the terminal with a loud blast of the horn.

Two rough-cut five-foot-tall granite pillars with rings that held a heavy chain marked the entrance to our property. Alta Coombs had been here to unlock and remove the chain and turn on the lights and the water heater. She somehow produced a playpen, which sat next to the ornate black wood-burning stove. With the crib mattress we'd brought, the playpen would transition to a bed by night.

I'd brought enough food from Brookline for a simple meal tonight, so I stored those items in the icebox. I noted that the newly installed bathroom, at the foot of the stairs, rendered the outhouse obsolete. Someone had cut the wild grass behind the house all the way down to Arey's Cove.

We pulled recliners and an old lobster pot, which served as a table, from the barn to the south of the house facing Arey's Cove. Our neighbor's small boathouse, strung with orange and yellow pot buoys, dwarfed by stacked lobster pots, sat at water's edge. The air was crisp and dry, with a faint aroma of pine and ozone from the sea.

The first thing we did the next day was drive to the lobster pool past town on the wharf. We picked out two large lobsters for dinner. Next, we dropped by Carver's Store for fresh corn and other produce. Constantin selected a white wine. I said hello to Mr. Carver, reminding him where our house was and who my parents were. He smiled in recognition.

After putting the food away, we made sandwiches and headed for a swim in a nearby quarry. Because of the sudden drop from granite ledges into deep water, Nina wore a life preserver. We found a sunny spot on a ledge about a foot above the water and settled there. A group of older children cavorted and dived off the ledges on the other side. I didn't think they were old enough to be without supervision and didn't spot anyone in charge.

"When we get back, let's check in with the Watsons," I suggested.

"Okay, I'll call," Constantin said.

"Be sure to let them know we've got a two-year-old," I reminded him.

He called late afternoon while I was feeding Nina. Although I couldn't hear the whole conversation, I heard enough to know it was an all-day affair Saturday.

Saturday, we parked our car at the Thoroughfare landing slip, flashed our headlights repeatedly until we heard the noise of an outboard motor, and saw the ferry/rowboat leave the North Haven side heading toward us.

Waiting on the other side, Tom Watson was a tall, ruggedly handsome man in his mid-forties, I guessed, with a mop of sandy hair and a boyish swagger that seemed to invite teasing. We drove to his side of North Haven, past his palatial two-story shingled house, and down a graveled one-lane road to his dock. His fifty-foot yacht, its hull painted black, was anchored in deeper water. We rowed to it in a dinghy and climbed aboard.

We were introduced to Tom's wife and two of their children, Olivia and Jane. Another guy, who looked like an "old salt," was busy checking rigging and getting the sails ready to haul aloft. I sat where I could keep Nina safely in my grasp. One of the Watson daughters, Olivia, about fifteen, took Nina below, so I relaxed and accepted a can of Heineken from Mrs. Watson.

The hired man pulled up anchor, and we motored out of the cove to the easterly side of North Haven, where, simultaneously, the sails were unfurled and hoisted and the motor was cut. A lovely breeze took us on a reach away from the island. Mr. Watson was enjoying himself at the helm.

His wife turned toward me, "Constance, or is it Connie?"

"I go by Consie." I tipped my head in my husband's direction. "He goes by Connie."

She laughed. "What fun you must have!"

"It comes up all the time," I said.

"So, how did you two meet?" she asked.

"In college. In Vermont," I said.

"Oh, look!" Tom Watson pointed to ten o'clock on the left horizon. "A seal."

A sleek black head glistened in the sunlight and watched us glide by and then disappeared. I slipped below to check on Nina. She and Olivia were playing on one of the bunk beds, peering through the porthole. Nina was sucking her thumb, which meant she was sleepy. We put her down and covered her with a soft blanket.

"I'll stay with her," said Olivia.

"Thanks," I said and climbed back on deck.

Constantin and Tom were in animated conversation about skiing somewhere in the Alps. Jane sat near her mother.

Suddenly, the wind shifted.

"Coming about," shouted Mr. Watson as he turned the wheel hard to his left.

There was the slapping of halyards and the creaking of the wooden mast as its sail-laden boom swung across the deck and the sheets were pulled taut and cleated. The gib sail was pulled in tight as we pointed the boat hard into the wind on a windward tack. She listed and groaned and gained speed. Those on deck pulled on jackets.

After tacking back and forth for about an hour, we came about and, with the wind behind us, ate lunch in relative calm under a dazzling sun. I awakened Nina and brought her on deck to drink her bottle.

Back at the Watsons' cove with the boat anchored, the hired man rowed several of us at a time to the dock, where we carried our belongings to respective vehicles. Mr. Watson and his man were the last to leave the boat. I watched as Tom Watson got up on the gunwales of the dinghy and rocked it back and forth, defying his age and gravity with balance.

We thanked Mrs. Watson for a delicious lunch and said goodbye. Tom Watson drove us to the North Haven Thoroughfare, where we summoned the rowboat operator to take us back to the Vinalhaven side.

As we waited on the dock, Mr. Watson turned to Constantin and said, "Here's my offer. You'll be *my* assistant. I only have one. I want you to think hard about this and get back to me pronto."

"Of course I will. Thank you for the sail, the lunch, everything," said Constantin.

I was stunned, speechless. Did I hear correctly? *His* assistant? That's one stop from the top! No more scrounging for dollars, I thought, relief washing over me. I tried to hide my emotions as I shook his hand, smiling sweetly.

162

I got into the rowboat and sat in the middle and Constantin handed Nina to me. Then he climbed in and we were off, waving to Mr. Watson as the boat carried us across the thoroughfare.

Sunday we cleaned up the house, stripped the bed, and called Alta Coombs before leaving to catch the morning ferry. Constantin would begin his new job Monday.

On the drive, I tried to sound Constantin out on Mr. Watson's job offer.

"Are you seriously considering Mr. Watson's job offer?" I asked.

"Of course."

"What do you consider the downside?" I asked.

"Not now, okay?"

I reluctantly dropped it, figuring it was a slippery slope: If I encouraged him and he took it and ended up hating it, he'd blame me.

"You've got time to mull it over," I said with encouragement.

"Mmmmm," he responded, lighting another cigarette.

⇒ 21 ⇐

With Constantin's steady job at the bank a "given," it made sense to own a house and not pay rent. I'd longed to live in the coastal city of Marblehead, about thirty miles north of Boston, because its old-town district was steeped in history, with a newer development facing the city of Salem and its harbor.

We began looking at Marblehead properties and zeroed in on No. 9 Pearl Street, a three-story 1700-era Federal with its original clapboard siding in the heart of old town. The pleasant middle-aged couple who owned it were moving out of state. By the third visit, I was in love with the house and the town, with its windy, twisted streets and various beaches. With many young couples and children of all ages in the neighborhood, it promised to be a friendly community. We made an offer on the $20,000 property.

On the morning scheduled for our closing, Constantin insisted on arriving at the bank in our old VW and wearing jeans.

"Dress down," he ordered me.

I put on faded jeans and a grubby sweatshirt. When we arrived, the excrow agent met us in the lobby and escorted us down a short hall to a small nondescript office. He was as unremarkable as his office. Constantin put his briefcase in his lap and extracted a large pile of ten-dollar bills, which he put on the desk. He began to count out loud—all 200 of them—drowning out what the agent kept trying to say. When he finished, he looked up, pleased with himself. We signed the papers and left the agent scratching his head.

We didn't own much furniture with which to furnish the house and had limited resources. Nonetheless, I plunged in. Abbey Carpet Company, in Brookline, held a once-a-year unclaimed-rug sale, and I made sure to be there when its doors opened at 7 that morning. A crush of women were already there; when the doors opened, we pushed in.

From a pile of 8-by-10 rugs roughly three feet high, I pulled corners back, revealing the rugs underneath, until I located three I thought I liked.

"Could you pull this one from the pile?" I asked one of the laborers standing nearby.

One by one, he and another man removed the rugs that were stacked on top. In this way I found three faded Orientals for a pittance.

On weekends I dragged Constantin to furniture auctions in New Hampshire and Maine, discovering that the best time to get a deal was on a rainy, miserable day. We bought a Queen Anne writing desk and a Colonial blanket chest for a pittance at an almost-empty Richard Worthington auction one wet Sunday.

On a late-summer weekend in Vinalhaven, I found two ceramic treasures, an early hot-water bottle, called a Henderson Foot Warmer, and a Hires Root Beer jug, both of which I bought for under fifteen dollars and later had fashioned into table lamps for the living room.

Being on Vinalhaven Island again must have pushed a memory button in Constantin's brain about the job offer Tom Watson had made in June. As soon as I opened the front door, he raced to the telephone to dial Mr. Watson's personal number, despite its being eight weeks later. Their conversation sounded amicable but short.

"He hired someone else?" I asked when I heard the handset drop onto the receiver.

Constantin nodded affirmatively.

What did he expect after not responding for two months? I speculated often about the reasons and deduced that it must have had something to do with my husband's fear of being overpowered by father figures like his own father, current president of Germany's AEG. Mr. Watson was an alpha male if I'd ever met one. But I didn't share these musings.

Back in Marblehead, we painted all the downstairs walls and woodwork and experimented by using off-white paint with different tints. To the off-white walls in the living room, I added a slight pink tint. The off white satin-finish woodwork had a faint green tint. The effect was to subtly differentiate the wood moldings from the walls without resorting to contrasting colors. It worked.

We hired a floor refinisher to sand and finish the original wide floorboards in the living room with three coats of sealer.

I ordered lined natural linen drapes with red tassels for three windows in the living room and vowed to learn to sew curtains for the rest of the windows in the house. We bought a predominantly white wool Moroccan rug with delineated black diamonds to offset the two red velvet sofas. I scattered the faded Oriental rugs throughout the rest of the house. Finding a large antique gate-legged pine table for the dining room and a beautiful early tavern table while browsing on Cape Cod, I also discovered a love for decorating and furnishing our eighteenth century house.

We began a difficult landscaping project of bricking a parking area on the street side of our garden and decided on a herringbone pattern. The whole thing was more involved than we thought, in that everything must slope toward the curb and the bricks had to be laid on a bed of sand. When it was finally completed, it was a real improvement to be able to park off the street. Walpole Woodworks erected a seven-foot-high cedar fence with a gate to separate the parking area from the yard.

We gradually met neighbors across and down the street, including Nancy and Bob McArthur and their three children. Nancy's sister was Tammy Grimes, the Broadway star. Directly across the street, Hope and John Hague lived in an immaculate house and garden with a white picket fence. Around the corner and up Mechanic Street lived Isabel and Bob Barach and their three kids. Up another street lived Bob and Mary Langston and their two children. Mary was a painter and became a lifelong friend.

Just when I was beginning to feel at home and getting to know neighbors, Constantin learned through the bank of an opportunity to work on a big project with a Mr. Kellogg in Dussledorf, Germany. It would mean going there for six months, leaving in November. I conceded that what was good for his career was good for all of us. We discussed renting the house but, after all the work and money spent getting it fixed up, decided instead to drain the water pipes and close it up until our return.

Dusseldorf was gray. Its buildings mirrored the heavens. Our furnished sublet was a hideous mixture of ornate Jacobean pieces and semimodern orange-stained wood tables and chairs. Someone from AEG, probably Pappi's secretary, found it. I missed Marblehead, our own barely lived-in house, and wondered what Nina and I would do here until spring. Was it the fate of all wives to follow their husbands to Timbuktu if need be and to put one's own life on hold?

Every day while Constantin was at work, Nina and I walked from the apartment to a nearby lake, where we fed the ducks. Along the way I pointed to objects and told her their names.

"Street lamp."

"Steet lam."

"Street." I emphasized the "T."

"Street."

"Good."

She repeated each word and pointed her tiny finger. It was very comforting to hold her small mitten-clad hand in mine and explore our slice of the universe.

I grew queasy and began to speculate that I must be pregnant. A second week of morning sickness was enough to prod me to visit a medical clinic, where my pregnancy was confirmed. Constantin's parents were ecstatic with the news and insisted we come for Christmas when the Dusseldorf office shut down for the Christmas holidays.

The Frankfurt house was buzzing with activity. An enormous Christmas tree sans decorations greeted us in the foyer. Open boxes of ornaments surrounded its base. Sweet cooking aromas emanated from the kitchen, prompting Nina to say, "Cookie?"

"*Ja*, darling, koo-kie," sang Mummi, as she led Nina into the kitchen to get one.

Two of my sisters-in-law, Doyle and Rehlein, were here, as was an older woman, who was introduced as Frau Radimaker, a seamstress. She'd come for a week or two to make clothes for Frau Boden and her daughters.

"I have lovely plaid wool for you," said Mummi. "Would you like Frau Radimaker to make a kilt for you after Christmas?"

Yes, indeed I would.

Pappi's chauffeur arrived with a huge box from the butcher. Among other items was the venison roast for our Christmas meal, which needed curing before cooking. This consisted of hanging the meat from a hook in the kitchen's ceiling until Christmas morning.

Tea and cookies were served in the breakfast nook off the foyer where we discussed plans for the following few days. Mummi had tickets to the Frankfurt symphony for Sunday evening, but we couldn't attend, as Constantin had to be back at work Monday morning in Dussledorf. We'd accompany Mummi shopping the next day for last-minute items, we assured her. She announced we would have high tea at Kronberg's afterward, and I knew she wanted to be seen in and around the fashionable shops with us.

Pappi discussed with his son, whom he called *Connie-lein* (little Connie,) what wine to serve with venison. He ceremoniously handed me the key to the wine cellar, and I led the way. On a knee-level shelf among ten rows of dusty wine racks, Pappi found the wine he sought, and we brought four bottles upstairs. Apparently, some of Pappi's wines dated back to Napoleon's reign and were irreplaceable.

In the afternoon, I learned how to make *blatterteig apfel strudel* from the cook. First I watched as she rolled out a puff pastry on a marble slab and then lifted it onto a baking sheet. She cut a smaller slice of a sponge cake, put in on top of the puff pastry, and drizzled rum on top. Apples, almonds, sour cream, and other spices awaited on the countertop. Reading her hand motions, I peeled and sliced the apples and dumped them into a bowl with the sour cream and spices. I poured the mixture onto the pastry, folded the puff pastry over the top and sealed all the ends. The cook took my hand in hers and, with a pastry brush, brushed the top with egg wash, sprinkling some almonds on top. I placed it in the middle of a preheated oven, which I guessed was about 375 F for about 25 minutes. This was my first attempt at baking, and the results were deliciously rewarding.

Mummi, *Connie-lein*, Nina, and I were in Pappi's chauffeur-driven Mercedes making last-minute shopping rounds in downtown Frankfurt. I was glad to get away from the house, which stank with the putrid curing venison. I couldn't imagine eating anything that smelled so revolting, but I was assured this is a normal process necessary to tenderize the meat.

Mummi dashed into her favorite jewelry store "to pick up something special" while we three stayed cozily in the warmth of the car listening to music on the radio. Next was a stop in front of an upscale children's clothing store.

"You can't go to Kronberg's in that awful jacket, darling," Mummi said, so Nina and I followed her inside. She chose a light blue woolen coat with a dark blue velvet collar. Nina shrugged out of her worn anorak and slipped her arms proudly into the coat sleeves. Mummi made arrangements to have the coat put on her bill while I took Nina to the car to show off her new coat to her father.

Finally, the three of us entered Kronberg's, an opulent Victorian tearoom with many small tables and ladylike upholstered chairs. The strains of a Viennese waltz floated softly through the great room while waitresses in black dresses with white aprons and caps scurried from kitchen to table carrying china and pastry-laden trays. We placed our order and looked around. Last-minute shoppers with boxes of gifts and shopping bags stuffed under chairs and tables crowded around their tables.

Our tea and pastries arrived. Nina and Constantin both had slices of chocolate cake, while I sipped tea and contemplated my pregnancy. I'd be full term around the middle of September.

Mummi looked around the room and smiled at the occupants of a table about twenty feet away, who nodded in recognition. I observed my mother-in-law's face while she was otherwise occupied. It was mannish: pronounced cheekbones and chin, thick eyebrows that traversed her brow in a straight line, a large, generous mouth. Her gray hair was cut in a chin-length bob and softly waved. She sported a green Tyrolean felt hat with partridge feathers and wore lots of jewelry on fingers and wrists. She removed a bracelet and handed it to Nina to play with.

My mother-in-law's most glaring fault was her inability to make others feel comfortable. While her daughters worked around these faults, filling in the gaps she left, Constantin found his mother difficult. They were two pieces of sandpaper always grating each other.

"What a wonderful place," I said to Mummi, waving my arm to include the great room.

Christmas morning we gathered in the sunlit drawing room to take our tea and coffee clad in dressing gowns and slippers. Instead of stockings filled by Santa, everyone had a table with gifts on it.

"Consie, there's your table." My mother-in-law indicated a small table set aside. On it were a pair of woolen mittens and matching scarf, a bottle of French perfume, and small black box, inside which sat a gold pinky ring with a cabochon emerald and a diamond on either side.

"It's beautiful," I cried as I slipped it over the little finger on my right hand.

"In honor of the child you carry," said Mummi.

"Very nice," said Pappi, examining my hand.

I showed it to my sisters-in-law and finally to Constantin, who smiled proudly.

On Nina's table lay a doll in a wood cradle with a diaper bag filled with tiny diapers and a small bottle. She was entranced.

So it progressed around the room. Each of us held our gifts aloft to the delight of all.

Constantin opened a box that revealed a V-neck yellow cashmere sweater. Another box held two pairs of argyle socks. He fingered an envelope and ceremoniously opened it, extracting a Christmas greeting with a business card inside. He flipped the card over and read what was scribbled, "1959

Mercedes 190 SL. Former test vehicle." He looked up at his father's face. Pappi's influence in this was evident in his pleased smile.

I must say I was getting used to wearing nice things, especially my new pinky ring. Material comforts weren't something I was brought up to expect, but they had grown on me. I mentally compared past Christmases at Green Gulch with this cheerful one. My mother was always depressed, usually trying to cover it up with a forced gaiety like a bright satin bow tied around a sopping blanket. She complained that there was too much to do, that we didn't help enough, that Christmas was too commercial. She seemed glad when it was over and we left for our respective lives elsewhere. The Bodens' Christmas was totally unlike those dreary, depressing ones at Green Gulch.

We left for Dusseldorf on Sunday morning, about 75 miles to the north. There was no time for Frau Radimaker to make my new kilt, but I'd left my measurements so she could begin. Being pregnant, I wouldn't be able to wear the kilt until next fall, so there was really no urgency; still, I wanted to take advantage of the offer.

Nina and I had passage on the *SS Statendam,* sailing to New York in June. I wished Constantin was with us, but he elected to remain a bit longer to wind up his project with Mr. Kellogg before flying to Boston.

The crossing was mild, but I still struggled to keep food down. I felt sorry for Nina, who had to put up with me as a roommate, because this was more than morning sickness: I felt deathly ill and vomited everything. Attempts to enroll Nina in scheduled children's activities were aborted by my having to crawl back to our cabin, where I hung to the sides of my bed while everything whirled. In desperation, I saw the ship's doctor. He put me on an antinausea medication, which calmed my stomach to the extent that I didn't miscarry and could keep broth and saltines down. Gradually, I added more solids until I was almost back to eating normally the day the ship docked.

Marblehead! It was summertime. We had shipped the Mercedes 190 SL from Stuttgart, and it had just arrived. At six months pregnant, I could just fit my belly under the steering wheel when I rocketed into Boston to visit my OB/GYN. Watching the RPM dial, I downshifted like a real performance driver. What a thrill this sleek piece of machinery was!

Marblehead was crawling with vacationers during the summer, especially during weekends. We met more local residents and invited couples for dinner on separate weekends. One young couple from MIT had a J-sailboat and entered J-boat class races in Marblehead Harbor. Another friend, Peter Fernald, who'd been at the business school with Constantin, turned out to be living in my grandfather's barn apartment in Needham. Through him, we had previously met Mary and Bob Langston, who lived nearby.

Despite all these positive things in our lives, our marriage sputtered along like a car with missing cylinders. A classic example was an evening when, as I served pasta with garlic and shrimp to our dinner guests and they plunged into the food and kept up an animated repartee, it was obvious that the only person *not* enjoying himself was my husband, who sat in stony silence with a disapproving grimace on his face.

I suddenly blurted, "Isn't it too bad that the only person *not* having any fun is the one who's paying for everything?"

Laughter exploded from our guests, which I think was nervous release. Constantin stiffly got up from the table and left the room.

There were other disturbing arguments in the weeks that followed, one of which culminated in his physical assault on me in front of Nina. At eight months pregnant, this had gone too far. The assault left me with black and blue marks on my arms and shoulders.

I made an appointment with a chiropractor for my physical aches and sought marriage counseling through the United Way of Boston, where I was referred to a group session in the evenings at a location on Beacon Hill. I told Constantin what night I was going and asked him to meet me there after work.

His response was, "It's your problem, not mine."

At the first session, the counselor asked where my partner was. I explained that my husband refused to attend. The counselor asked for my husband's work telephone number, which I gave with renewed hope.

During the second session, I learned that Constantin stonewalled, even as the counselor accused him of "sabotaging your marriage and impeding progress." There was no point continuing, so I dropped out.

The Brookline chiropractor, Dr. Miller, was kind and rather attractive and said he'd never treated a pregnant patient, but I felt safe in his competent hands. I explained how my pain had come about, and he listened sympathetically. The manipulation brought amazing physical relief to my aching body with each visit. Over the ensuing weeks of therapy, I felt a growing attraction.

One afternoon, I told him how I felt and asked, "Does this often happen in your practice?"

"Occasionally," he calmly said, "but you're the first pregnant one."

We both laughed at the sheer idiocy of the situation. I was his last patient that day, he told me. Would I like to drive to the Charles River and sit awhile to watch the sunset?

"I'd like that very much," I said.

On the way there, I told him about my unhappy marriage and how things had progressed to where they were now. We parked next to an empty picnic table facing the banks of the Charles on the Boston side. I wanted to touch him, and did. We kissed. As much as I was able, I twisted my body so that my side could press against the length of his without my stomach being impaled on the gearshift. He fondled my nipples, producing shudders of pleasure. We were half undressed in the bucket seats of his sports car when I suddenly glanced at my watch. It was 6:30. I'd left Nina with a baby-sitter and was already an hour late. What if Constantin didn't go directly home from work?

Pulling away, I gasped. "I have to leave immediately. I'm sorry. My daughter—she's with a sitter. I should have been home by now."

I pulled myself together, rolled down the passenger window, and waited for him to turn the key in the ignition. Dr Miller's frustration was evident, but I was too traumatized by what I'd just done to offer a meaningful apology. We drove back to his office in silence.

At home, Constantin and I avoided bringing up "trigger" issues with one another. This truce held little hope of revealing the roots of his anger, my sexual frustration, or why we both felt as if we were living with the enemy.

In the weeks before giving birth, I replayed what had almost occurred with Dr. Miller, which had more to do with what wasn't happening in my marriage than anything else. I hadn't realized until then how much of a powder keg I had become or what exactly to do about the escalating mess.

⇒ 22 ⇐

Hans Ulysses Boden was born September 18, 1962, at Boston Lying-In Hospital, weighing close to nine pounds. The delivery was normal, with no complications like those accompanying Nina's.

A nurse's face hovered over my bed.

"What did I have?" I asked.

"You gave birth to a baby boy," she said.

"Oh, thank you, thank you," I cried.

"Honey, I had nothing to do with it," she left to bring me the baby.

Because Constantin said to me on more than one occasion that I'd have at least seven girls before giving birth to a boy, I almost believed him. The first thing I did while holding my son was to undo one side of his diaper to see for myself. Yes, he was a boy. Now that I'd produced a boy, would I be more valued?

When Constantin arrived, we named our baby Hans, after his father, and Ulysses because we had to break the naming cycle of Hans Constantin or Constantin Hans that had gone on for too long. We both admired Homer's *Ulysses* and liked the name.

My mother called to congratulate us and promised to give me the services of a daily housekeeper three hours a day for a month.

"That's wonderful," I said. "Thank you."

I examined my body, which felt and looked sleek. It amazed me how the female body can grow a fetus from a small egg into a complete baby, give birth, and shrink to normal proportions in a matter of days. My attraction to Dr. Miller had reawakened my sexuality and made me feel like a woman again, but I avoided dealing with this obvious signpost because its implications were too threatening to my marriage.

On my first night at home in Marblehead, I was shocked to learn that Constantin had invited company for dinner without consulting me. I refused to entertain and remained in bed upstairs with growing resentment. Let him figure it out! When he finally came to bed upset at me for not keeping the silver polished, I wanted to hit him with something hard and blunt!

I nursed Hans every two to three hours. Day and night were inseparable, except that during the night I kept the radio tuned to a news station. One night I heard that President Kennedy had authorized the use of 3,000 federal troops to integrate the University of Mississippi. Civil rights were taking front stage.

Ida, the lady from the housekeeping service, who came every morning, made sure I had a good breakfast. She also pushed a dry mop over the wood floors, washed the dishes, and helped with Nina. When she left at noon, she always had some form of lunch started for us. Grateful for her ministrations, I wished she were a permanent fixture in our lives.

Hans was a hungry baby, and by the time Ida's month was up, I was adding cereal to his menu. Although Nina adored her baby brother and spent hours cuddling with him, alone with Nina and Hans all day, I felt exhausted and depressed. It was an effort just to get dressed in the morning, especially after nursing several times during the night. I contemplated going back to group counseling at United Way, where at least I would be able to talk about my feelings, but I was too exhausted to put any plans into motion.

Increasingly worried, I called my stepuncle, Joe Wheelwright in California, a psychiatrist who'd founded the Carl Jung Society of San Francisco, and told him my symptoms. He suggested I see a colleague affiliated with McLean Hospital, in Belmont. I wrote down his name and a backup doctor's name.

I made an appointment with Dr. Mueller for a day the following week at McLean Hospital. I listened to the secretary give me directions from where I lived on the North Shore. Having made an appointment to be evaluated lifted my spirits somewhat. Finding a baby-sitter and introducing formula to Hans before the appointment was a welcome challenge. Hans tolerated the formula. I called the agency that had sent Ida to inquire about mature baby-sitters. They assured me they could provide reliable, experienced sitters.

"I'll need someone for four hours next Tuesday," I said. They called me back to confirm the job.

I bundled up the kids. Pushing Hans in his pram, we walked up to Red's Pond amid the fluttering fall leaves to feed stale bread to the ducks. Soon we were surrounded by aggressive gulls that swooped like dive-bombers stealing scraps from the ducks.

The drive to Belmont in my slow-moving dix-chevaux Citroën took over an hour. I found the main gate to the hospital and the red brick building called Minot House among many buildings on its large campus. I gave my name to a receptionist.

"I'm here to see Dr. Mueller," I said.

Dr. Mueller was tall, thin, and dark-haired and had a German accent. He shook my hand and led me into his office. I nervously explained how depressed and tired I felt with a newborn son and a three-year old daughter. He had a gentle probing manner. Soon I was telling him how Constantin had invited dinner guests the night I came home from the hospital with the new baby and how angry he was that I hadn't kept the silver polished.

"You sound pretty upset at your husband," he observed.

"*Upset* is an understatement!" I declared.

I recounted my efforts to enroll us in group therapy at United Way and the disappointing outcome. Somehow the fifty minutes were up before I could run out of things to tell him.

He suggested we make another appointment, during which I would be given evaluative tests that would help chart a course of treatment. He advised me not to self-diagnose and not to worry too much. I made an appointment for a week later.

On the way home I pondered the coincidence of my attraction to a Dr. Miller and a psychiatric session with a Dr. Mueller. Cosmic jokes? I definitely felt as if a weight had been lifted, even if I didn't know where all this was going.

I arrived home in time to feed both children and put Hans to bed before preparing our dinner. When Constantin arrived from work, we sat down to an uneventful supper, and I brought him up to date on my appointment that afternoon.

"Dr. Mueller is German," I said.

"Does that matter?" he asked.

"Not to me. I guess it's just a coincidence."

"What did Dr. Mueller say?" he asked.

"Mostly he asked questions. I'm taking tests next week."

"Oh. Is this a two-time, three-time or more occasion?"

"Why? I mean, I don't know. I'm the patient, not the doctor."

"You look fine to me." He looked at me with a pasted-on smile.

"It's how *I feel*. I'm depressed. Tired. Don't you care?" I asked in bewilderment.

"Don't accuse me of not caring," he snapped.

"Let's drop it, okay?" I rose to begin clearing our plates from the table.

"Fine."

In pajamas, Nina ran to her father with a book she asked him to read. "Please Daddy, *Goodnight Moon*." She held up the book. He picked Nina up and carried her into the living room.

We sold the Mercedes 190 SL for a good sum and used the money to meet the gap between bills and Constantin's salary. Fearful that something really might be wrong with me, I made "to do" lists, which helped me accomplish the simplest of routines such as grocery shopping and putting gas in the Citroën. No matter where I was, I could burst into tears without warning.

When the day arrived for my second appointment at McLean's for the testing, I was both relieved and anxious. The tests were interesting. In the thematic apperception test, the administrator showed me a series of ambiguous pictures and asked me what had led to the event shown, what was happening at the moment, what the characters were feeling and thinking, and what the outcome of the story was. Another was the Rorschach test, with inkblot-like forms. I was asked to describe what I saw in them. Then, left alone, I took two more, an IQ test and one that seemed to be trying to find out what my interests were. When I'd finished all the tests, I made another appointment with Dr. Mueller for the following week before heading home.

The two-hour drive there and home gave me time to digest things. I hadn't said a word about Dr. Miller to anyone, but I thought about what had almost happened all the time. It was apparent that my attraction to him terrified me. If consummated, an affair would threaten my marriage, the children, and everyone's financial security. On the other hand, Constantin's and my communication skills were reduced to accusations and blame or prolonged silences, and I was dying in this marriage. Constantin refused marriage counseling. It wasn't a happy impasse.

I continued weekly psychiatric sessions with Dr. Mueller, who prescribed medication for my postpartum depression and, although hopeful about my prognosis, remained concerned. He was careful in what he said to me, but he was also candid. One day I told him my suspicions that I was a hopeless schizophrenic, just biding time until committed. He recounted a story about two frogs who fell into a container of milk. One frog, knowing it was hopeless, dropped to the bottom and drowned. The other frog kept swimming, keeping his head above the surface. After a long while, his churning legs turned the milk to butter, and the frog climbed out. I planted this story in my heart and held on to it for dear life.

My motherly concerns for Hans and Nina sustained me. These instincts came from a well deep inside where I never worried about responding inappropriately to my children's needs. I knew the right thing to say and do. Why didn't I have the same sense of self-preservation or self-esteem? Dr. Mueller and I would explore this in therapy in the months ahead. Currently, I was treading milk and holding my own in a fragile balance.

One day after the engine in our Citroën caught fire, the fire department hauled it away, and we bought a used Ford station wagon that seemed gigantic by comparison. It was certainly safer.

When 1962 came to a close, I was glad to say goodbye to it. While not looking forward to the future yet, I had stopped dreading the present. I had a nascent awareness that it was up to me to shape my own life, which felt good.

By February I'd enrolled in a secretarial course at Katherine Gibbs in Boston. My parents were paying the course fees and the costs for the baby-sitter. Although only two hours three times a week, it got me into the real world, with its limited opportunities for nonprofessionals and college dropouts like me.

While I was making steady efforts to become self-sufficient in the real world, Constantin offered only resistance. He called the secretarial courses "an expenditure of futility." With every step forward, I felt him pushing me back two.

I discussed this observation with Dr. Mueller, who suggested that my husband might feel threatened by my efforts to be independent. Perhaps that's why I had no bank account and had to depend on Constantin's weekly allocation of cash to buy food and gas. With this awareness came a liberation of sorts. I no longer felt like a victim, just someone temporarily impeded.

One evening while Constantin was taking a shower, I rifled through his wallet and removed a $20 bill, which I hid in my bureau drawer under socks. I felt like a thief, but a justified one.

April brought crocuses that miraculously poked through snowbanks and mud to reach the sun's rays. Nina, who was almost four years old and curious about everything, bent over to stare intently at a crocus beside our front doorstep.

"It's alive," she pronounced.

"Yes, you're right. It is. Soon all the buds will come out on the trees," I added.

By May, all the trees were in bloom, and we'd seen the last snowflake of the year. Martin Luther King delivered his "I Have a Dream" speech, which ricocheted around the world, and Nina would celebrate her fourth birthday on the 16th.

Today we were off with Hans in tow to do food shopping. The coming weekend, Judd Goldfedder was invited for dinner. I remembered that his father was a bigwig at the Heinz Company in Los Angeles and that he and his wife, Maris, had bought a house in Lexington during Judd's attendance in the master's program. They'd since sold the house and moved back to Los Angeles. I wondered what had brought Judd to Boston.

I bought ingredients for beef Stroganoff with noodles and sour cream and for a Boston lettuce salad with vinaigrette dressing, and I picked out a ready-made cherry pie for dessert. It was fun to set the handsome antique gate-leg table with our wedding silver, linen place mats, and napkins. It was also enjoyable to anticipate company for dinner and wear something other than my everyday jeans and shirts. I chose black pants and a red velour top with a cowl neck. On my feet, I wore black ballet slippers. I put on the gold-and-ruby earrings my mother-in-law had given me.

Judd arrived on time and handed me a bouquet of yellow tulips, which I put in a vase on the dining table. We introduced Judd to both children and drank cocktails in the living room. After I put the children to bed, we adjourned to the dining room. Lacking serving dishes, I served each plate in the kitchen and brought them and a salad bowl to the table before sitting down. So busy with the meal, I missed the core of Judd and Constantin's conversation but gathered that it had something to do with banking.

During dinner we talked about casual things and life in general in Marblehead. The red wine was good with the Stroganoff. I served coffee and pie with a dollop of sour cream. The gentlemen retired to the living room, leaving me to clear the table. I felt good about the meal and the evening in general.

Suddenly, I was aware of raised voices coming from the living room. Judd's voice I recognized because it was a deep bass.

"It was not! Look around you. She has taste and class. You're wrong. Wrong!" Judd shouted.

I walked into the living room and saw Judd standing, facing Constantin, who was seated. "You're discussing me?" I asked incredulously.

Judd's eyes dropped to the floor. Constantin was seated in his favorite chair, and his mouth wore that pasted-on smile as he dismissively waved me toward the kitchen with one hand, saying, "It's the wine talking, not Judd. He doesn't know what he's saying."

Judd shouted, "You bastard! I never did like you. Now I know why."

Judd suddenly swiveled to face me, grasping my hands in his. "Please excuse my outburst. Your dinner was delicious. Your house is lovely. You are lovely. Now I have to leave."

He dropped my hands, opened the front door, and walked out without another word. I stood silently facing the closed door and wondered what in the world had just taken place, but somehow I knew it was momentous.

After cleaning up in the kitchen, I resolved to find out what had happened between Judd and my husband. Upstairs, I found Constantin in bed with the lights out. I turned on the bedside light on the table on my side of the bed, undressed, and climbed in.

"What made Judd so angry?" I asked before turning out the light. He turned away from me and grumbled that it was too late.

⇥ 23 ⇤

The next morning, Constantin and his car were gone. There was a note saying he could be reached in an emergency at the Hochgebirge Club in New Hampshire. I wondered if there could really be enough snow to ski at this time of year. Why did he leave without asking or telling me?

Judd telephoned around ten in the morning to thank me again for dinner. I told him Constantin had disappeared skiing. Judd coughed into the receiver and asked if he could invite us for lunch.

"How nice. But Hans' lunch is on me, à la carte," I told him.

"Be there by noon," he said.

We drove north in Judd's large rental car to Essex, where we stopped at Woodmans in the Rough to eat clams, lobster, and corn on the cob, sitting on benches at long wooden tables. Nina would eat only a hotdog and French fries; Hans drank his juice. On the way home, I nursed Hans in the back seat while Nina sat next to Judd enjoying the outing with a gentleman other than her father.

Back at home in Marblehead, I invited Judd into the living room and excused myself to put both children down for naps. I made us tea and called Judd into the dining room.

"What happened last night?" I asked, looking directly into his eyes as I served his tea.

"Your husband was disrespectful to you. I took offense."

"What did he say?" I asked.

"I'd rather not say." Judd shook his head and then lifted the mug to his lips.

"But if I'm to believe you?" I implored.

"It's better you don't," he said in a monotone, dropping his chin to his chest.

"Judd, please."

He looked at me, collected himself and blurted, "He called dinner 'Catastroff.' Get it? Catastroff, not Stroganoff."

"But I thought the meal was pretty good, didn't you?" I asked nervously.

"See? You question yourself. Your feelings are hurt. I shouldn't have told you."

Judd reached across the table and took my hand in his. At this tenderness, my eyes welled with tears and spilled down my face. I looked up at his friendly, warm face.

"You're a classy lady. Don't ever question that," he said.

I swiped at my tears. "Thanks for the vote of confidence." I was beginning to realize how much confidence I lacked. "Judd, I had no idea he, Constantin . . . even in my own house!"

Judd squeezed my hand. We hugged. He asked if he could see me tomorrow. I thought it was better that we didn't and told him so. I needed time to sort through my feelings and try to figure out what to do about my unraveling marriage.

Nina, Hans, and I tried to spend Sunday as routinely as possible, but without Constantin, the day dragged on. Nina kept asking where Daddy was. I got a phone call in the afternoon from a voice I didn't recognize. At first I thought the person had reached the wrong number. When the caller identified herself the second time as Maris Goldfedder from Brentwood, California, I registered that it was Judd's wife.

"Leave my husband alone! I'll kill myself if you don't," she threatened. Then she hung up before I had a chance to respond.

I hadn't done anything, but I still felt guilty and upset, which might have been her intention. What in the world had Judd said to her? I didn't even know where he was staying in Boston or how to reach him.

Constantin didn't come home until after dark Sunday evening, and then it was only to pack a few things and leave again. He was throwing underwear and shirts into a duffel bag on the bed.

"Where are you going? What's happening?" I asked.

"What's it look like?"

"Like you're leaving. What about us? Will you leave us any money?"

He pulled his wallet out of his back pocket and extracted a wad of bills. He counted out the usual weekly amount and placed it on the dresser. "Here."

"What will I tell Nina?"

"Tell her I had to go on a trip."

He zipped the duffel, lifted it and headed down the stairs and out the door, grabbing his jacket from the hall closet on the way. I followed frantically and watched as his car backed out and the headlights swung to the right up Pearl Street and out of sight.

I needed to talk to someone, but who, and what would I say? Although our marriage had been in a silent détente with no recent fighting, it was wrong to up and leave without a word. Now this. These weren't the actions of a responsible husband.

I debated calling my mother in California, but I decided not to "cry wolf" unless I knew specifically what to ask for in the way of help. She was battling her own cancer demons. What were my options? Getting an attorney was probably step No. 1. Peter Seamans, who lived in Marblehead and was a partner at the Boston firm Peabody & Arnold, was the kind of person I'd trust. Married with five children, he was respected in the community and had deep New England roots. With no money, no attorney, two minor children to feed and clothe, and no prospects for earning a living, I was in a very vulnerable position.

The next day brought near-panic when I realized again that I alone was responsible for my two small children. I had diminishing assurance that Constantin felt anything resembling responsibility toward them or me. Whatever I decided to do, I needed to do it fast.

Midmorning I received a call from Judd, asking how I was doing. I informed him that his wife had called me from California threatening to kill herself if I didn't leave her husband alone. There was silence on his end of the line.

"Judd, are you there?"

"Whoa. Did you just say what I *thought* I heard you say?"

"What did you tell Maris?" I asked. There was a clunking noise from his end, as if he'd dropped the receiver. Maybe it had rolled against a hard object before he lifted it to his ear.

"I need to see you. What are you doing now?" he asked.

"I'm talking to you. When we hang up, I'll feed the children, then put Hans down for his nap. Then there's laundry to do. Why?"

"I'm coming. I'll be there in about an hour and a half." He paused for a response. Hearing none, he said, "I'm on my way," before hanging up.

I realized too late that I should have stopped him. He seemed to precipitate small explosions: Friday night's dinner that ended in a shouting match, followed by Constantin's exodus that weekend; then Maris' threatening call; my husband's reappearance Sunday evening only to pack a duffel bag and leave in a hurry with no explanation. I felt vulnerable, insecure—barely coping. This stew didn't need another volatile ingredient like Judd Goldfedder.

When Judd arrived all bumbling and emotive, I showed him the cool, reserved side of my personality as I folded laundry from the dryer.

"I owe you an explanation," Judd blurted.

"Well?"

"I told Maris I was in love with you," he said.

"You don't even know me," I said incredulously.

Judd moved closer to me. I picked up a pile of folded laundry and started up the back stairs.

"I don't expect you to understand," he said to my back.

I stopped on the stairs, turned around, and faced him. "Judd, this is the worst time in my life. My marriage is coming apart. I'm struggling to keep things together for Nina and Hans. The last thing I need are your fantasies or your wife's crazy threats. Please, just leave."

When I came back downstairs, Judd and his rental car were gone. I felt enormous relief at not having to respond emotionally. I spent the rest of the day with the children, doing routine, ordinary tasks that made life seem safer and more predictable.

I telephoned my parents to tell them what was happening and to ask how Mom was recovering.

"I'm feeling much stronger," she said.

Rather than showing my turbulent feelings, I struggled to sound matter-of-fact and together, telling her the children were fine even though it was a mixed-up period for us all. I let Mom know that I needed an attorney and mentioned Peter Seamans' name. Could they help me pay for legal representation? My mother was pretty calm throughout our conversation and said she'd call me back after discussing it with George.

Constantin joined us to celebrate Nina's fourth birthday in Marblehead mid-May. These days, he frequently dropped in, never calling beforehand to confirm. He usually brought one or two loads of dirty laundry with him. I mistakenly viewed these visits as a sign that he missed us and wanted to come home, but he was carefree and happy each time he left. His visits were excruciating for me because our situation couldn't be more ambiguous and I had a low threshold for ambiguity. From the beginning, I knew that he hated his domineering, self-centered mother, but I was nothing like her. These comings and goings left me feeling abandoned each time.

During a therapy session with Dr. Mueller one day, I was shocked when he suggested that my husband might be trying to get rid of me.

"What do you mean?" I asked.

"Why else would he move out?" Dr. Mueller asked.

"Stress? To capture his old lifestyle?"

"What kind of lifestyle is that?" he asked.

"I don't know. But if he wanted to get rid of me, why hasn't he started formal divorce proceedings?" I argued.

"Maybe he likes to have his cake and eat it, too."

"What?"

"You know, *not* totally upset the apple cart but do what he wants when he wants."

"You mean move out, leave us in limbo, and enjoy life as a single guy?" I blurted.

"Not a bad deal for him, all things considered," Dr. Mueller concluded.

Dr. Mueller's perceptions, if they were true, left me feeling boiling mad on one hand and like a stupid dumbbell on the other. All the way home, I cursed my stupidity and naiveté. I needed to toughen up and smarten up—fast!

My parents agreed to cover any legal fees. In fact, they'd already spoken to Peter Seamans.

"I'll call Mr. Seamans right away," I told them.

They wouldn't be going to Vinalhaven Island until the following summer, because they hoped to travel to Russia that fall, so I was encouraged to use our house on Vinalhaven.

I made an appointment with Mr. Seamans at Peabody & Arnold for the following Tuesday. When I arrived at the law offices, I was directed through a paneled hallway decorated with old sailing etchings in handsome frames to a seating area with leather sofas and upholstered chairs. I made myself comfortable until Mr. Seamans found me.

Peter must have been six foot four and had a full head of tousled graying hair. He moved like a big machine of such velocity that, once in gear, was impossible to stop or redirect. In four strides he was inside his corner office while I was catching up.

The office overlooked Boston's harbor. After exchanging pleasantries, I brought Peter up to date on my marital situation and confusion over

Constantin's sudden recent departure. I recounted how Constantin had refused to join me in marriage counseling and that I was an outpatient at McLean's Hospital for postpartum depression and I gave him my husband's work number at First National Bank of Boston on Milk Street. I also dropped the name of my aunt and uncle's architectural firm, headed by Uncle Joe, because I wanted to make him aware of my family's Boston roots.

Finally, I said, "I have absolutely no money. Constantin gives me cash for food and incidentals, but that's it. What if he just disappears?"

"You don't have a joint bank account?" he asked.

"No."

"And Constantin's a banker?" He looked at me with a perplexed expression.

"I know. Stupid, right?"

Peter then explained what he proposed: a separation agreement. He gave me a brief overview of what this document accomplished. As a lawfully married woman, under the laws of the Commonwealth of Massachusetts, I had rights that included alimony and child-support payments from my husband. The amounts were to be spelled out in the separation agreement. Signed by both parties, the agreement would then be legal and binding, meaning I could use the court's power to enforce it if need be.

"Basically, he can't walk out without providing money and housing for his minor children and you to live on."

"What if he decides to go back to Germany?" I asked.

"Whoa. Slow down. I don't think that's going to happen. He's got too much invested here. I know his boss at the bank. Let me snoop around a bit."

"One more thing, Peter. Did my parents make a financial arrangement with you?"

"Not to worry. It's taken care of."

He arose from behind his desk, which was my cue to leave. We shook hands. Peter then led me out the office door and down the hall through the lobby to the bank of elevators. He waved goodbye as I entered the down elevator.

Why, I wondered, if married women with children had such rights, wasn't I aware of it? Was this a failure of my education and upbringing or a result of my hardheadedness? Believing I was one step from the gutter due to dependence on my estranged husband's moods and whims, I was ecstatic to learn Massachusetts would give me rights to child-support payments and alimony. Halleluiah!

In June, President Kennedy visited Berlin, where he enchanted the German crowds with his *"Ich bin ein Berliner"* speech. I telephoned our Maine caretaker, Alta Coombs, to ask her open the Vinalhaven house. I managed to rent our Marblehead house for two weeks in August during race week, which brought in what was to me a lot of cash.

On the island, we bought whole fish directly from the fish factory on the main wharf, and I made a variety of broiled and fried fish dishes and chowders. At a place called The Basin, outgoing tides exposed a boulder-strewn shoreline with gleaming midnight-blue mussels, which we gathered by the bucketful. I learned to make rhubarb pies from Alta Coombs and delighted in the rejuvenating rhubarb patch on the west side of the house. We adopted a stray cat, which we named Yum-Yum.

Time passed quickly on the island, away from wreckage of my marriage. The noise of the wind as it whipped up whitecaps in Arey's Cove and slammed a screen door, and the drone of bees collecting pollen as we picked wild blueberries on Carter's Hill were happy sounds. My children's laughter at the delight in our summer world was all the music I needed.

Back in Marblehead, fall brought a first birthday for Hans and preschool for Nina, who seemed all grown up. I learned that our separation agreement was being stalled because Constantin kept sending it back to the drawing board. Irrationally hopeful, I viewed his stalling tactics as a sign that he wanted to remain married until, through the grapevine, I learned that he had spent much of the summer at Uncle Joe and Aunt Peggy's house in Brookline and had been seen hanging out at The Country Club with a woman named Katherine Colt.

In November, President Kennedy was shot and killed as he rode in his motorcade in Dallas. Profoundly shocked, I came to realize the fabric of my once-safe world was disintegrating around me. First, the demise of my own young marriage; now, the president, a scion of the most powerful Massachusetts family, shot dead in one of our cities, which I thought happened only in Third World countries. The bittersweet image of Jacqueline Kennedy holding John-John's hand in the Rotunda was etched in my brain forever.

By Thanksgiving, these feelings matched the raw weather through which the children and I soldiered on. Nina was excited and nervous about her first solo singing performance in Tower School's holiday pageant. I sat as close to the stage as I could and marveled at how radiant she was while singing, "Que Sera, sera, Whatever will be will be." My smile felt a mile wide and I hoped my vociferous applause wasn't viewed as the overenthusiasm of a stage mom.

In December, in an effort to brighten the holidays, my neighbor Linda and I took our girls to a matinee performance of *The Nutcracker Suite* in Boston, leaving the babies with a sitter. Afterward, I got Linda to drive by the address I'd found in the phone book for a Katherine Colt, the woman rumored to have been seen with Constantin. Linda knew my suspicions about my husband and agreed to drive slightly out of our way.

As we drove past the apartment complex in Cambridge, I told Linda, "It's so dark. Go slow. Slower."

Suddenly, I spotted Constantin's parked car. "There it is. Goddamn! Sorry, kids, Mommy didn't say that."

"Mommy, I heard you," said Nina.

"I said the bad word so you would know never to use it," I explained, sounding like the kind of grownup I loathed.

"Are you sure it's his car?" asked Linda.

"For reasons that I won't go into now, which are obvious, yes, I'm sure," I said, hoping this didn't compute with Nina, while craning my head to look at the receding line of cars.

Seeing his car parked there had the effect of a tsunami of nauseating waves washing through me. I knifed in half, gripping my knees to my chest. I buried my head between my legs, wishing we hadn't driven this way.

"Are you okay?" Linda asked.

"No," I murmured, "but I'm glad you're here."

"Mommy, what's wrong?" asked Nina.

"She doesn't feel well," Linda said. By the time we got home to Marblehead, I had recovered enough to pay the baby sitter, find something to feed to Nina, put her to bed, and check on Hans. A new problem surfaced as I closed the door to my bedroom. How would I ever sleep in this bed again, which I wanted to rip apart with my bare hands and set on fire? I had never experienced fierce emotions like this and was thankfully too tired and wrung out to do anything but collapse onto the bed.

The next time Constantin arrived with dirty laundry, I quickly loaded both children into my car and drove off—anywhere where I wouldn't have to be in the same room.

"Next time, call if you expect to visit," I yelled at him from the driver's-side window.

We wandered the aisles of Penny's Supermarket, absently tossing items into the cart. While waiting for an order of meat and fish to be weighed and wrapped, I stared at the overhead fluorescent light fixture, realizing that I had exhausted my tolerance for the status quo. Exhausted and depressed, I couldn't continue without help. What should I do?

With Christmas only a few weeks away and no plan for me or the children to join Constantin on his Christmas visit to Frankfurt, I decided to telephone Eugene Garbatti, my father-in-law's old German friend, in Connecticut for advice.

He listened to my desperate litany and said, "Call your father-in-law. He's the only one who can control Constantin."

"All right."

"Telephone him and tell him exactly what you just told me, and good luck!"

✦ 24 ✦

Three days before Christmas, the aircraft was preparing to land in Frankfurt, Germany. After calling my father-in-law ten days before, I received three round-trip tickets, and Peter Seamans had taken us to Logan International Airport the night before. Now, Hans was sound asleep in my arms, and Nina was transfixed by her view of the clouds and the fast-approaching ground.

I was at wit's end: Constantin wasn't giving us enough money to live on, and he had failed to sign various versions of a separation agreement. Leaving us in Marblehead, he'd flown to Germany the week before.

Unsure about my reception, I was still hoping to find some solace under Frau and Herr Boden's roof. I was also banking on their falling in love with Hans and Nina.

Pappi's chauffeur was waiting outside customs holding a placard that spelled *Boden*. He took our luggage, and I carried Hans and various satchels of diapers and formula to the black Mercedes sedan.

Constantin was positively icy to me and overjoyed to see his children, deserving an Academy Award for his ability to deliver opposing emotions so precisely. He acted as if I had done something wrong to *him*. I supposed my initiative in getting here was what really ticked him off, and I was certain he didn't appreciate looking like the cad he was. We three were given bedrooms on the third floor away from Constantin's on the second.

At dinnertime, my husband disappeared rather than join us. Constantin's twin sister, Dorothy, was visiting. During dinner, aware of how painful and different this visit was from previous ones, I burst into tears.

"I'm sorry. I'm so sad and tired. I don't know what's wrong with me."

Dorothy brought me a box of tissues and held my hand.

"You're so thin, Consie," she said.

Mummi said, "Something's not right. I just knew it. Letters arriving with a woman's handwriting. He's a bad, bad boy."

"Let's not jump to conclusions," said Pappi. Turning to me, he said, "Consie, maybe you'll feel better after a good night's rest."

"Yes, I'm sure I will." I saw through blurry eyes and picked at the food on my plate. "Things haven't been right since Hans was born," I explained. "Constantin refused marriage counseling, and he moved out. I can only reach him at work. It's not right, just not right." I began to sob and clumsily left the dining room without finishing my meal.

When the three of us came downstairs the next morning, I noticed that the double doors to the dining room, which were usually open, were closed. Muffled voices emanated from within. Nodding toward the closed door, Dorothy whispered that Pappi and Constantin were in discussion. We repaired to the breakfast nook. I ordered cereal for Hans. Nina, Dorothy and I ordered eggs, toast, and orange juice.

"Did you sleep well?" Dorothy asked.

"Yes."

"Consie, we thought you and the children weren't coming," said Dorothy.

"I was never invited," I whispered.

"I see," said Dorothy, looking uncomfortable with this information.

Hans slapped the top of his high-chair tray, mouthing sounds between mouthfuls of cereal. He reached for the spoon. I gave him my finger to hold instead. He reached for the bottle of milk and knocked it to the floor. Nina hopped down to retrieve it.

"Thank you, sweetie," I said. I was aware of how confusing it was for both children to experience their parents' estrangement, their father and grandfather behind closed doors while we breakfasted on the other side of those doors. How could they not sense the enormous tension between Constantin and me?

After breakfast, it was decided that Dorothy, Mummi, the children, and I would drive into town to see the Christmas decorations in the shop windows, picking up some food items on the way home. The men were on their own for the day.

That evening, all of us dined together. Constantin was cautiously civil. When Pappi announced the "arrangement" he and Constantin had planned, I understood why: Constantin would take Nina and Hans home to Marblehead the day after Christmas while I'd remain. The plan was for me to go to the Lech Ski School for two weeks in Austria, resting and gaining back some of the weight I'd lost. Mummi promised to outfit me in appropriate ski and après-ski clothes before sending me off to have "a wonderful, wonderful time," she chimed.

When I asked how Constantin would take care of the children when he had a job to go to, Pappi said, "That's *his* problem."

Constantin smiled confidently at his father's comment. I was beginning to grasp this very European way of coping with the crisis. If the offender was sent home with his infant children to take care of as well as his professional job to do, he wouldn't have time or means to play around. If the injured party (me) was given R&R and a new hairstyle, perhaps the marriage could be saved. Mulling this over, I felt relieved that something had been decided, because I was too worn out to do anything but acquiesce to any reasonable plan.

Later that evening when most had gone to bed and others were having a nightcap in the drawing room, I spied Constantin's briefcase lying on the hall table by the front door. I snatched it and ran up the stairs to my room on the third floor. The briefcase was locked. I looked for a sharp tool or a screwdriver in the hall shoe closet. Nothing but a metal shoehorn, shoes, polish, rags, and brushes. I palmed the shoehorn and crept back down to the kitchen, where I found an ice pick and a small paring knife. Flying up the stairs to my room, I locked the door and began to pry the lock open. If incriminating letters were in here, I wanted to read them.

The left-side lock on the briefcase opened easily, but the right lock was stubborn. I used the paring knife to pry the tongue away from its locking slot. Wedging the shoehorn into the space between the tongue and its slot and twisting with all my strength, I separated the hardware. The whole brass lock tore away, pulling pieces of leather with it.

Nestled beside a passport and airline tickets were two envelopes addressed to Constantin in the same hand; the envelope revealed a Cambridge, Massachusetts, postmark. I pulled out the fluttering pages and read:

> Sweetheart,
>
> By now I hope time with your parents and sisters will be a source of renewal. I miss you! Tons already. G says to say hello, and Rush wags his tail at the mere mention of your name.
>
> I was musing—why not get rid of that lawyer and use our

191

family's attorney? He's with the best Boston firm, by far. When you're back, I'll personally introduce you to him. Lunch downtown, so each of you can walk there?

I'll be leaving for R.I. on the 24th. Excited that Lenny will be home this Christmas.

Well my dear one, that's all for now. (smiley face)

Your K2

How dare she! Trying to get him to dump his attorney and use her rich family's lawyer and law firm. I was livid as I extracted pages from the other envelope. More of the same.

Since seeing Constantin's car parked at her apartment, I learned that she was from Rhode Island. The Colts made their money in Colt Manufacturing, in Providence, Rhode Island, purveyors of the ubiquitous Colt 45 firearm. Katherine, the youngest child, graduated from Sarah Lawrence College, currently worked in Cambridge and was single.

I waited until past midnight before quietly taking the mauled briefcase, its contents accounted for, back down to the hall table. If confronted, I would deny breaking into it.

Throughout the next day, no one mentioned the obviously ruined briefcase on the hall table. From where I sat in the breakfast nook, I saw Constantin's reflection in the mirror as he stood looking down at his briefcase on the table, but he didn't say a word. How could he inquire about its damage without having to reveal its contents?

Later, Mummi noticed the briefcase and muttered, "Very strange. Yesterday not like zat."

Thankfully, by noon, the briefcase had been removed.

The immaculate electric train wound through the Alps to Lech Zurs am Arlberg, Austria, my destination. The small village nestled in a valley between mountains was right out of a picture postcard, with steepled churches, guest houses, and hotels laden with snowy roofs emanating smoke from chimneys. A horse-drawn wagon waited by the tracks harnessed to a Clydesdale horse. The driver stacked baggage and skis in the back and took us to our respective lodgings.

My reservations were at Frau Standheimer's, a small guest house in the middle of the village, accommodating not more than seven guests. My package included meals and full participation in the famous Lech Ski School, which started the next day. Dinner was communal, wine was extra, and after the long travel day, my bed beckoned.

After a hearty breakfast at Frau Standheimer's, I meandered to the Ski School headquarters, not far away. I was put in Group 6, the beginner's group. Eight of us stood at the bottom of what looked like a gentle slope and were told to climb up it on skis. Johannes demonstrated how to go up a hill on skis with herringbone strides, using poles to advantage. Johannes encouraged, then corrected us in a loud Austrian voice, which I understood more by tone than by translation. By the time I got to the top, I didn't think the slope was so gentle. One by one we were now instructed to ski down the same slope. Many of us fell and then struggled to get upright again. All morning we worked our muscles on the same slope. By lunchtime, my thighs and upper arms were screaming *stop*! By nightfall, I crawled into the eiderdown-duvet-clad bed and immediately fell asleep.

The next day was the same, but with only seven of us. The eighth person had either died or decided to be a ski bunny. A half-hour before quitting time, Johannes introduced us to the rope tow adjacent to the baby-baby slope. One by one we hitched a ride to the top of the tow and skied down. I felt as if I'd conquered the Matterhorn. Johannes told us walking uphill for two solid days had made our leg muscles strong. He said this in Austrian, slapping his strong thighs and pointing to ours.

Days three and four were spent learning and perfecting a snowplow stop on any downhill, gradual or steep. We looked like a bevy of baby ducks as one by one we followed Johannes and tried to do what he did. Day five introduced us to our first chairlift and taught us how to descend an icy bank without getting killed. Friday we graduated to the Level 5 group.

On the weekend we free-skied and lounged around at outdoor cafes. Evenings I donned a pair of black wool après-ski pants and one of several fancy tops, over which I wore Mummi's red fox jacket. My après-ski boots were gray walrus hide. In crowded nightclubs, I danced the twist, which was all the rage, as were The Beatles.

Week two in the Lech Ski School was more strenuous and challenging. We practiced skiing over moguls—small bumps in a ski run. The trick was to turn while on top and then slide down on parallel skis. I fell again and again but was less afraid of hurting myself. By the end of the second week, we'd all graduated to Group 4. I mastered "skating" on skis on a flat surface and learned how to parallel-turn and slide to a flashy stop. We seven were now considered "intermediate" skiers.

Before I knew it, the train was carrying me back over the Alps to Friedrichshafen, Germany, and from there another train took me to Frankfurt.

I was flying home via London on a British Airways flight. As the aircraft approached Boston's Logan International Airport, we dropped altitude over the harbor and touched down on a snow-free runway. The passengers filed through the jetway to luggage, then to customs, where my suitcase was inspected and cleared.

I wasn't surprised to see six-foot-four Peter Seamans on the other side of the customs barrier rather than my husband. Although I warmly hugged Peter, his presence seemed to be a negative prophecy about the current state of my marriage

"Hi, Toots!" He hugged me back, relieving me of ski boots in their metal carrier.

I couldn't help wondering what had transpired legal-wise during the three weeks I'd been in Austria and Germany, but I saved questions until we were in the car, heading north.

"You look great. That tan brings you back to life."

"Austria was wonderful. I learned to ski—even skated up to the après-ski bar!"

"Wow." In a more serious tone, he said, "What I'm going to tell you isn't pretty, but listen to me, okay?"

"Okay." I settled back as the car climbed the ramp onto the Mystic River Bridge toward Revere.

"Constantin's attorney is a friend of mine. We go way back. Anyway, Jack thought what your husband was planning was pretty awful--unethical, in fact, so he tipped me off. You follow?"

"Uh-huh."

"Constantin wasn't going to let you back in your Marblehead house. He claimed that because of your mental condition, you would disrupt the children. You follow?"

"Mental?"

"Yep. Like in delicate or unstable. Apparently he convinced your aunt, Helen Richardson, into agreeing to take you in at her place on the North Shore."

I was stunned. I hardly knew my Aunt Helen. "Go on," I told him.

"If he can keep you from returning to the Marblehead house, he can claim you abandoned your children. Then he stands a chance to get sole custody."

"Oh, my God!"

"So, anyway, that's why Jack tipped me off. That's why I met your flight and why I'm delivering you to your house in Marblehead."

"What happened to the plan to send me to Aunt Helen's?"

"No idea. Today I told Constantin that I'd meet your flight and give you a ride home. Had to stay in town late anyway, blah, blah, blah, that I wanted to talk to you about settlement issues. I think he bought it."

"Did he say anything about my staying with Helen Richardson?"

"No. I think I caught him off guard."

The realization that Constantin could be so nefarious and manipulative had the same effect as having a pitcher of ice water dumped over my head. Suddenly, the thought of remaining married to him seemed a worse danger.

"Now, here's what I want you to do. Listen up."

"Do?" My mind suddenly refocused on the highway turnoff sign we took toward Danvers and the North Shore.

"Just listen. You'll be all sweetness and lovey-dovey, got it? You and he have a new start. You're in love with him. You cook his favorite foods. You snuggle up to him in bed—the whole nine yards, got it?"

"Yes," I replied. "But why?"

"I predict he won't be able to live this lie, so *he'll* be the one to leave. I know he's been seen openly with another woman."

"Katherine Colt?"

"Yes. So you know?" He sounded relieved.

I told Peter about the mauled briefcase and the letters inside.

"We'll flush him out. You just play your part, okay, Toots?"

"What if he doesn't leave?"

"Then maybe you two can start something nice. Maybe I've got it all wrong, but let's play it my way for now, okay?"

"Okay. Peter, if he leaves, I want a divorce immediately. No, first I want to change the locks."

Peter put his giant hand over mine and squeezed.

⇢ 25 ⇠

The reception upon my arrival home was cool but polite. I learned that a Mrs. Martin, whom Constantin had found through First National Bank contacts, had been coming daily to take care of Hans and cook supper for the children, leaving when Constantin arrived from work. She would come the following day as well.

"That's really not necessary now that I'm home," I said. "I'll telephone Mrs. Martin in the morning."

"Suit yourself," he answered.

This first night home was strained and I was tired, but I tiptoed to both children's rooms and softly kissed them. Looking at their sleeping faces and stroking their warm bodies, I prayed I'd be strong enough to do what was in their best interest. Then I crossed the hall and closed the door of our bedroom. When I crawled into my side of the king-size bed, Constantin turned toward the wall. It was a relief not to pretend closeness.

I awoke early due to jet lag. By the time I had my second cup of coffee in the kitchen, Constantin and the children were stirring. Both children and their father, who was dressed for work, found me there.

"Look who's here!" said Constantin.

"Mommy," cried Nina as she ran to hug me.

"Ma-ma," said Hans, dragging his blanket behind him.

"My babies," I cried happily. "Oh, I've missed you!" I buried my nose in each of their necks and breathed deeply.

I grabbed the oatmeal box for Hans, poured milk into a saucepan and turned the stove to "low." Nina would have a grownup breakfast, which meant whatever her father or I ate.

"I'm leaving," Constantin said, turning his back to us.

"Without breakfast?" I asked.

He turned his head, smiled his terrible fake smile, waved goodbye to the children, and was gone.

We three ate breakfast in our sunny kitchen while I described skiing down the highest Austrian slopes.

"Is Mrs. Martin coming?" asked Nina suddenly.

"Yes, she is. I want to meet her. Did you like her?"

"She's old," said Nina. "She's nice."

"I'm glad she's nice. But now I'm home, so I'll take care of you."

"Oh," Nina said.

I'd decided to let Mrs. Martin arrive this morning so that she and I could establish a relationship. God only knows what she'd heard about me. I also wanted to be filled in on the kids' activities and to thank her.

I greeted Mrs. Martin at the front door, introduced myself, and brought her into the kitchen, where I offered her a cup of coffee.

"Yes, thank you." Mrs. Martin slipped her arms out of her winter coat and let it drape over the back of her chair. "Nina is invited to Bobby Barach's birthday party tomorrow."

"Oh, good. We'll get him a present today, right, sweetie?" I said to Nina. "What time is the party?"

"Lunchtime. Anne Barach came over yesterday and they played upstairs for two hours," she said.

"The children like you so much, Mrs. Martin. I hope you'll be available to baby-sit from time to time," I said, hoping to forge a working future relationship. She assured me that she'd like nothing better.

The next few days ran smoothly while Constantin was at work and the children and I fell into our daily routines.

The minute Constantin arrived home from the bank, the atmosphere became charged and uncomfortable. I noticed that he overtly competed with me for Nina's attention. For instance, after I helped her tie her shoelaces, he called her over.

"Let Daddy teach you, Nina-B," he coaxed, untying the laces we had just tied so that he could show her how to retie them.

I didn't react. No longer feeling vulnerable or trusting, I was somehow able to play my part as his loving wife convincingly, but it felt as if I was watching myself rather than being *inside* myself. I made a mental note to schedule an appointment with Dr. Mueller, whom I hadn't seen for over six weeks, to bring him up to date. I had a feeling I'd need support before this situation was resolved.

The following weekend, Constantin and I hired Mrs. Martin to baby-sit while we headed to New Hampshire to ski. He must have figured that if I accompanied him, it would look like he was making an effort at reconciliation—to the lawyers, anyway.

After two weeks in Austria, I couldn't wait to exercise my new skills. The lodge was full, and the slopes were topped with at least a foot of packed powder.

The sleeping arrangement at the Ski Club Hochgebirge is dormitory-style by sex, which was fine with me. I didn't even see Constantin at breakfast Saturday morning, so I skied Canon Mountain all day by myself, which was also fine. Being in Europe alone had certainly given me confidence.

Sunday, two couples approached me about joining them for the day on one of several intermediate runs. Patsy, Sam, and I decided to tackle the North Face. Before we started, Constantin and I agreed to meet at 4 to leave for home. I was sad that my husband wasn't even curious enough to ski with me, but I was still having a good time and didn't need his approval or attention to enjoy myself anymore. On the drive home, we chatted like distant relatives, which, I guess, is what we were.

A few nights later as I lay on top of the covers in a lovely silky nightgown, I smiled invitingly as Constantin crossed the foot of the bed on his way to the bathroom. Instead of joining me, he came out fully dressed, crossed the room toward the door, and told me, "I can't stay here." And he left. I heard his car start, back up, and climb the hill.

No tears this time, no agony of rejection like I'd experienced over the past two years. Peter Seamans had been right. *He* left. Now *I* wanted custody of the children and a divorce.

The following morning, I called Peter. "I've already gone through the worst," I told him. "I don't really feel that sad. I want it over."

"I understand. I've prepared a summons for you to look over and sign. It gives your spouse thirty days to respond to the petition for dissolution of marriage. The petition spells all the bare-bone facts."

Peter agreed to drop a copy by my house on his way home.

The same week, I received a telephone call from a broker with Hunneman Real Estate, asking if I'd let her list my house. In midsentence, I slammed the phone into its cradle and burst into tears. Talk about ambulance chasers! How did word get around so fast? I wandered through the house letting my eyes caress the walls I'd painstakingly painted and papered, the floors we sanded, the rooms that were meant to be filled with laughter, not tears.

Another telephone call surprised me. It was Sam Johnson, who had to remind me that we met skiing at Ski Club Hochgebirge a few weeks ago. "You left an alarm clock there, and I brought it back."

"I did?" I had no recollection. "Gee, thanks."

"When are you going to be in town next?" he asked. "We can meet for a drink and I'll bring it."

"Well, I don't know, but I'll be in town to sign some legal papers. How about my calling you when *I* know?"

Sam gave me both his work number and his home number before we hung up. Trying to remember what he looked like, I could only picture a figure on skis wearing dark blue pants and jacket with a white woolen hat and leaning on ski poles.

After signing divorce-related papers, I met Sam at Nick's bar in the theater district, a short walk from the garage under Boston Common. I recognized him immediately even though he was wearing business attire. Shy of six feet, he had a deep mellifluous voice. We slid into a red leather banquette around a table and ordered dry martinis.

"Thanks so much for the alarm clock," I said, wondering where it was. "Where is your friend, Patsy, right?"

"Yeah. She's in Buffalo. She lives there."

Our cocktails arrived along with a bowl of peanuts.

"Cheers," said Sam, hoisting his martini glass eye level.

"Cheers." I raised mine before taking a dainty sip. "I just signed divorce papers at my attorney's office downtown."

"You did? Your husband, Constantin, was with you that weekend, am I right?"

"Technically, yes. I hardly saw him all weekend." I downed the cold gin and munched on the olive. Sam caught the waitress's eye, held up two fingers, and pointed to our empty glasses.

I continued, "It's a long story, and I don't want to talk about it."

Sam placed his right hand on top of my left one and said in a whisper, "I have a confession."

I looked at him, my eyebrows raised.

"I don't *have* your alarm clock."

"I don't understand." My look was a question.

"You didn't leave one." He squeezed my hand. "I wanted to see you again. I made it up."

"Oh." I gasped.

Our martinis arrived and I quickly took a swallow. It slid down like cold velvet and spread through my insides with sudden heat. Sam invented a believable fib so that he could see me again. Knowing this did wonders for my tattered ego. Still, he and Patsy had seemed to be a couple when we met that ski weekend.

"So, Patsy," I continued. "She's in Buffalo?"

"Yes," said Sam.

"Aren't you two dating?" I asked.

"We've known each other for about eight years," he said.

"And . . . "

"She's Catholic, a virgin, so no, we aren't technically a couple the way you mean it."

Sam put his hand over mine and squeezed. I leaned toward him and kissed him on the mouth. Apparently, the feeling was mutual. I wanted more of this and told him. We agreed to meet at his house on the North Shore. He drew me a map to his place and slipped it into my hand.

→ 26 ←

Sam's place was a small one-bedroom house in the middle of about a half-acre near the shoreline on a peninsula called Nahant. He had inherited the house when his mom died. Unmistakably a bachelor's pad, I noted a model sailboat on the fireplace mantel, two oars hanging on a wall, and a case of beer next to the fridge. A framed display of four different rope knots hung above the kitchen table. Sam was wearing faded Levis and a wrinkled flannel shirt. His feet were ensconced in worn Top-Siders. An old plaid sofa faced the hearth, in which a fire was burning. Sam took off my jacket and hung it from a hook behind the door and then pulled me into an embrace. After we kissed I gently unfastened myself.

"So who is Sam Johnson?" I asked.

His arm swept around the room and then indicated the ocean seen beyond the windows.

"All this is part of who I am," he said, "and what's out there is a bigger part."

"Really? "

"If you'll promise to sit down and let me make you a drink, I'll tell all," he said. "What's your pleasure? Gin? Whiskey? Beer? Old-fashioned?"

I settled myself on the sofa. "Can you really make an old-fashioned?"

"You bet. My other career: bartender."

Sam went to the kitchen, where, because the house was so small, I could watch him. He moved like a gymnast, balancing as he moved from one corner to the other, reaching all the way across the kitchen to grab an object. I was mesmerized by his grace.

"This 'bigger part' of who you are has to do with the ocean, right?"

An ice-crushing machine muffled his answer. He repeated, "I crew in professional races—Bermuda, World's Cup."

Sam brought two old-fashioneds and joined me on the sofa. "I was born in the wrong century," he said, "to the wrong family."

"How so?"

"You can't make a living crewing. You *need* money. But I'm the best crew there is."

"You've probably heard of my maternal great-grandfather, C. Oliver Iselin, who won the America's Cup—three times, I think."

"No! Your grandfather?"

"*Great*-grandfather. He was a great sportsman and yachtsman. My branch of the family has all that blue blood but no money. Can't you tell?"

"What happened to the money?"

"I don't know. Only what I've heard, that fortunes were made building the Panama Canal and in international banking. By the time it filtered down to our generation, it was almost all gone, So what *do* you do to earn a living?"

"Any job that pays the bills—between sailing gigs."

"That bad, huh?"

"That bad."

This line of questioning had the effect of clamming him up, so I switched subjects.

"Do you ski a lot?"

"Occasionally."

"I just learned to ski in Austria. Just before I met you."

Sam lowered his arm from along the top of the sofa so that it was in contact with me, and his hand cupped my shoulder.

"I love your smell," he said, nestling his face into the curve of my neck and breathing deeply. He turned me toward him.

"Will you let me undress you?" he asked tenderly.

This melted any resolve I might have had to not sleep with him on a first date.

"Nobody's ever asked me that before." Inhaling a deep breath, I turned toward Sam to help the removal of my clothing. He was gentle and skilled. He kissed me while unbuttoning my shirt and unzipping my jeans. When I wriggled out of the jeans and panties, he bent over to kiss my exposed stomach. While he removed each item of clothing, his hands never left my body. When I was sitting next to him au naturel, he lifted his old-fashioned and said, "Here sits a beautiful woman! Look at her, but look only because tonight she is all mine."

Sam shed his clothes. I wasn't shy or nervous being naked with him. It felt as natural as breathing. He led me to the bedroom, where we fell onto the bed and clasped one another along the whole length of our bodies. My skin felt electrified as it slid against his. I fanned his face with my hair and blew little puffs of air into his ears. He slowed me down, taking his time. By the time he entered me, my body knew its own needs and showed him. I cried tears of joy. Afterward, we fell into a peaceful sleep. When I awoke, we embraced and whispered loving words before I pulled on my clothes and headed home with the sun setting over the Boston skyline.

The most amazing realization was what I'd discovered about my body and its capacity for pleasure. It was obvious what had been missing in my marriage. Never having made love with a man who knew what he was doing, how could I know otherwise?

This put everything into perspective. The furthest thing from my mind was my soon-to-be ex-husband. I wasn't even interested in revenge, so deliriously happy was I with the discoveries I'd made with Sam. When he called after work and Mrs. Martin arrived to baby sit, my car flew almost by itself to Nahant.

When I saw Dr. Mueller, there was so much to tell him that I had to break my news into segments over several sessions before he was fully up to date. While I found it difficult to talk about sex, I desperately wanted to know how a woman can give birth twice and know so little about her own ability to be sexually aroused and fulfilled. I skirted the issue, wishing I could be more direct and less embarrassed. Dr. Mueller seemed embarrassed, too. I wished he were a woman and could explain female things.

Peter Seamans informed me that Constantin's girlfriend had skipped town for London out of fear that I would name her as a correspondent in our divorce proceedings. He advised me not to, because ugly accounts would surface in the society section of the Boston newspapers, which could backfire on the children and me. Believing my lawyer to be a sensible man, I took his advice. Secretly I could almost taste the satisfaction of sullying her reputation.

We listed the house with a local broker—I refused to list it with those bloodsucking realtors Hunneman & Company—and it sold in two days for the asking price. After paying off the mortgage, Constantin and I split the profit.

I signed a lease on a cheerful two-bedroom apartment on the waterfront called Henry Bay's and began sorting through belongings, trying to decide what to take that would fit. The small apartment wouldn't accommodate our king-size bed, the one I had wanted to rip into shreds, so I was happy when Constantin claimed it. Before I could sell any of the furniture especially bought for our Pearl Street house, Constantin took what he wanted, including the gate-leg dining and tavern tables. I kept reminding myself that love wasn't about "things."

One evening after Sam and I had washed the dishes after eating lobster and corn on the cob, he playfully tackled me to the floor, where we embraced and he looked deeply into my eyes.

"I hate telling you this," he blurted, "but Patsy and I are going to be married July 15."

In disbelief I blurted, "You can't marry Patsy. You love me!"

He kissed me passionately and said, "I can't change the wedding date."

Convinced it was all a bad joke, I shouted, "Are you crazy?" Tears sprang from my eyes as I finally absorbed that he wasn't joking.

"How long have you and Patsy been engaged?" I demanded, standing and backing away from him.

"We didn't have a date set until last week."

"And you've never slept with her?"

"No, she's a virgin."

"Sam, this is sick. How can you marry *her* when you love *me*?"

"I love Patsy, too. We wear the same shoe size," he explained lamely.

I faced him and declared, "Don't expect to see me ever again!" before turning and walking briskly to my car.

After dragging myself to the next therapy session and recounting my woes, Dr. Mueller suggested that Sam might be driven by the Catholic whore-Madonna complex, on which he elaborated.

"Women you have sex with are whores. Virgins are ones you marry."

Sam telephoned every day. Although I refused to speak to him, the sound of his voice brought instant tears. As his marriage date approached, I kept busy packing our belongings into moving boxes, putting physical as well as emotional distance between us. Every day I took the children to one beach or another. Sam even called on his wedding day *and* on the first day of his honeymoon. I hung up as soon as I heard his voice.

I'd been so certain that Sam and I were meant for each other, and the outcome had totally knocked me off balance. Now I was questioning my ability to judge any man's motives or character.

One afternoon while watering the lawn in a bikini, I watched as Constantin arrived to pick up the children for the weekend. When he got out of the car, it was obvious that he had a hard-on. What a complete surprise! If I hadn't felt so upside-down, I probably wouldn't have considered the sudden shift of tectonic plates when, a week later and out of the blue, Constantin asked me to stop divorce proceedings and give it a go again. He wanted to move into the apartment with the children and me.

This time I was the one who wasn't sure it was worth the effort. Indecisive at first, I ultimately figured I didn't have much to lose. I made my conditions crystal clear: One, we must both attend marriage counseling; two, no more mentioning of Katherine or letters or anything else involving her. He agreed to all and we set a move-in date. I researched and found a marriage counselor, Dr. Robert Maltzman, with a practice in the neighboring town.

I purchased sheets for the new queen-size bed, and with help from local movers, we four moved in. Nina's bubbling happy face—happy because her daddy was living with us again—made *me* happy. We bought the children bunk beds for the small second bedroom, along with two white mice in a small cage with an exercise wheel.

During our first session with the marriage counselor, Constantin revealed that he was suspicious about the new sheets and pillowcases.

"Our old bed was a king. This one is smaller, so our old sheets don't fit," I explained.

Dr. Maltzman zeroed in on Constantin's suspicions.

"Are you worried that the bedding isn't new?" he asked Constantin.

"Well, she had an affair," said Constantin.

Dr. Maltzman asked if I had anything to say.

"The affair is over. It had nothing to do with the new sheets or the new bed."

"I hear that this is really about trust," said the therapist.

I nodded in agreement, while Constantin crossed one leg over the other and looked at a spot on the wall.

We were trying to be more considerate to each other, especially in front of the children.

During September, we saw Dr. Maltzman on a weekly basis; although I had hopes for these sessions, I sensed that Constantin resented being there. These hopes were shattered one September morning. It was Nina's and my routine to choose her school clothes together and for me to lay them on a chair before lights-out the night before. This routine saved time and confusion during the morning rush. On this particular morning, Nina, in the yellow dress we picked out the night before, had gone to her father saying, "Mommy won't let me wear the blue dress."

Constantin called me urgently and I came running, thinking it was some sort of emergency.

"Constance, I order you to change Nina's dress!" he told me, handing me the blue dress.

Incredulous, I spat, "You've *got* to be kidding." Nina's expression was triumphant. I turned and walked out of the room, trying to regain my composure. In one moment he'd undermined me irrevocably in my daughter's eyes.

I planned to bring this up in our next marriage-counseling session, which was canceled because of a scheduling conflict with Constantin's new responsibilities as a bank-loan officer. These included some travel and consulting with midlevel bank managers at branches in Connecticut and Rhode Island.

Constantin invited me to join him on a day trip to a bank near Hartford. We climbed into the VW Bug and headed south on the Massachusetts Turnpike, which followed a gently rolling landscape, fall leaves painting splashes of crimson, orange and yellow, dotted with weathered houses and outbuildings.

At the Hartford branch offices, Constantin said he'd be less than an hour, so I elected to sit in the car and wait. While waiting, I opened the glove compartment, hoping to find something to occupy my time, a New England map perhaps. Out fell a slew of letters from the U.K. addressed to Constantin at the bank's Milk Street address in Boston, all from Katherine.

I pulled the contents out of one envelope and read, "Your bossy wife won't let you." A few lines down she wrote, "Why don't you put your mistake of a marriage and Constance where she belongs? The past."

Of the two conditions, one was now broken. When he returned to the car, he immediately saw the letters strewn about the driver's seat. My face felt as if it was on fire and I wanted to murder him.

"Take me home," I demanded. He didn't say a word as he gathered up the envelopes, fired up the engine, and headed back the way we'd just traveled while nervously lighting cigarettes.

Two hours later, he dropped me at the apartment and drove off. Mrs. Martin was there with Hans while Nina was on a play date at the Barachs'. I paid Mrs. Martin without explaining why I had returned sooner than expected. After she left, I gathered all my husband's clothes, shoes, and underwear and threw them into two suitcases and an empty moving box. I dumped his shaving equipment and other toiletries into three empty grocery bags and stacked all his belongings outside the front door, facing the parking lot. With Hans under one arm, I grabbed my car keys and drove to pick up Nina at the Barachs', just around the corner from our old house.

When Constantin got home from work and saw his belongings stacked outside, he banged on the front door, which I'd bolted. "You can't come in," I shouted.

"You can't do this to me. I have a cold," he whined.

How I dealt with the end of our marriage was one thing, but what to tell Nina and Hans? I piled both kids into the car and drove to a thrift shop, where I bought an entire set of used crockery. Standing at one end of our long narrow hall, I threw each piece at the opposite wall, where they smashed into shards. Over the racket I yelled that when you are angry, it feels good to break things and it doesn't hurt anyone. By the time the whole set lay in myriad pieces on the floor, I was laughing and crying, while Nina and Hans, mouths agape, didn't know how to react.

Divorce was inevitable. I wanted a marriage founded and based on trust, not deceit. Believing that I was the better role model for the children, I declared my intentions to ask and fight for legal custody of both children from the Massachusetts courts.

Fast-forward three months: We signed a formal separation agreement that gave me legal custody of the children and detailed the amount of child support and alimony I would receive. Constantin arranged a trip during which he would live in Idaho for the required amount of time to be divorced from me. Katherine returned from London, I presumed, to continue her relationship with my soon-to-be-ex-husband.

My mother had invited me and the children to spend two weeks at the ranch and had generously paid our airfare. My spirits perked up as the date of our trip approached. Mom explained that she and George wouldn't be there when I arrived, because they'd be at a cattle show. Mildred, their maid, would be there to help in any way she could, and my parents would return shortly.

As the children and I walked down the narrow concrete path to the kitchen, my brother Turo, who was unofficially in charge, said, "I don't know why you came. The folks aren't in a good space. Gee, if I were you, I'd turn around and go right back home, pronto."

This unfriendly greeting diminished what little self-esteem I possessed. Because he was my older brother and lived in the next town, I assumed he must be more in touch with Mom and George than I. His remark certainly eroded my confidence at a time when it was in short supply, leaving me wondering why Mom had invited us.

Mildred, a soft, round motherly woman, greeted me with a warm hug and made a fuss over Nina and Hans. I tried to appear cheerful and upbeat, although what I was feeling was far from that. I hoped a good night's sleep would calm my nerves and ease the stress.

It was fun to show both children a working ranch, the vegetable garden, and the handsome Herefords, some with calves. Mildred's cooking produced calls for second helpings from everyone.

On the third day there, I received an upsetting phone call.

"Constance," Constantin's voice sounded tiny, far away. "Stop me!"

"What?" I asked, not understanding.

"Just stop me from doing this!"

The hand I was holding the telephone with began to shake. I dropped the phone into its cradle and collapsed into a chair.

"You look like you've seen a ghost," said Mildred. Both children watched with alarm.

"That was my husband. He's in Idaho to divorce me. He just told me to stop him. Can you believe that?"

Mildred put her plump arm around my shoulders. "Ain't no worse business than man business," she said. "Women's lot."

Moments later, I felt as if I was suffocating. The more oxygen I gulped, the worse it became. I rushed to the door for outside air. With alarm, Mildred picked up the telephone and, checking a list posted on the wall next to the phone, dialed a number. Mildred explained my symptoms to the voice on the other end.

"Uh-huh. She's gasping, like can't get no air. . . . Uh-huh. Okay. I'll try that. We'll come by later."

Mildred hung up, rummaged in a drawer, and produced a small paper bag. She put it over my mouth and nose.

"Breathe. Breathe. Hold it close. Make a tent."

I complied and, after about fifteen minutes, felt better.

Mildred calmly said, "You having a panic attack is all."

By the time Mom and George had returned and been filled in by Mildred, who'd been scared to death by my panic attack, Mom asked with concern, "How are you, Consie?"

"Much better, thank you. Dr. Moore explained what panic attacks are and how to curb them. You breathe in carbon dioxide to counter the effect of gulping too much oxygen."

"I hear Constantin called you."

"Yes. He asked me to stop him—stop him from getting our divorce. How?"

"I don't think you should talk to him again," said my mother.

"Turo's greeting didn't help either," I added.

"What was wrong with Turo's greeting?"

I repeated what Turo had said and how it made me question whether I should have come at all.

"Funny, that," she said while gazing into the distance, seemingly in deep thought. "You never think the one you *most* trust could have ulterior motives."

I realized Mom was saying she'd never questioned Turo's motives but just realized she should have. It was suddenly crystal clear that Turo was trying to sabotage my visit, probably so he could always be No. 1. From now on, I would be much more cautious about trusting my older brother.

The rest of our visit was peaceful and fun. One evening Mom crawled on the living-room floor with a cowhide over her back and "mooed" while chasing Nina and Hans, who shrieked with delight.

Another night, we who slept on the ground floor awoke to the strong smell of skunk. Collectively making our way to the kitchen, George investigated and deduced that a skunk had come through the dog door in the laundry room, where it unleashed its potent weapon before leaving. We opened all the doors and windows, unearthed fans from closets, and blew in clear air. By 5 in the morning, punch-drunk, tired and silly, we collapsed in a heap on the floor.

Constantin and Katherine married in January of the new year. She bought them a large house on the exclusive Sargent Estate, in Brookline, whose grounds had been designed by the landscape architect Frederick Law

Olmsted for a small fortune. Our three-story authentic Federal house in old-town Marblehead cost one-fifth of that.

In the spring, Martin Luther King marched from Selma to Montgomery, Alabama. Over the summer, President Lyndon Johnson authorized the first U.S. combat forces to fight in Vietnam. Bob Dylan released *Like a Rolling Stone*, and *My Fair Lady* won big at the Academy Awards.

Learning to live on my only income, child support and alimony called for extreme fiscal discipline. I discovered the more affordable day-old produce bins at Penny's, as well as reduced-price meats and fish. These tasted just as good and had the same nutritional content as more costly items.

Marblehead had one used-clothing store for children, where I took outgrown items for trade-ins on slightly used clothing. I bought an almost-new red wool coat for Nina for the winter. We were fortunate that my parents continued to pay Nina's tuition at Tower School so she would have continuity with teachers and friends.

The reality of my limited financial resources was magnified each weekend that the children spent in their father and Katherine's affluent surroundings. Constantin and Katherine kept clothes that Nina and Hans were allowed to wear only at their house.

Six-year-old Nina argued, "If I lived there, I could have all the leotards I want." She hoped I would give in and let her live with her daddy.

"When you're more grownup, I'll consider letting you live with him," I told her.

One Friday afternoon, in our 1960 Ford station wagon packed with children, suitcases, and snacks, we headed south to visit my younger brother, Phil, and his fiancée, Judy Benet. Phil had just completed his two years of service with the United States Coast & Geodetic Survey as a lieutenant junior grade, stationed in Norfolk, Virginia, on two vessels, the Explorer and the Whiting. Phil had begun graduate work in oceanography at the University of Rhode Island and lived in Saunderstown. This was our first visit.

Five miles from home, the passenger-side rear tire blew out. I steered the car lopsidedly to the shoulder and inspected the damage. Not good. A kind motorist pulled over behind us. The man put his hazard lights on and approached the Ford.

"A bit of a problem, huh? Got a spare?"

I shrugged, opened the trunk, and lifted the carpet covering the tire well. There was a spare and a jack, neither of which I had the faintest idea how to use. I watched with relief as the man set about jacking up the car, removing the flat tire, and putting on the spare.

"You'll need to get it patched before you go on," he said, acknowledging the packed car and fussing children.

"How long will it take?"

"Depends on how busy they are." The man tightened the nuts on the wheel and stood, holding the jack apparatus and the flat tire. He put the jack back in the wagon and laid the tire on top of the carpet. "I wish you better luck for the rest of your trip," he said, waving at the children.

We drove to the next gas station, where a young mechanic took the flat tire into a bay. The children and I arranged ourselves on chairs inside the small glass-fronted office in a corner near a table with a coffee machine and magazines. Thank goodness I'd brought snacks, which I doled out from my canvas tote bag. The mechanic, whose nametag said "Bill," told me the other three tires were no good.

"They're as bad as the one that blew."

"How much would it cost for four new tires?" I inquired.

While waiting, I silently compared the Ford with my ex-husband's well-kept Mercedes sedan and Katherine's almost-new Volvo. The unfairness was infuriating. An hour and four new tires later, I wrote a check for an amount that was our food budget for the whole month. I'd figure out what to do later. At least we wouldn't get killed on our way to my brother's.

The drive south to Rhode Island was pretty, with flattening fields delineated by low stone walls as the road paralleled the shore. We easily found Phil and Judy's house from Phil's precise directions and piled out, apologizing and explaining why we were late.

After the last few tumultuous months, it was relaxing to spend a quiet weekend with my brother and his wife-to-be. It was comforting to know they'd be within easy driving distance for the foreseeable future, and I vowed to make the effort to get together more often. We took walks on the beach, cooked out on a small hibachi on the lawn, and listened to Bob Dylan records. By the time Sunday rolled around, the children and I were relaxed.

⇢27⇠

Dominating the national news was a growing and widespread anti-Vietnam War movement, with 15,000 people demonstrating against it in Washington, D.C.

On the personal front, there was a growing voice inside telling me I needed to be able to pay my own way and not rely on marrying because of financial insecurity. It was a soft whisper steadily gathering volume.

When I learned that I could transfer only seven academic credits to complete my bachelor of arts degree at Tufts University, in Boston, I reapplied to Bennington College. There I'd already accumulated two solid years toward a degree. The response to my inquiry to the dean of admissions informed me that Bennington College didn't encourage those who had decided to interrupt their four years of college to continue unless the absence had been due to serious illness.

I angrily questioned Bennington's logic and plugged my determination into a more forceful letter. "Would they deny members of the armed services if the reason they left college was to fight in Vietnam?" I asked. The G.I. Bill helped many to complete a higher education. I argued that the decision to marry and have children was a life-altering commitment but shouldn't stop a lifelong learning process from continuing. "Investing money, effort, and two years into Bennington College should not be a mistake," I wrote. How I would actually pay the tuition if they gave me the green light was something I hadn't figured out.

One evening I was invited for drinks across the parking lot at Henry Bay's apartments, where we lived. Bill was a good-looking guy about my age whom I'd nodded to while coming and going but didn't know.

After putting both kids to bed, I stayed a while to make sure they were asleep before walking the short distance to Bill's apartment on the second story facing the water. Bill made our drinks while we chatted about current affairs and settled in with our drinks on his sofa.

Suddenly I heard and recognized Nina's panicked cries: "She's gone! Wake up! She's gone!"

In my hurry, I spilled the drink as I raced down the staircase and crossed the parking lot. Inside my apartment, I enveloped a sobbing Nina in my arms and tried to soothe her with promises that I'd never ever leave her or Hans. We rocked back and forth until she fell asleep in my arms. So much for a casual drink next door.

While waiting for the dean of admissions at Bennington to respond, I enrolled in an evening course at the Boston Museum of Fine Arts School. My Plan B: to accumulate academic credits so I could either transfer to a four-year school or graduate from the museum school. I took Anatomy, which was mostly drawing from live models, and Graphic Design, which involved too many hours of creating repeated designs (as for wallpaper or fabric)—I felt as if my mind was in a perpetual repetitive loop.

When my lease at Henry Bay's was up and the rent was raised, I was forced to find more reasonable quarters. After stumbling upon a wonderful three-story brick mansion on Salem Common for $250 a month, heat included, we moved to Salem, about five miles from Marblehead. The large living room had interior folding shutters on all its windows, and each of the four bedrooms was generous. The only problem was our paucity of furniture, giving the house a barely lived-in look.

I wanted my children to have as normal a childhood as I could provide, and a pet would be a wonderful addition, so I was on the lookout for free puppies who needed a home. Providence arrived in the form of a poster on a telephone pole advertising free dachshund puppies to the right family. I called the posted number. There were three squirming puppies from which to choose. We picked a gregarious, lovable female and named her Piffin after my first childhood dog.

My struggles to get Bennington to readmit me continued and the file thickened. I continued taking a course each semester at the museum school. Eventually I drifted downstairs to the basement to sample my first course in motion-picture production, and it was instant love. The course was offered only in the daytime, so I arranged for Mrs. Martin to come on Wednesdays.

My first film was a period piece about an opera diva's debut, shot on 16mm color film. We gained permission to shoot at the Isabella Stuart Gardner Museum, a replica of a beautiful fifteenth century Renaissance Venetian Palace. The actress who played my diva couldn't sing, so I dubbed a recorded aria onto the final soundtrack. With its ambiguous plot, the visually beautiful ten-minute film didn't win any awards, but I loved everything about the collaborative process that gave it birth.

Another California trip to visit my mother was on the horizon just for me this time. The kids would spend Thanksgiving with Constantin and Katherine at her family's house in Providence, R.I., while I would fly to San Francisco the Wednesday before the holiday and stay through Monday.

Mom wasn't doing well. Her breast cancer, in remission for four years, had metastasized to her brain. She'd just completed five weeks of radiation with hopes for remission. I hadn't been away from the children since that two-week ski trip to Austria, and it felt unnatural without them. Everything about California felt unnatural to me this time, from the lack of snow in its coastal climate to the flaky group of people Mom and George had apparently gotten involved with who called themselves Synanon.

Mom rapturously described Synanon as "the most wonderful drug-rehabilitation program that truly works."

"Chuck Dederich founded it," she said. "You'll love him."

"But I don't *have* a drug problem," I said.

"We don't either. We're 'square' members who play the Synanon Game," explained my mother, which made no sense at all.

The day after Thanksgiving, the whole family drove from Marin County to Synanon's headquarters, in San Francisco. We arrived, parked the car, and made our way upstairs to a fairly large room with windows facing the San Francisco Bay. Turo and his wife, Jane, arrived separately. Eventually, twelve of us gathered in a circle facing one another. The "game," as it unfolded, was a no-holds-barred, uninhibited exchange in which participants were encouraged and goaded into a heated debate about their most vulnerable, private secrets and emotions.

As the agitator kept boring in on one poor woman, she confessed her shame about doing "tricks" to support her former drug addiction. She broke down in wracking sobs and was then praised for being honest.

Next, he asked Turo, "Have you walked Jane past any bars lately?" Snickering flitted around the circle, then silence. Jane was a former alcoholic, so the pointedly hostile accusative question was pretty damning. My brother looked uncomfortable but maintained a neutral face while all eyes were on him.

Jane said, "He only did that once," which redirected everyone's attention to Jane.

"So far," said the agitator with a smug smile.

This went on for about an hour, hitting on everyone in the circle, including me. Since I was an unknown commodity, the only visible flaw was my weight, though at 150 pounds, I was by no means obese. I noticed that my parents were treated deferentially, almost like royalty, and wondered why.

I eventually learned that Mom's most recent will, with George's blessings, left her half of Green Gulch Ranch to Synanon, with a caveat that Synanon would keep the ranch agricultural—no development.

At the "game's" conclusion, Chuck Dederich made his appearance. He was a burly, heavy-set man around forty or fifty with bushy eyebrows and a wide mouth, and my mother introduced us.

"Well, what do you think?" he asked me.

"I'm speechless," was the most honest answer I could think of. He laughed a real belly laugh and continued around the room like a politician shaking hands with his constituents.

A few days later, Mom announced that she, George and I were going to Synanon's other facility, its house in Point Reyes, for a session with Betty Dederich, Chuck's wife. Mom and I would join other women in a women-only "game," over which Betty would preside.

Even though mixed marriages were becoming more frequent, when I met Betty I was surprised that she was African-American, since Chuck was Caucasian.

The women-only game began in a similar fashion to the first I'd attended. Nine people sat in a circle facing one another in a barnlike room with clerestory windows.

Betty turned to me and asked, "Why did you come today?"

I thought she was being friendly. "My parents brought me."

"Why? Where's your husband, your children? I understand you have two children? Where are they?"

"They're with their father—my *ex*-husband. Mom invited just me for Thanksgiving. I live on the East Coast," I said to further explain.

"I see," said Betty. "How are you getting along as a single mom?"

"We're surviving. I'm applying to schools—I *must* complete my bachelor's, but I can only go part-time. It's all I can afford."

"I see." Betty turned to my mother. "Hope, what are you and George doing to help?"

"We're paying for Nina's—my granddaughter's—private school"

Betty turned to me. "Why did you get married in the first place?"

"I was kinda lost." I'd *been* lost ever since the Arizona school I went to closed.

Betty asked Hope, "Why was Consie lost?"

My mother looked momentarily stuck. "She always wanted to live with her father. When she was 10, I let her decide where she wanted to live. She chose her dad's."

"You let a ten-year-old choose which parent to live with?"

"Yes. I wanted her to be happy," said Hope. "She adored her father."

"You were pretty sure she'd choose her father then, right? Were you hoping she would? Didn't you also tell me that her father was an alcoholic?"

"I—we—didn't know." My mother looked nervous.

"So, besides letting a young child make life-altering decisions they shouldn't have to make, you were also 99.9 percent sure you'd be sending her off to live with a man you divorced because of his drinking, right?"

My mother cast her eyes down. Her shoulders slumped forward listlessly and the corners of her mouth turned down.

"But she never went to live with him," explained my mother, making this sound like a reprieve.

"Why?"

"He died suddenly in Tucson before Consie could go."

"Oh. So then you were stuck with her, right?"

"No. I didn't *feel* stuck. She was—*is*—my daughter. I wanted her to be happy. You've twisted this."

"Weren't you concerned about sending a ten-year-old girl to live with an alcoholic, even if he was her father?"

"I didn't think of it that way. I thought of how much Consie adored her father."

"As her mother, you failed her," concluded Betty.

The other women in the room either nodded or muttered "Yeah" in agreement.

I felt extremely uncomfortable watching my mother take this emotional beating, even if what they said was true.

"I was difficult. I *did* choose to live with Dad," I confessed.

"That's not the issue, honey," said Betty. "You shouldn't have had to choose in the first place."

Another chorus from the women.

I wanted to get the spotlight off my mother. I was afraid of the backlash that was bound to occur and that I'd be blamed for making my mother look bad, even though I didn't directly cause this. I'd learned this the hard way, just like the lesson I learned after supposed tryst I'd made with an Army guy that Easter Sunday when I was in the eighth grade. For that I was banished to boarding school.

Ancient history.

Right now I felt I couldn't endure any more hurt or humiliation. What I needed was support and a comforting shoulder, not this woman berating my mother in public. I began to cry.

"Hope," Betty continued. "You need to ask Consie for forgiveness."

The women's chorus approved. "Yeah. Um-hum. Do it!"

My mother got up from where she was sitting and stood over me, looking down. Her face was a tight mask, her eyes small slits, her mouth turned down at the corners.

"Ask her," said Betty.

"Will you forgive me?" asked Mom in a small voice.

Although I didn't believe for a minute that she was sorry or believed she'd done any wrong, I nodded my head and said "Yes," hoping this would end our mortification.

On the way home in the backseat, I heard my mother tell George that it had been an awful meeting and that she'd explain more later.

My as-yet-unexpressed question was, how and why did two intelligent, educated people like my parents get involved with such a group to begin with? They didn't have drug or alcohol problems. None of their children did. What drew them and kept them in to the point where my mother, who was dying from breast cancer, left her half of Green Gulch Ranch to Synanon?[1]

---

[1] *The Cult Observer Report*, Vol. 1, No. 2, September 1984, 16; The International Cultic Studies A ssociation, ICSA, Bonita Springs, Florida 34133.

Synanon is still pressing its controversial drug and alcohol rehabilitation program on the public despite years of conflict with critics and ex-members as well as with the IRS, which has withdrawn the organization's tax exemption.

Synanon, which changed under founder Charles Dederich into a totalitarian cult, recently ran a full-page ad for its services in a special alcohol and drug abuse supplement of the *Chicago Sun Times* (July 10). An unsigned story extolling the virtues of Synanon, and without reference to its history, also appeared in the same edition of the *Sun Times*. All this while thirteen Synanon associates surrendered in Los Angeles Superior Court to answer charges that they destroyed evidence subpoenaed in connection with the celebrated "rattlesnake" case, which began in 1978. (Four of Mr. Dederich's lieutenants were found guilty of placing a rattlesnake in the mailbox of California attorney Paul Morantz—it seriously injured him—who was representing two former Synanon members in lawsuits against the group. Mr. Dederich, also accused in the affair, pleaded no contest.)

→28←

Phil and Judy were married in a small ceremony over the summer in Vin-
alhaven, Maine. Frank Sinatra, who was fifty, married twenty-one year old
Mia Farrow in Las Vegas. United States bombs rained on Hanoi, while the
Mamas & the Papas' *Monday, Monday* was heard on every café's jukebox.

News from Green Gulch Ranch wasn't good. The cancer was now in
Mom's lungs, making it a struggle to breathe. Her few letters showed a
wobbling hand. Mom and George hoped that Laetrile, an extract from
apricot pits likened to vitamin B, would be the miracle panacea even though
the FDA had banned it. George took my mother to the Laetrile clinic in
Tijuana, Mexico, for treatments.

Feeling helpless, needing to do something, I volunteered as a nurse's aid
at Mary Scott Hospital, in Marblehead, where I emptied bedpans and held
the hands of patients I didn't know.

By October of 1967, she was gone. Parking both children with the
Barachs, I flew to California for a weekend. While George wandered the
ranch with a vacant look, I sorted through my mother's belongings and
made decisions about them. In her everyday, banged-up leather purse along
with her driver's license, some Kleenex and a few bobby pins, I found a love
letter she'd written to George. Knowing she was dying, she thanked him for
the wonderful life they shared. She told him how truly happy he'd made her
and asked him not to grieve and especially not to spend the rest of his days
alone. She was generously giving him permission to love again. Grateful
to have had the privilege of finding the letter, I gave it to George before
carrying the boxes filled with her belongings to the barn.

My mother left each of us five children $13,000 and everything else to
George. After George passed away, my mother's half of the ranch would go
to Synanon.

As soon as Synanon digested the content of Mom's will, its lawyer, Dan
Garrett, contacted my stepfather to notify him that Synanon planned to

develop and build apartment houses on top of the ridge overlooking Tennessee Cove and the Golden Gate Bridge and would start the engineering and grading phase immediately.

George was ballistic. "You agreed, Dan. No development, period. How can you go back on your word to Hope?"

"You can't be an Indian giver, George," Dan replied.

"You want to bet?" said George.

What ensued was a nasty fight, in which George's attorney found a technicality with which to break my mother's will. Another clause in her will said that if, for some reason, Synanon didn't get legal title to the ranch, her half of the ranch would revert to her five children, share and share alike. For reasons I'll never understand, and although Synanon was disqualified, not one of the five of us inherited any piece of Green Gulch Ranch.

What now took center stage and had become a financial possibility was the completion of my bachelor's at Bennington. I made an appointment with Wallace Stevens, the director of admissions, regardless of whether he wanted to meet me or not. I practiced my spiel during the four-hour drive.

When I arrived, I was surprised to see a diminutive man crouched on a sofa, almost hidden by plump cushions.

"Wa-wa-wa-well, hello," he stuttered, rising off the sofa and offering an outstretched hand.

"Mr. Stevens, hello." We shook hands.

"Si-si-si-si-sit down." He motioned to an armchair facing the sofa.

"Mr. Stevens, I'm a determined person, and I want to point out what a mistake Bennington made the day Alan Arkin and I were told to take a leave of absence. You know, the movie actor, Alan Arkin?"

Mr. Wallace's eyes suddenly focused on me with a startling urgency.

"Well," I continued, "I'm sure Alan has no plans to leave the college money. Now *I'm* a different story. I plan to become a filmmaker, and I'm certain that you'll want to help me achieve my goals. Am I right?"

He nodded. "Wha-wha-wha-wha-why don't you speak to Isaac Whitkin, ho-ho-ho-who's head of the art department."

And so I was admitted on a provisional basis to start that spring semester. Each week, I commuted the 200 miles from Salem and another 200 back to take art courses over a two-day period. My local baby-sitter, Jane, a Salem High School senior, came after school on the days I drove up. She fed the children, put them to bed, and spent the night. The next morning, Jane got everyone, including herself, off to school.

I attended one class the first day and spent the night in a rooming house. I took another class the next morning before driving back to Salem, hoping to get home before the children.

Around this same time, I met Peter Van Wyck, a divorced man my age who lived in nearby Essex in a house he'd built. We met on a Saturday afternoon, shepherding our four kids on a baby ski slope in New Hampshire. I learned that, like me, Peter had been brought up before the war in the Connecticut town next to ours. At the end of the day, I gave him my telephone number.

Peter called, expressing a desire to know me better. He was a handsome, dark-haired, athletic guy with a strange speech impediment: Every other word, it seemed, was *um*, and he mispronounced certain words—*cleats for pleats*, for example. Peter worked for Hunneman & Company in its Boston office, which had multiple divisions, including commercial and residential real estate. Not knowing exactly what Peter did at Hunneman, I was aware that he owned undeveloped property in Essex, and we were invited to visit his house, sitting on several acres with a horse and a barn.

Something that eventually turned me off was his reference to OKD. When I looked at him blankly, he translated. "Our kind, dear." I guess I was supposed to feel relieved that we were from similar backgrounds, ethnicities, and social status, but the term and all it implied revolted me.

As I got to know Peter better, I also warily observed his two badly behaved boys, Stephen and Nicholas. They whined constantly while Peter's threats to spank them escalated along with the volume of his voice.

"I want Cheerios," wailed Stephen.

"No," said Peter. "Any more of that and I'll spank you."

"I want a doughnut," screamed Nicholas.

Peter laughed at Nicholas, which encouraged him to demand more.

"Doughnuts, Daddy. Daddy, doughnuts," he implored.

Peter lunged for Nicholas, grabbing him by his waist and lifting him off the ground, shaking him, Peter's mouth a rictus grimace. Nicholas' screaming invited physical punishment.

When things quieted down, I suggested, "Reward *good* behavior, Peter. Ignore whining. They'll stop if it doesn't get them anywhere."

Sadly, Peter never caught on.

At Peter's suggestion, I consulted with Dr. Eleanor Wait, Ed. D., thinking her testing and profiling might help me sort out professional options. I was given two IQ tests, the Murray Thematic Apperception Test and the Thurstone Interest Schedule profile.

In the four-page developmental-study results, I was dumbfounded to learn I scored in the ninety-eighth percentile and was classified "superior" on the Stanford Binet Intelligence Scale. Convinced my intelligence was *sub*par—and that that was why my mother didn't love me as much as she did the boys—this had a stunning effect on my self-confidence.

Dr. Wait thought I needed to establish a sense of basic trust in a few significant people because many interactions I'd had with both men and women had led me to doubt the reality of faith and goodwill as essential components of satisfactory social living.

Imagine my excitement upon arriving home one evening to see a big Hollywood production in full swing on Salem Common right outside my house! Although I'd never been on the set of a major feature film, I knew immediately that it was one by the large klieg lights, the many trailers parked around the perimeter, and the Hollywood "trees" (long branches strapped to aluminum poles) being waved in front of the lights to cast dramatic leafy shadows.

I ran inside, asked Jane to stay with the kids for longer, grabbed and loaded film into my Leica, filled a small silver flask with bourbon, and approached the roped-off area on the common.

A man told me, "This is off-limits, ma'am."

"Oh, hi. I live right there." I turned and pointed to our house. "Do you think I could visit awhile? I'm a film student, and it's my first big production." I fluttered my eyelashes.

"Well, okay, if you'll stay in the background." He lifted the rope.

I watched two men laying tracks for a dolly shot nearby and walked closer to the lights to hear the director.

"Roll camera!"

"Camera rolling. Speed."

"Action!"

An actor ran down the street past several klieg lights. I saw two cameras and cameramen as they panned with the action.

"Cut!" yelled the director.

This scene was repeated again and again. Between takes, the runner's head dropped to his heaving chest while his arms rested on his hips.

Another guy came up to me and said somebody told him I had something to warm him up with. I handed him the flask and asked his name.

"David. I'm the key grip."

"What's the name of the film?"

"*Tell Me That You Love Me, Junie Moon.* Otto Preminger is the director, and Liza Minnelli's the star."

He took a swig, then another before handing it back.

"Look, I live there." I pointed out my house. "I've got two kids and dinner to make, but I'll come again tomorrow, okay?"

"Sure. Just say the key grip said it's all right."

"Thanks. Bye."

The next night, armed with a full flask, Levis, and a warm jacket, I encountered the same security person.

"Hi. Remember me?" I asked

"Yes, ma'am."

"The key clutch said to tell you to let me in."

A big smile spread across his face. "Key clutch, you say?"

I nodded.

"Hey, David," he yelled

When David arrived, the other guy tipped his head toward me. "She says that the key clutch said it's okay to let her in."

They both cracked up while David held the rope so I could slide under. He whispered softly, "Honey, I'm the key *grip*, not key *clutch*."

At that moment, the assistant director interrupted us. "Excuse me, but you can't take film on the set." He stared at the camera around my neck and held his hand out to take possession of the film. I rewound the film, extracted the cartridge and handed it to him. He firmly escorted me to the edge of the roped-in area and said "Goodbye" while lifting the rope to make sure I left.

I turned and waved to David and the other guy. They called in unison, "Bye-bye, key clutch."

When Bennington College accepted me as a full-time student, I made arrangements to relocate to Bennington and enroll both children in local public schools. To facilitate finding a place to live there, I asked Alta Coombs to stay with the children in Salem until school let out and everyone could move to Vermont. She planned to come to Massachusetts by bus, which was an event in itself, since she'd never been south of Portland, Maine.

Peter Van Wyck offered to buy a small house in the town of Bennington that Nina, Hans, and I could live in. I was hesitant about the implied strings of such an arrangement until Peter explained that it would be a good financial investment for him and that my rent would be low. Still, I saw it as an opportunity for Peter to have control over my life, which I didn't want. On the other hand, our living conditions might be much nicer than what I could afford to pay for on my own. My lawyer's advice was that as long as Peter and I were crystal clear about our expectations, go for it.

The week Alta arrived and settled in, I found a fairly new three-bedroom ranch at the right price on Jefferson Heights, just a half-mile above Bennington's city center. Peter and the real estate agent made the necessary arrangements via telephone and mail; all I had to do was sign a yearlong rental agreement with Peter.

One Saturday three weeks later, Alta, Piffin, a small moving company, the kids, and I drove to Vermont. When I asked Alta about her time alone with Nina and Hans, she told me they'd had a visitor.

"Who?" I asked.

"Katherine Boden," she replied. "She was real nice, real 'nice-nasty' is what we call it."

"Why did she visit?"

"She came while the kids were in school, so it wasn't to see them. She was trying to get me to say bad stuff about how lonely it is in that big house with two children, like you done left us."

"Oh, I'm sorry, Alta."

"I didn't fall for it. Went along with her until she left."

"Thank you for your loyalty." I reached over and clasped her hand in mine.

The first two nights in the new house, Alta slept in Nina's room, while Nina and I shared my queen-size bed. On Monday we took Alta to the Greyhound terminal for her trip home to Maine. We made sure she had snacks and enough money to spend a night in a Rockland hotel if she missed the last ferry to Vinalhaven. We waved farewell as the bus pulled away from the terminal.

Over the summer, I located the two schools Nina and Hans would go to and met their principals. Nina would be in fifth grade in an intermediate school, while Hans would enter third grade in the primary school. We registered at the library and walked home from downtown so they'd know how to in case either one should miss the bus.

I telephoned Gloria Gil, an alumna of Bennington College whom I met at a summer camp on parents' visiting day last summer. She and her husband were founders of the successful and well-known Bennington Potters. Gloria was as warm as David was aloof. She invited us to stop by the Bennington Pottery store on Sunday to give us the cook's tour.

We found Bennington Potters in an impressive former barn that was now a modern showroom. Some shelves were lined with less-than-perfect merchandise called "seconds," while the majority of shelves showcased the line of dishes, bowls, and cups in a variety of patinas. Judging by the traffic on this Sunday, sales were brisk and steady.

We three sat on railroad ties holding the retaining wall of the courtyard and watched people meandering by.

"Mom, when can we get my new bike?" asked Hans.

"It'll have to wait until tomorrow. Nothing's open here on Sundays."

"This place is," he countered.

"Some places are. Bike shops aren't."

"What about my new school clothes?" asked Nina.

I explained that unlike Boston, this was a small town and most stores were closed. "We'll go tomorrow," I promised.

Nina heaved a resigned sigh, which I interpreted as her wish that we'd never moved away from Massachusetts.

"I bet you'll make some good friends here, sweetie," I said, pulling her close. She gave me a wan smile that blossomed when I suggested getting ice-cream cones.

For the remainder of the summer, I was kept busy unpacking and arranging our belongings and restocking our kitchen with a few new small appliances, a blender, and copper-bottomed saucepans.

For my studio, I bought a large used easel and set it up in the basement. I bought clip-on portable lights and hung them from ceiling joists. I converted an old service tray on wheels into a painting cart with a thick glass slab. On a bench I lined up jars of turpentine, oil, brush-cleaning solvents, and containers for brushes and palette knives. Finally, I found an enormous framed, full-length mirror at a garage sale and dragged it into the basement. When I envisioned painting the human figure, I realized it would have to be my own reflection.

For the first time in a long time, I felt like captain of my own ship, heading on a steady course rather than adjusting due to winds that blew from my ex-husband and Katherine. I liked being away from their constant scrutiny. My future, once so predictably mired in poverty, now had new hope. With a completed bachelor's degree, I would surely gain meaningful employment and be self-sufficient.

Hans began to hang out at the Gils' house, and before long, the Gils' son, Michael, and Hans became inseparable, spending entire days playing Monopoly.

Nina invented a game she played with Piffin. She would hide somewhere in the house and then call "Ready." Piffin would search for Nina in each room, including the bathroom and closets. When Nina was discovered, Piffin would bark and jump joyously in circles.

One lazy afternoon I showed Nina how to make my mother's delicious recipe for spaghetti with meatballs in tomato sauce. We made garlic bread and salad. That evening Nina proudly served her first meal to Hans and me. The three of us were building happy memories.

August arrived and with it the children's yearly summer visit to their father's for two weeks. As prearranged, I delivered Nina and Hans to the Boden's house on Codman Road, in Brookline. I expected that Constantin or Katherine would reciprocate by driving them back to Bennington in two weeks' time.

Returning home in a leisurely fashion, I stopped at various spots of interest to break up the all-day drive. Produce stands along the road offered the freshest corn, lettuce, and tomatoes, and at one of these I sat on a bale of hay and crunched into an apple.

At home I read in bed until my head rolled forward onto my chest. The following morning, I didn't get up until the sun was high and Piffin's whine told me she needed to go out. I padded across wood floors to let her out the back door and watched from the kitchen window until she came back in. Sipping a fresh cup of coffee, I turned on the television and watched a horrible story that was on every news channel. A cult had apparently killed Sharon Tate and others in Los Angeles. At first I was compelled to follow the story's gruesome trajectory, but then I turned the TV off.

All week I wrapped my temporary freedom like a luxurious silk cloak around me, savoring each moment. I missed the children, but I needed this time to myself and knew they were coming home in another week.

On the date the children were due home, no one called to confirm their time of arrival. When I telephoned Constantin and Katherine's house, no one answered. By evening it was clear that the children weren't coming. I started imagining that an accident had befallen them. These imaginings escalated to full-blown paranoia: Constantin had kidnapped the children and taken them to Germany. I'd lost them!

Increasingly fearful, I called my Boston attorney, Peter Seamans, at home.

"The kids were supposed to be home today. No one answers at Codman Road, and I'm frantic. Peter, what if he's taken them to Germany?"

"Listen, Toots, calm down. He's got too much at stake here in Boston to do that. I'll make a few calls in the morning. We'll find out where he is."

"Thank God you're my attorney, Peter."

"Get some sleep."

"Call as soon as you know anything, okay?"

"Right-o."

By the time I heard from Peter again, it was midmorning of the next day, and what a story! Apparently, Constantin was on vacation from the bank until tomorrow. Peter tracked the children to the Belash household in Milton, where Constantin had parked Nina and Hans over the weekend while he and Katherine flew to the music festival in Salzberg. Mrs. Belash sounded quite upset that the children had been virtually dumped on them. She had no idea how to reach the Bodens in case of an emergency.

"So," said Peter, "I'm going to hit him with a subpoena tomorrow at the bank. He'll have twelve hours to return Nina and Hans to you in Bennington or he's cooked."

"Do you know what time you'll do this?"

"Trust me, you'll have the children by tomorrow evening at the latest."

In a terse phone call the next day, Constantin said he planned to arrive in North Bennington around four o'clock with the children. I coolly thanked him.

I watched from the front-room window as the Mercedes approached, swung a "U" so it was headed back down the hill, and stopped. The children exploded from the back doors, running up the path to our front door. I flung the door open and embraced Nina first, smelling the warm blond head sprouting pigtails, then Hans, his face pure joy at seeing me as my arms enfolded him.

Nina raced into the house calling "Piffin," and Hans turned to wave goodbye to his father, who was hurling the children's bags onto the lawn in a heap. He gestured a goodbye flick with one hand, jumped into the driver's seat and threw the Mercedes into forward gear.

I was stunned at Constantin's rude, angry behavior. Didn't he realize I'd be frantic when the children weren't returned on the agreed-upon date? Why fly to Europe for the children's last vacation weekend, leaving them with semi-strangers? Why be angry for insisting he live up to our custody agreement? Who did he think he was? How did these actions affect the children?

The more I thought about this, the more relief I felt that I was no longer legally tied to him.

⟫ 29 ⟪

We three settled into our routine school lives, out the door before 8 a.m. and usually in bed before 10 p.m. Most of my classes were during the children's school hours, so I was home by the time they got back from school midafternoon. My in-home painting studio afforded me parental overview of Nina's and Hans's after-school activities while also allowing me to work. Considering the grueling two hundred mile commute I'd endured the previous semester, it was an easy transition.

Living expenses in Vermont were more easily curbed because our lives were simpler. With combined alimony and child support of $500 a month, we got by. Still, as I paid our bills, I complained to myself that a first-class stamp cost six cents. Consciously gambling by not buying myself medical insurance, I felt secure in knowing that the children were covered under their father's policy.

October brought "leaf peepers" and early frosts. Janis Joplin died suddenly of a heroin overdose. "Oh Lord, woncha buy me a Mercedes-Benz."

I'd been right to be suspicious of Peter Van Wyck's business-only motive for buying the house we rented on Jefferson Heights. He thought the least we should do is invite him for a visit.

"We can't offer you a guest room, Peter. There isn't one, but you are welcome to visit. I'll reserve you a motel room in town."

"That's a total brush-off!"

"I don't mean it to be, Peter."

"Why not show your appreciation for me then?"

"By?"

"You know how I feel about you. Don't pretend you don't. Not everyone would buy you a house."

"Peter, you didn't buy *me* this house. We were clear from the get-go that this was a business deal. No strings and no obligations, except the lease. I do pay rent on time."

"But you *know* how I feel."

"I don't, actually. I'm not ready for a relationship with anyone. I only want to finish my undergraduate degree. That and the children are all I can handle. I'm sorry."

"You could have said so before."

"I'm saying it now."

Peter slammed the receiver and the line went dead. It was obvious that he thought I'd used him.

I heard from several sources that Gloria and David Gil's marriage was rumored to be on the skids because of David's alleged affair with a Bennington dropout who worked at the Pottery Barn. Knowing firsthand how painful this situation was, I resolved to be as supportive to Gloria as she'd let me be. I gave her plenty of opportunity to bring this up during weekly lunches, but Gloria still behaved as if everything was hunky-dory.

Hans rode his bike to the Gils' almost every afternoon to play Monopoly with Michael, while Nina's new friend, Jessica, frequently came to our house in the afternoons. I loved hearing the giggling, happy girls playing.

My classes were challenging. In Sidney Tillim's Painting Tutorial, I was working on a still life of draped fabric on a table with onions and an earthen jar. Peering over my shoulder at the canvas, Sidney said, "Don't be afraid to use a ruler to establish a straight line. You can soften the line with a brush later, but architectural elements like doorways are perpendicular." Sidney described his own work as large representational pictures of historic figures and events.

The college was a magnet for artistic glitterati, including Kenneth Nolan, who was referred to as the greatest colorist since Matisse; Jules Olitski, the color field painter; Barnett Newman, the American abstract expressionist; and the sculptor Anthony Caro. While the aforementioned were constantly in the media, Sidney Tillim, although an accessible, thoughtful teacher, seemed to be the odd man out, a dinosaur among skyscrapers.

In Photography Studio, I was trying to learn Ansel Adams's Zone System of film exposure and development. Adams developed the Zone System to cope with the drawbacks of the exposure meter. If you followed the meter's reading, every scene would have the same middle gray density. Adams' approach was to "expose for the shadows, develop for the highlights." However, the detailed data I was required to meticulously record on each exposure quickly bogged me down.

For my major project in Photography Studio with Neil Rappaport, I decided to take a series of black-and-white photographs of the vast railroad yards in Albany. I grew up riding trains and loved the steel tracks that had the promise of exotic destinations, other lives.

I spent a whole day in Albany shooting five rolls of film and two more days processing the negatives and printing proofs. The proofs were okay, but I wasn't satisfied. On a rainy day I went back to shoot more film. The overcast sky and diffused light added drama by rendering minute details such as a discarded milk carton in the foreground and a man in a dark jacket crossing the tracks in the middle distance.

With light gleaming off the steel tracks, the prints came alive. The shots I liked the best depicted a horizontal landscape of many rails merging into the distant horizon.

For my final project I chose ten negatives to print and mat from over two hundred. Rappaport, who was working on a series of photographs of Vermont granite quarries for a book, congratulated me for a well-done project

The semester was over. Suddenly Christmas arrived. I'd bought a family-membership ski pass at the tiny mountain about ten miles from home. It had a rope tow and one short chairlift, which was perfect for the kids to learn on. Each night before lights-out, I attached a list to the feet of their beds spelling out what each must wear. In the morning I wouldn't start the car until all the items on the lists had been checked off.

Peter Van Wyck invited the three of us to join him at the Ski Club Hochgebirge over New Year's, and I accepted. That's where I'd first met Sam Johnson seemingly a million years ago. Peter and I arranged to meet there on New Year's Eve. I was glad we'd be in dormitory rooms, so the question of sleeping together would be a nonissue.

We left on Wednesday and arrived in Franconia past sunset. Peter was already there. The kitchen was fitted with two large refrigerators that could hold enough food for twenty guests. We wrote our names with indelible markers on the grocery bags as we placed them in one of the refrigerators, and then we took our duffels upstairs. The second story had been converted into three large dormitories, men's, women's, and children's. Peter and Hans would be in the men's dorm, Nina and I in the ladies dorm.

Surprisingly, the club wasn't full. I spotted three couples and two single older men meandering around the first floor. Four people played cards. Another couple sat on a small sofa, the man reading and the woman knitting blue wool yarn.

⇢ Swimming Upstream ⇠

In the kitchen I made preparations for supper, pork chops with baked potatoes and sliced tomatoes. As I brushed mustard and soy sauce on the pork chops, Peter handed me a cocktail. We joined others in the living room while the potatoes baked. Nina and Hans were assembling a puzzle near the fireplace.

"My name is Peter Van Wyck, and this is Constance Boden and her children, Nina and Hans," said Peter to the others.

"Welcome," said the woman knitting the blue wool. "I'm Anna, and this is my husband, Paul."

Paul looked up, smiled, and resumed reading.

"Hello," said a male member of the foursome playing cards. "I'm Scott, and this is Mary." He nodded across the table at the woman wearing red pants and a red sweater and holding a fan of cards that obscured all but her eyes.

"Hi," said Mary suddenly, lowering her cards to reveal a megawatt smile.

"We are the Swifts," announced the other male at the card table. "I'm Rodney, and this is my wife, Rebecca." He tipped his head in her direction. "For twenty-five years!"

"They aren't interested in how long we've been married," whispered Rebecca.

"Oh, we certainly are!" I said, not knowing why.

Smiles all around.

Peter turned to the couple on the sofa. "Would you mind baby-sitting so I can take Constance for a New Year's Eve celebratory drink a little later on?"

"We have our own plans," said the bookworm husband.

Peter got up and walked over to the foursome playing cards. "Would any of you be willing to cover for us if we have a New Year's drink later on?"

I was embarrassed by Peter's aggressiveness and intervened. "Peter, it's not that important." I tried to distract him by pulling him into the kitchen. "We can celebrate right here in front of the fireplace," I suggested.

Peter mumbled something that didn't sound encouraging. I set the table and asked the children to wash their hands. We four ate the meal I'd prepared and discussed what ski slopes we'd tackle the next day. The children were excitedly looking forward to it, while I was just hoping to get through New Year's Eve without unpleasantness.

After washing, drying our dishes, and putting them away, I joined the others in the living room. I noticed that Peter was missing. On the pretext of needing something from my car, I looked in the parking lot and saw that his car was gone. So, if he doesn't get his way, it's the highway—literally.

After reading to and putting both children to bed, I decided not to stay over the long weekend and telephoned my stepbrother, George, and his wife, Caroline, in New Canaan, Connecticut. After explaining the dicey situation with Peter, they invited us to come down tomorrow.

That decision made, I made a cup of tea and sat in front of the fireplace, mesmerized by the flames. My watch showed it was past 9. The children would be disappointed about not skiing, but they loved their cousins Quinto and Sophia.

All the others had either gone to bed or were out somewhere. In the bookshelf, I'd found a mystery and had begun to read when, with a blast of icy air, Peter rushed through the front door and slammed it behind him.

"Where did you go?" I asked.

"Out."

"That's not very considerate, Peter."

"So, I'm a turd."

"I've decided to go to George and Caroline's in the morning," I told him.

Suddenly, he was standing over me, yanking me off the chair. He dragged and pushed me out the door into the freezing cold and threw me down on the icy ground. Astride me, he punched my face and my ear. I used my hands to cover my face, but his blows continued, and he grunted with the effort.

"Stop, Peter, stop. You're hurting me!" I screamed.

Suddenly, two men pulled Peter off me, hauling him upright. One of the men pinned Peter to the building; the other helped me into the house. I tasted my own blood, and there was a loud ringing in my right ear. Limping up the stairs to the bathroom, I washed my face gingerly and put tissue on the cut near my left eye. I crawled into the bunk below Nina. Out of fear and exhaustion, I was able to dissolve into blackness.

The next morning in the bathroom mirror I saw a swollen face with a black-and-blue eye. Downstairs, I faced my children and the other guests at the breakfast table. Nina and Hans stared at my face, but none of the guests' eyes would meet mine.

"I'm all right and very sorry about last night's disturbance," I said to everyone.

"Peter Van Wyck has been thrown out of the club," a man said.

"The children and I are leaving after breakfast and going to my brother's," I said.

We packed our few belongings and took them to the car. Feeling guilty about being part of such an ugly episode for club members, I ran the vacuum cleaner over the living-room floors before taking leave.

During the drive to Connecticut, I explained to Nina and Hans what had happened and why we'd left and were going to New Canaan.

"Will you ever see Peter again?" asked Nina.

"No."

"Why did he do that?" asked Hans.

"He's a very angry, unhappy man, sweetheart."

"He sure is," said Hans. "Will you get all better?"

"Yes, I will. These are just bad bruises. They'll fade."

We drove in silence.

⇒ 30 ⇐

During nonresident term, I worked on my paintings and photographs and spent more time with the children. By the time spring term rolled around, everyone was tired of the slush, cumbersome outerwear and heavy boots. I couldn't wait to put away our woolens; however, in Vermont it wasn't safe to count on warm weather until after Memorial Day.

Everyone was equally sick of the unwinnable war in Vietnam, with its toll on servicemen and the American psyche. In April 1970, when it was announced that President Nixon had ordered the invasion of Cambodia, smoldering antiwar sentiments erupted on college campuses. Events escalated at Kent State University, in Ohio, where four students were shot and killed and nine others were wounded by the National Guard. A photograph of Mary Veddhio screaming over the body of Jeffrey Miller appeared on the front pages of newspapers and magazines throughout the country.

In an emergency meeting, Bennington College administrators, students and faculty unanimously decided to suspend classes in protest of violence against students at Kent State. The development office was mobilized to coordinate strike affairs and generate press releases. Existing staff turned their efforts toward supporting this position. I was proud that the college took a stand rather than adopting a business-as-usual attitude, and I volunteered to assist in any way.

In the days that followed, the impact of the Kent State shootings triggered a nationwide student strike that forced hundreds of colleges and universities to close. Brandeis University was New England's hub for strike activities. Part of my new job as a volunteer was to be in daily contact with Brandeis to learn of any marches or rallies in the Boston area and to disseminate information locally.

Chris Bellini, assistant to the director of development, agreed to work with the strike committee. Chris helped me write a broadsheet outlining the college's position, including a synopsis of how and when these decisions were made. With President Bloustein's input and eventual approval, we printed hundreds of the broadsheets and delivered them to various locations around the college.

Suspended classes had a sobering effect. I was paying tuition from my inheritance from my mother. When that was gone, that was it. Tuition for one year ate a third of it. I wondered if I could afford *not* to complete classes this semester. Thankfully, the faculty had agreed to meet one-on-one with students until the summer break. In addition to coordinating strike activities with the college, I made sure I completed necessary course work for all four classes in order to graduate.

Time spent working on projects in the development office with Chris was very pleasant. Chris had a friendly personality coupled with a thoughtful intelligence. His frame was slim, coordinated. He had an angular face framed by longish, wavy brown hair. Soon we were taking pleasant lunch breaks and strolls around campus, during which we discovered we had lots in common. In his previous job, he worked for the curator at the Corcoran Gallery, in Washington, D.C. Drawn to painting but having to make a living, he wrote public relations and other materials for the development office.

One Saturday, Chris, the children, and I visited the Clark Museum, in Williamstown, Massachusetts, which had an outstanding collection of French Impressionist paintings. Afterward, I brought Chris by our house for tea. I ended up showing him my photographic works, and then we decided to eat at the diner in Bennington. Unlike adults who condescend to kids, Chris had a genuine curiosity that made children respond to him. Leafing through the menu, he suddenly turned to Hans. "I wonder, is a hot dog really a hot *dog*?"

"No, silly. It's called 'hot dog' because it's long and close to the ground, like our dog, Piffin."

Chris guffawed.

"What's a chicken-fried steak?" I asked. "Does the chicken fry the steak?"

"Come on, Mom!" wailed Nina.

"If they have cold slaw, can you order *hot* slaw?" asked Chris.

Our laughter continued throughout the meal.

Over the summer months, Chris and I saw one another often, but I wondered why he never tried to kiss me. Wasn't he attracted? This gnawed at me to the uncomfortable point that I wrote to sound him out. Although I was afraid of being rejected, I had to know. I didn't want to invest feelings where they were unwelcome. Handing him the letter, I suggested that if he was too uncomfortable to respond in person, he could write.

Twenty-four hours passed and I still hadn't heard from Chris. I stuck close to home all day and, on my single trip to the college, gave a wide berth to the development office to avoid embarrassment. The next day Chris telephoned to suggest we meet during his lunch break on a walk to Jennings.

It was a lovely walk from The Barn through meadows, by a pond and up a slight incline to the low stone wall in front of once-formal gardens, where we parked ourselves. Chris spoke hesitantly and a bit circuitously about an old girlfriend. His hands fidgeted and his arm gestured in a wide arc when explaining why things hadn't worked out with Jenny in Washington, D.C. I pressed on with more questions until I finally realized he was trying to tell me something without telling me.

"Are you trying to tell me you're still a virgin?" I asked.

I heard a huge sigh, then "Yes." His head fell to his chest.

"Is that all?" I asked, relieved that it wasn't because he found me unattractive.

On the Big Day, when we had my house to ourselves at midday, we sipped glasses of Champagne and climbed into bed.

"Everyone has a first time," I said soothingly, noticing Chris's jumpiness. He laughed nervously. We embraced and kissed. I drank in his taste and ran my tongue down his neck to the hollow of his throat. He groaned in pleasure. I blew softly in his ear and told him how much I wanted him. Instinctively, nature took over.

Over the summer, we met often at midday, when he could slip out of the office on his lunch break. Our lovemaking improved. "Practice makes perfect" should be every lover's mantra.

While the children spent August with their father and stepmother, Chris and I visited my stepfather at Green Gulch Ranch. I'd discovered through experience how important it is to see how a prospective partner relates to one's family and vice versa.

When we got there, I was shocked at how shabby the house looked, especially the kitchen, with bottles of vitamin pills stacked on the table and used tea bags littering the countertops. Could things have deteriorated so quickly in two years? I asked George if Mom's cleaning lady still came.

He seemed preoccupied. "What did you say?"

I noted how diminished his vigor and equilibrium had become. When he registered my concern, he rallied. "Oh, I know, it's a mess, isn't it?" he said, waving his arm to encompass the room. "I'm hopeless, you know," he told me with a twinkle in his eye, ever the extrovert I had grown to love.

Our trip was cut short when Chris made a routine phone call to his office at Bennington College and learned that his job as assistant to the director was no more. In shock, Chris insisted we leave the next day to try to salvage whatever remained of his career.

We drove nonstop to Vermont, consuming packages of No Doz over the seventy-odd-hour drive.

Although concerned about Chris's situation, it was a relief to be home in Jefferson Heights, preparing for my final year of undergraduate studies. After spending August apart, I looked forward to seeing my children. Within a week, Chris found another job, as a reporter for our local rag, the *Bennington Banner*, but he was disillusioned about what had happened and I didn't blame him one bit.

For my senior thesis, I decided to paint a five-by-three-foot self-portrait. Trying a variety of poses, I ended up choosing to stand behind a 35mm Leica camera mounted on a tripod in front of an easel on which sat a large figurative painting. I shot a roll of black-and-white film into my mirror image, developed the roll and picked one shot to be blown up. I marked this eight-by-ten into horizontal and vertical grids and marked the large canvas into proportionally sized grids to facilitate the drawing of each section. It was a challenge.

Michael Gil and Hans resumed their ongoing game of Monopoly at the Gils' house after school. Nina checked out volumes of books from the library, sometimes reading each one twice, which concerned me. Was her school engaging her sufficiently? I signed her up for piano lessons at the van der Lindes' Sonatina Music School, which I hoped would help her overcome shyness, and wished there were money for a piano for her to practice on.

George called to say he'd like to come for a visit in October. Flattered and a bit surprised because he'd never gone out of his way on my behalf, I offered to put him up. Both children would have to sleep in one room during his visit.

Chris and I became friendly with Helen Feeley, widow of Paul Feeley, the painter, who lived in the old firehouse in North Bennington that used to be Paul's studio. We often dropped by for cocktails and sat on the deck cantilevered over the Wallomsac River. Helen worked in the alumni office at the college and already knew Chris, and she mixed a mean martini while making caustic remarks about nearly everyone. I vowed never to get on her bad side.

I admired her ability to sew. One afternoon, she was appliquéing a jacket with silks of every hue, which she pulled out of a basket as we sipped our cocktails.

"Chris, do you like the *Bennington Banner*?" she asked, peering over bifocals.

"Yes, I've gotten over being fired. I think I'm happier in a newsroom rather than the uptight development office."

"Good. And you, Consie?"

"I'm almost ready to start my final canvases," I told her. "Also, my stepdad called saying he wants to visit here next month. I'd like to introduce you. You both lost spouses the same time period. Would you consider dining with all of us?"

"I'd love it," said Helen.

We thanked Helen for the cocktails, and I headed home to make dinner for the kids and myself, wondering just what I'd set in motion between Helen and my stepfather.

On a crisp fall day, George arrived from Albany in a rental car. Hans, Nina, and I rushed from the front door to welcome him.

We had the weekend to catch up before school resumed. I planned to bring him to Pat Adams' Color Workshop on Monday. George had accepted an invitation to speak about founding the Polaroid Corporation with Edwin Land in the 1930s and was eagerly awaiting an audience.

After breakfast the next morning, George left to run an errand. He reappeared with a new small gas-powered lawn mower in the back of his car.

"I didn't realize you needed one or I would have gotten it sooner," he said.

"How kind of you!"

Nina ran to hug him.

Hans joined us on the front lawn, where we admired the lawn mower. Just then the postman delivered our mail. Among mostly bills was a letter for Hans from Katherine, whose handwriting I would have recognized anywhere, postmarked "Boston." Hans opened it and began to read. He gave up shortly, handing me the letter, asking for help. I began to read it out loud.

> Your mother is selfish to move all of you to Vermont, without considering what is best for you.

I folded the letter, telling Hans I'd finish reading it later.

"George, could I speak to you alone?" I asked. When we were in the kitchen I showed him Katherine's letter.

"I was reading it to Hans because he couldn't make out certain words. Isn't it just awful?"

"It's worse than awful. Consie, you stay here. Nina, Hans," he called, "I have something important to say to you."

When the three were gathered, he shut the door between the kitchen and the living room. I could barely hear him through the door. "What your stepmother has written in this letter is poison. If your mother had written it, I'd spank her, and she would deserve it! If you ever get another letter like this, speaking badly about your mother, you call and tell me. I'll tell our attorney to put a stop to this. Am I clear?"

"Yes, Gramps," said the children in unison.

When George opened the door, I saw two grave faces that had taken what Gramps said seriously. I was flooded with relief that he'd stood up for me against this dirty assault.

We introduced Helen to George, and they hit it off. In fact, George was invited to Helen's the following evening for dinner. When he hadn't come home by 10, I went to bed until the buzzing of the front door bell awakened me at 2 a.m. Opening it, I found a sheepish George.

"Sort of a reverse role, don't you think?" he said apologetically before creeping to his room.

He was still asleep the next morning when the three of us left the house, so I left a note telling him what time I'd be home.

George said, "Helen's quite a woman. I just may ask her to marry me."

I didn't take him seriously, because I'd heard this before. He'd fallen for several inappropriate women since Mom died, including one thirtysome-thing California mother of three.

However, the next day when Helen called me into her office to announce their intention to marry, I was stunned. While I thought this was too fast, I told her I wished them both the best.

George planned to fly immediately to the ranch to prepare for a visit from Helen planned for a few weeks later, while Helen would stay to arrange the engagement party that would follow her trip.

I was looking forward to meeting Chris's parents, who were planning to visit from Buffalo the following weekend. I'd put out feelers for a sitter so I could join them Saturday evening for dinner at very fancy Four Chimneys Inn.

When Saturday rolled around, I got a panicked call from Chris in the morning, saying he had to see me right away.

"Come on over," I told him.

Ten minutes later, Chris got out of his car with a grim slash where he usually had a smile.

"What's wrong?"

Chris's eyes flashed to mine, then to Nina's and Hans's, then back to me.

"Sweeties . . . " I ushered both children toward their bedrooms. "Chris and I need to talk alone for a bit." I hugged each and went to the living room, where Chris had collapsed in an armchair, his head cradled in his hands.

"My parents refuse to meet you," he said.

"What? *Why?*"

"You're 'damaged goods,' they told me. A divorcée."

"Oh, how awful."

"I've told them dinner is off. I won't go unless you're included."

"Thank you," I murmured. "Do they know my husband walked out on me?"

"Yes. I explained everything. They know I love you. They won't budge. I can't believe this is happening."

"Chris, *you're* not shunning me. I wanted to meet your folks, but maybe it's better this way. Let's forget it."

"I'll never forget—*or* forgive them."

I knelt beside Chris and took one of his hands. "Look at me, Chris."

His eyes met mine. He looked so miserable. "This is about them, not us," I said. "They're old-fashioned. It's not about me, or you. Try not to take it personally."

After he left, I telephoned the sitter to cancel.

After several weeks, and although I'd forgotten about Chris's parents' visit, something odious infiltrated my psyche. I couldn't stop thinking about the nine-year difference in our ages or about being the only woman Chris had "been with." *Nine years may not be noticeable now, but when I'm 50 and he's 41, will I seem old to him? Can he know he loves me if he hasn't made love with anyone else?* These fears grew exponentially with my anxiety about what to do and where to live after the fast-approaching graduation ceremonies.

The next time I saw Chris, we were sitting in his Volkswagen in front of my house after a dinner date. Sensing my malaise, he asked what was wrong. Since trying to pretend everything was copacetic hadn't worked, I voiced my fears.

"What if a year from now you meet a woman your age and have *those* feelings?" I asked. "You'll be curious, and if we're married, you'll resent me."

"What if it snows purple flakes?"

"You aren't taking this seriously!"

Exiting, I slammed the passenger-side door. So many things were converging: the critique of my three paintings by the celebrated New York art critic Clement Greenberg, how to support myself and the children, where to move, Chris's and my relationship.

A welcome respite from all this pressure arrived in the form of an invitation from Chris to picnic under blossoming apple trees, where he unfolded a tablecloth, uncorked Champagne, and poured it into plastic flutes. We spread pate and cheese on a baguette and lay on our backs, looking up through the canopy of white blossoms. Freeze frame.

Life had a way of screaming forward. The children's schools would soon close for summer vacation, and they would spend July with their father. I was pretty sure I'd move back to Boston over the summer to look for work. As I became more resolute about this course of action, Chris became more and more attentive. One evening he telephoned to say he had to see me and asked if he could come by late?

"How late?"

"I'm finishing a story—an eleven o'clock deadline."

When I heard his car door slam, I opened the front door. A stark-naked Chris ran across the lawn and into the living room. Speechless, I

241

tossed him a pillow from the sofa, checking nervously to see if we had woken up the children.

"What on earth?"

"You're always saying I'm not demonstrative enough, so"—he raised both arms to the ceiling—"here I am in all my glory!"

The day that my senior critique with Clement Greenberg arrived, I was too involved with transporting and hanging canvases in the Carriage House to be as nervous as I ought to have been. The rumor mill overflowed with Mr. Greenberg's importance in New York's art and literary world. In the 1950s, Clement Greenberg had introduced Helen Frankenhauler, a Bennington graduate, to the New York art scene, where she studied with Hans Hofmann before becoming America's most innovative and successful abstract American expressionist. Her canvases now commanded tens of thousands of dollars. The main reason I wasn't more intimidated by the imminent proceedings was that my paintings were only a steppingstone to my real love: film. I was determined to become a filmmaker.

By early afternoon, the Carriage House was packed. Graduating students milled around the first floor, anxiously awaiting their critiques, while spectators crowded the second-story gallery.

I presented three canvases, the dominant one a nearly life-size self-portrait. It depicted me standing in front of a painting on an easel, my hand holding the remote shutter-release cable to my Leica camera, mounted on a tripod. In the portrait, I seemed to be asking myself whether I was a painter or a photographer? I called it *The Bridge Painting*. The second large painting depicted four semiclothed figures on the marshes in Essex, Massachusetts. The third was a still life with an eggplant, a white jug, and a red tablecloth that shimmered like silk.

Mr. Greenberg approached. He stepped up to the self-portrait, then backed up several feet, threw a glance at the two other oils, and focused again on the self-portrait.

"Shapes and areas geometrically simplified. The color flat and bright—undifferentiated. Little attempt to show value difference, relying on the pattern which lures the viewer into the picture."

I wondered what all this meant. Did he like it?

"The arm of the man in the painting is at a downward angle." He gestured with his right hand. "Echoing the right arm of the woman standing—a duality of shapes and direction. Repletion again of the man's white pants in the woman's white pants. Against these soft-edged clothed figures, sharp geometrics come into focus with the squares of the floor, square painting on the easel, and so on. The vertical linear elements set off the figure, who by virtue of color and size dominates the scene and creates an original and vigorous painting."

Ignoring the other figurative painting, he walked closer to inspect the smaller still life.

"Here the vivid lyric quality of the red tablecloth provides an anchor for familiar objects, a Vermeer white bowl, a jug and undulating vegetable forms. Contrasting this, the architectural frame and white background mass spiral to the weightless air surrounding the scene."

He stopped, turned, and proffered his right hand. I shook it. While I'd listened closely to his words, I didn't grasp their meaning. Relief poured over me as I realized he hadn't trashed my work; in fact, his handshake was a form of congratulation. Smiling, I moved to the perimeter of the room while the next senior stepped bravely forward.

At Bennington's commencement ceremony, the speaker was author Anais Nin. In the high eighties, the weather was partly cloudy, threatening thundershowers. The small group of seniors assembled in the quadrangle in front of The Barn at 10 to don our gowns.

I felt palpable excitement as families of graduates and loved ones mingled. Nina, Hans, and I formed a triangle on the outer edge and searched for Uncle Joe and Aunt Peggy, who were coming from Boston. This was the happiest day of my life: completing undergraduate studies as a single mother of two children and living on limited means. I didn't care a hoot about Anais Nin. My own life's drama was about to unfold, and I was ready! I wanted to pinch myself to make sure I wasn't dreaming.

Suddenly, on a grassy knoll, I spotted Aunt Peggy in a leopard-print shirtsleeve dress and Uncle Joe beside her.

"Aunt Peggy," I called, "over here!"

Then the ceremony began. We marched two by two across the grass to President Blaustein, who shook our hands and gave us our rolled-up diplomas tied with ribbon. As I reached out my hand to shake his, he leaned over to plant a kiss on my cheek.

"I get to kiss all graduating mothers," he said.

→ Constance Richardson ←

I heard a piercing whistle. Turning, I spotted Nina, her blond braids swinging, holding her thumb and forefinger to her mouth, with which she blew another celebratory whistle. I hadn't known she could do that!

I cradled the diploma in one hand, relishing the moment, before I continued across the lawn to join my fellow graduates, not realizing that my picture would be on the front page of the *Bennington Banner* the next day.